MEN ENGAGING FEMINISMS

feminist educational thinking

Series Editors:
Kathleen Weiler, Tufts University, USA
Gaby Weiner, Umea University, Sweden
Lyn Yates, La Trobe University, Australia

This authoritative series explores how theory/practice and the development of advanced ideas within feminism and education can be fused. The series aims to address the specific theoretical issues that confront feminist educators and to encourage both practitioner and academic debate.

MEN ENGAGING FEMINISMS

Pro-feminism, backlashes and schooling

BOB LINGARD
and
PETER DOUGLAS

OPEN UNIVERSITY PRESS
Buckingham · Philadelphia

Open University Press
Celtic Court
22 Ballmoor
Buckingham
MK18 1XW

email: enquiries@openup.co.uk
world wide web: http://www.openup.co.uk

and
325 Chestnut Street
Philadelphia, PA 19106, USA

First Published 1999

A catalogue record of this book is available from the British Library

ISBN   0 335 19817 1 (pb)   0 335 19818 X (hb)

Library of Congress Cataloging-in-Publication Data
Lingard, Bob.
    Men engaging feminisms : pro-feminism, backlashes and schooling
/ Bob Lingard and Peter Douglas.
    p.   cm. – (Feminist education thinking)
  Includes bibliographical references and index.
  ISBN 0-335-19818-X (hb)
  ISBN 0-335-19817-1 (pbk.)
  1. Sex differences in education.   2. Men's movement.   3. Feminism
and education.   I. Douglas, Peter, 1963–   II. Title.   III. Series.
  LC212.9 .LS3 1999
  306.43'2–dc21   98-41548
                                                                         CIP

Typeset by Type Study, Scarborough
Printed in Great Britain by St Edmundsbury Press Limited, Bury St Edmunds, Suffolk

For Nicholas Lingard and Benjamin Douglas

Contents

Series editors' preface

At the end of the twentieth century it is not a new idea to have a series on feminist educational thinking – feminist perspectives on educational theory, research, policy and practice have made a notable impact on these fields in the final decades of the century. But theory and practice have evolved, and educational and political contexts have changed. In contemporary educational policy debates, economic efficiency rather than social inequality is a key concern; what happens to boys is drawing more interest than what happens to girls; issues about cultural difference interrupt questions about gender; and new forms of theory challenge older frameworks of analysis. This series represents feminist educational thinking as it takes up these developments now.

Feminist educational thinking views the intersection of education and gender through a variety of lenses: it examines schools and universities as sites for the enacting of gender; it explores the ways in which conceptions of gender shape the provision of state-supported education; it highlights the resistances subordinated groups have developed around ideas of knowledge, power and learning; and it seeks to understand the relationship of education to gendered conceptions of citizenship, the family and the economy. Thus feminist educational thinking is fundamentally political; it fuses theory and practice in seeking to understand contemporary education with the aim of building a more just world for women and men. In so doing, it acknowledges the reality of multiple 'feminisms' and the intertwining of ethnicity, race and gender.

Feminist educational thinking is influenced both by developments in feminist theory more broadly and by the changing global educational landscape. In terms of theory, both post-structuralist and post-colonial theories have profoundly influenced what is conceived of as 'feminist'. As is true elsewhere, current feminist educational thinking takes as central the intersecting forces that shape the educational experiences of women and men. This emphasis on the construction and performances of gender through both discourses and material practices leads to an attitude of openness and questioning of accepted assumptions – including the underlying assumptions of the various strands of feminism.

In terms of the sites in which we work, feminist educational thinking increasingly addresses the impact of 'globalization' – the impact of neo-laissez-faire theories on education. As each of us knows all too well, the schools and universities in which we work have been profoundly affected by the growing dominance of ideas of social efficiency, market choice, and competition. In a rapidly changing world in which an ideology of profit has come to define all relationships, the question of gender is often lost, but in fact it is central to the way power is enacted in education as in society as a whole.

The books in this series thus seek to explore the ways in which theory and practice are interrelated. They introduce a third wave of feminist thinking in education, one that takes account of both global changes to the economy and politics, and changes in theorizing about that world. It is important to emphasize that feminist educational thinking not only shapes how we think about education but what we do *in* education – as teachers, academics and citizens. Thus books within the series not only address the impact of global, national and local changes of education, but what specific space is available for feminists within education to mount a challenge to educational practices which encourage gendered and other forms of discriminatory practice.

Kathleen Weiler
Gaby Weiner
Lyn Yates

Preface

The last few years have seen a great upsurge of writing on boys and men and masculinity, so it should come as no surprise that a contemporary series on *Feminist Educational Thinking* would take up this topic. And indeed one of the contributions made by Bob Lingard and Peter Douglas in the present volume, is that they do address this new set of developments as a phenomenon to be examined as well as taking it as a set of agendas requiring new theories and practices. As they say in their own introduction, the issue of boys and men in the context of discussions about gender and feminism is not a simple or unitary one: it includes engagements *with* as well as engagements *against* feminism, it raises questions about the psychological as compared with the social framing of identities, actions and policies; and it confronts the issue of differences within feminism and feminist agendas.

What Bob Lingard and Peter Douglas have sought to do here is to take up, in the form of a series of essays, some different facets of contemporary developments: developments in theory and popular culture; the different versions of the men's movement; the changing structural arrangements of education; achievement statistics and the 'what about the boys?' debate; and case-studies of programmes for boys in schools. In each of these essays they show the reader very clearly the evidence of change and new developments relating to feminism, men and boys – drawing on examples across many different countries. At the same time, gradually, they begin to draw out some of the tensions, problems and issues the 'man question' poses for feminism: sometimes by its diversionary force and by making things seem other than they are (the achievement statistics debate, discussed in Chapter 4, for example); sometimes by its invisibility (for example, as in Chapter 3, when changes in the organization of schooling are seen as simply about efficiency and as having no gendered implications); and sometimes by the intrinsic difficulty of what needs to be encompassed (what they call the 'recuperative' psychological concerns *together with* the social and political projects for change, a discussion that threads through Chapters 1, 2 and 5).

The book begins with a chapter which should leave the reader with no doubt about the pervasiveness of the boys and men issue as a phenomenon of contemporary (meaning the current decade) life. Bob and Peter draw on examples across newspapers and magazines, television, films, fiction; they track men's conferences and organizations across many different countries; they show above all the cultural salience of this issue at this historical moment. They also, in this chapter, discuss some different emphases within feminism and argue that neither feminism of equality nor feminism of difference adequately deals with the agenda for men. They consider whether their own position should be labelled 'pro-feminism' or 'pro-feminist', acknowledging both theoretical and practical, political, relational elements to this type of questioning.

In Chapter 2, the authors identify various strands of the men's movement, including conservative forms of 'men's rights' alliances, more psychologically-framed (and sometimes religious-framed) movements of male bonding, to movements that self-consciously work as an adjunct to feminism. In terms of some agendas for 'feminist thinking', Bob and Peter discuss in this chapter the difficulty of combining the personal and the political, and the need to attend to the diversity of men.

Chapter 3 is a discussion of the changing shape of the organization of schooling and its gendered effects. This chapter is largely based on developments in Australia, but cites many echoes elsewhere of the trends it notes. It argues that there is at work a 'retraditionalization' of the education workforce: one which is no longer based on an essentialist view that certain jobs are women's work and others are men's prerogatives, but where this same hierarchical output is being produced by an apparently gender-neutral emphasis on 'performativity'. They discuss here too the ways the emotional labour in education is increasingly an unacknowledged burden on women.

In Chapter 4 the writers, in their own words, 'deconstruct' the 'what about the boys?' backlash. In this chapter they bring together a wide-ranging discussion of the types of claims that are being made in the media, and a detailed look at the evidence on achievements. Their analysis provides an excellent case that important evidence of the lack of achievement of many groups (of girls as well as boys) is being written out of the media, and that the disaggregated statistics tell a quite different story from the one being used to feed a 'backlash' climate.

In Chapter 5, Lingard and Douglas discuss some current examples of approaches to programmes for boys in schools. The discussion here is linked very clearly to analyses of different forms of both feminism and of the men's movement discussed in Chapters 1 and 2 of the book. They argue, for example, that to approach sport and physical education for boys through the lens of the 'recuperative' (psychological needs) men's movement would lead to a different set of activities than if these programmes were framed as 'pro-feminist' ones. They also discuss one form of 'pro-feminist' work with boys, the 'boys' talk' programmes, and again point to some difficulties in bridging rational-political and psychological-needs agendas.

The conclusion of this book argues for a 'politics of alliance' between men and feminism, and for the acceptability of both 'strategic essentialism' and 'strategic pluralism' in its repertoire of action. It is a conclusion which does not set out a model, or 'the answer', so much as it lays the grounds for continuing further the sensitive discussion of theory, political and cultural change, and education reform that these essays provide.

Lyn Yates

Acknowledgements

There are many, many people who have contributed to our thinking about men and feminisms in education. Their contributions to our argument will be very evident to them. We would like very much to express our thanks by acknowledging them. Lists of this sort, however, are always dangerous, to the extent that some are inadvertently omitted. We apologize to those who have been omitted and sincerely thank those who are listed for their support.

Jill Blackmore, Leonie Daws, Pam Gilbert, Rob Gilbert, Elizabeth Hatton, Miriam Henry, Ian Hextall, Barbara Kamler, Jane Kenway, Pat Mahony, Lyn Martinez, Daphne Meadmore, Peter Meadmore, Martin Mills, Fazal Rizvi, Judyth Sachs, Roger Slee, Sandra Taylor and Lyn Yates have provided support, intellectual nourishment and friendship for a long period and will see much of their influence at many points throughout the text. Brigid Limerick has also been a catalyst for our pro-feminist theorizing. Allan Luke has been a very supportive head of department/dean during the time of the development of the arguments of this book; he has also always provided intellectual stimulation. Paige Porter offered similar support before him in that role and also contributed to our thinking about pro-feminism. Indeed the Graduate School of Education at The University of Queensland has been a very good environment in which to work and many friendships, particularly those of Don Alexander, Carolyn Baker, John Knight, Allan Luke, Peter Renshaw and Merle Warry have contributed to that situation.

Discussions and working with the members of the gender equity unit within the Queensland Department of Education have been most beneficial, as well as being enjoyable and stimulating. Those who work there – Kay Boulden, Lyn Martinez, Maree Hedemann and Maree Parker – epitomize the very best of the Australian femocrat tradition – intellectually informed, politically aware and strategically smart. Lyn Martinez's writing and thinking about feminisms and schooling deserve to be better known. Eleanor Ramsay, now a Pro-Vice-Chancellor at the University of South Australia, also represents the very best of that femocrat tradition, and has contributed in a most generous way to our development as pro-feminists, as has Linda Apelt.

While we were working on *Men Engaging Feminisms*, we were privileged to have access to two manuscripts in progress: one by Jane Kenway, Sue Willis, Jill Blackmore and Leonie Rennie (now published by Allen and Unwin as *Answering Back*) and the other by Rob and Pam Gilbert (now published as *Masculinity Goes to School* by Allen and Unwin). These two very good studies also contributed to our thinking and in our view represent the very best of feminist and pro-feminist scholarship coming out of Australia.

During the writing of this book, Bob supervised Martin Mills's PhD thesis on Masculinity and Violence. As is usual in most pedagogical relationships around PhD supervision, Bob learnt as much from Martin and his research as vice versa. Those discussions and the reading of Martin's work have contributed to our thinking and to the book. Furthermore, Martin generously commented on the full manuscript and we were able to improve the argument through taking account of his comments.

Teaching a Master's subject on Gender and Education with Carolyn Baker and Carmen Luke was also an educational experience for Bob. The men of the pro-feminist community activist group, Men Against Sexual Assault (MASA), and the women who informed and worked with them, helped Peter develop his thinking around the issues.

Many people have commented on various chapters of the book in draft form. Vicki Crowley and Deb Hayes commented on Chapters 1 and 2 and helped improve their arguments and clarity with hard-headed but encouraging criticisms. Miriam David and Jim Ladwig also provided most useful feedback on those two chapters. Michael Flood provided very helpful and constructive comments on Chapter 2. Discussions with Jill Blackmore and Judyth Sachs contributed considerably towards the argument presented in Chapter 3. Several people commented on what has become Chapter 4 of this book. They are: Kay Boulden, Miriam Henry, Lyn Martinez, Martin Mills, Paige Porter, Eleanor Ramsay and Sandra Taylor. This chapter was also given as a seminar at QUT, Brisbane at the invitation of Anne Hudson-Hickling. These individual responses and those at the seminar helped immeasurably. Ian Hextall, Ron Frey, Martin Mills and Lyn Yates, one of the series editors, read the entire manuscript and were helpfully critical in their readings. Some of the issues were also discussed with Pat Hextall, while Pat Mahony provided ongoing support and critique and invited a presentation at Roehampton Institute of Surrey University from the book.

We would also like to thank Gaby Weiner for asking us to write the book, a request we took as a compliment in itself; Lyn Yates for being very supportive during the time we took to complete it; and Shona Mullen for her ongoing encouragement, support, and indeed, patience, while she waited for us to complete this manuscript. She appeared always to exert the appropriate balance between pressure and support. All the staff at Open University Press have been great to work with.

There are many others who have helped along the way, as well as others who have contributed to our thinking. These include Nick Burbules, Bob Connell, Cameron McCarthy and Leslie Roman. Merideth Sadler made sure the manuscript was in an acceptable state when it was submitted and as is usually the case with much of our writing, Merle Warry did a wonderful editing job. We wish to thank them both most sincerely. Carolynn and Nicholas Lingard have always been more supportive than is warranted during the writing of this book.

1 Men engaging feminisms in education

Men's relation to feminism is an impossible one. This is not said sadly nor angrily (though sadness and anger are both known and common reactions) but politically. Men have a necessary relation to feminism – the point after all is that it should change them too, that it involves new ways of being women *and men* against and as an end to the reality of women's oppression – and that relation is also necessarily one of a certain exclusion – the point after all is that this is a matter *for women*, that it is their voices and actions that must determine the change and redefinition. Their voices and actions, not ours: no matter how 'sincere', 'sympathetic' or whatever, we are always also in a male position which brings with it all the implications of domination and appropriation, everything precisely that is being challenged, that has to be altered.

(Stephen Heath 1987: 1)

Introduction: the focus of the book

This book – *Men Engaging Feminisms: Pro-feminism, Backlashes and Schooling* – is about men's responses to feminist reforms in schooling. As such, it is concerned to document the various masculinity politics which have emerged since the 1970s as feminism has ensured that men are aware that they too have a gender. It outlines the playing out of such masculinity politics in educational systems, in both policy and practice. We use the word 'engaging' in the title because it can mean a close and supportive relationship, but is also used to refer to participation in war and thus when used in conjunction with 'feminisms' seems to pick up on the two ends of the continuum of positions that men have taken in relation to feminisms.[1] We use 'feminisms' so as to indicate the multiple theoretical and political stances that exist today under the broad category of feminism.

Written by two men from a pro-feminist perspective, *Men Engaging Feminisms* seeks to open up a dialogue about schooling and the changing gender order and changing gender relations, while also desiring to contribute to a more equal gender order in the future.[2] The picture painted throughout of men and feminist reforms in schooling is not based strongly enough on an empirical research basis. More research and theorizing are required. An invitation is thus extended to the reader to take the arguments and the research further. We have tried to write a book which will have meaning for educators in Europe, North America, Australia, New Zealand and other parts of the world. In Australia we have both been involved in the politics surrounding issues to do with men and feminisms in education, as well as related policy and academic debates, and worked with programmes in schools for boys concerning masculinity. Despite our Australian location, however, we have attempted to engage a broader literature and where possible, utilize evidence from elsewhere. Given this situation, the essay is the genre in which we have attempted to negotiate a passage through our knowledges and experiences of men and feminist reforms in education. As Wark (1997) has noted:

> What the essayist offers the reader is then not the last word on any particular speciality. The essayist makes introductions. This is why the essayist is a 'friend', someone who can make connections among those with whom the essayist is acquainted. The essay attempts a kind of 'hypertext'. The essayist's judgements are always based on incomplete information. They are an invitation to the reader to pursue a connection further. The essayist doesn't pretend to an overview or synthesis of everything. The essay is rather one particular way of negotiating passages through knowledge and experience.
>
> (Wark 1997: xx)

We thus see the essays in this book as opening up the area under consideration for further research, theorizing, conversations and argument.

Since the early 1990s the issue of men and feminist reform agendas in schooling has become very closely intertwined with questions to do with boys and schooling.[3] Thus, the book also deconstructs the evidence which is usually mobilized in the so-called 'What about the boys?' debate, a debate which, according to Mahony (1996: 1), has 'reached epidemic proportions when viewed from an international perspective'. For example, before the 1997 national election in the UK, the British Labour Party produced a much publicized education consultation paper, entitled 'Boys will be boys? Closing the gender gap' which was purportedly 'about tackling the growing problem of boys' underachievement' (Morris 1996: 1). An inquiry was conducted into boys' education in the New South Wales schooling system in 1994 for similar reasons, as well as because of the negative social consequences of particular practices of masculinity as indicated in boys' bullying behaviour, suspension and expulsion rates, proclivities for 'at risk' behaviours, and so on (O'Doherty 1994). A deconstruction of the data on changing patterns of male/female school performance rejects the essentializing of girls and boys, of young women and young men in that debate. Which boys are we talking about – middle-class boys, working-class boys, Black boys? Which girls are we talking about? Such analysis also rejects the stance of 'presumptive equality' which underpins most 'What about the boys?' calls, an assumption which simply equates females and males as equivalent but different populations (Foster 1996), neglecting the power differentials between them. Some gains have been made by females in respect of retention to the end of secondary schooling, in access to university and in academic performance, but still on a terrain which valorizes what we might call technical rational versions of masculinist school subjects such as the maths and the sciences. Factors other than the feminist reform project, such as the collapse of the female teenage labour market and changes in adult labour markets, have also contributed to these changes. As Chapter 4 demonstrates, these data need disaggregation and nuanced readings, as well as location within historical context.

The contemporary call for a focus on boys' schooling is usually accompanied by the assumption that the feminist reform agenda generally and in schooling specifically has achieved its goals (Yates 1997). When set against the data, this assumption indicates a backlash is at work, particularly if one accepts Faludi's (1991) narrow conception of backlashes as episodic and historical occurrences in response to the perception, correct or otherwise, that 'women are making great strides' (Faludi 1991: xix), with small gains here often read as 'great strides'.[4] There is another backlash element at work if one understands that at the same time as many of the 'What about the boys?' protagonists reject that girls and women are in any way disadvantaged as a group, they are attempting to mount an argument that boys are the new disadvantaged in schooling and that feminism has contributed to this situation. We also know that the conversion of these (limited) educational gains (for some girls) into post-school gains for young women in relation to careers, income and life trajectory are still somewhat limited when compared with the pay-offs for their male counterparts. Furthermore, it is doubtful if girls and women feel any safer now as they go about their everyday and everynight activities than they did in the past. The evidence on schooling also indicates a considerable amount of harassment of girls by boys (and of boys by boys and of female teachers by boys). Despite this situation, there is a way in which for young and successful men and women, educationally and in career terms, there is something of what Walby calls a 'gender convergence' (1997: 2) under way for those from middle-class backgrounds. At the same time, there are economic and life trajectory polarizations between generations of women (Walby 1997) and polarizations among young males, and among young females, as globalization of the economy and a politics of post-welfarism together produce redundant populations and underclasses (Bauman 1997). There is a pervasive insecurity in the population at large, along with a new individualism, which together encourage various forms of backlash against claims of group disadvantage and calls for redress through state policies and targeted funding.

We also demonstrate another form of backlash at work in contemporary schooling (Chapter 3): what we call 'structural backlash' to refer to the way in which the contemporary restructuring of educational systems has re-instated men and new forms of entrepreneurial, rather than older style pater-nalistic, masculinity (Whitehead 1999), at the core of policy making in education. At the same time, teaching has become even more feminized and subject to the gaze of the more masculinized centre through the depredations of a culture of performativity (Lyotard 1984) which emphasizes outcomes and produces a self-surveilling performative self. Middle management – heads of department – and teachers in schools carry the burden of the emotional fall-out of these restructured, leaner and meaner, outcomes-focused educational systems, which make new and increased demands upon the emotional labour (Hochschild 1983) of those (largely women) who fill these positions. A new emotional economy within educational systems and schools is the result. The increased feminization of teaching has also been 'blamed' for the supposed deteriorating performance of boys in schooling. The most extravagant manifestation of this argument has been the description of school culture as 'sissy culture' by one British journalist (Shakespeare 1998) and as the explanation of the (questionable) assertion that boys are falling behind girls in school performance. What is different from earlier episodes of backlash is that this structural backlash has occurred under conditions of formal equality articulated by affirmative action, anti-discrimination, equal opportunity legislation and the like; our analysis of structural backlash argues, however, that the condition of substantive equality between boys and girls, men and women has not been achieved, in schooling or elsewhere. Structural backlash inhibits the potential gains of this legislation, while this legislation itself has become the focus of a sustained politics of resentment, particularly in the United States. Feminisms, including the weakest liberal form, are on the defensive.

The book also documents what has been done about masculinities and boys in school programmes (Chapter 5). These policies and practices are underpinned by different versions of masculinity politics (Connell 1995), stretching from progressive pro-feminisms through masculinity therapy, which focuses in a self-absorbed fashion upon the injuries and costs of masculinity, to reactionary men's rights stances which constitute men and boys as the new disadvantaged. The perspective adopted throughout this book is pro-feminist – a position easier to describe than practise. Pro-feminism sees the need to change men and masculinities, as well as masculinist social structures, while recognizing the hidden injuries of gender for many men and boys. Pro-feminists also support feminist reform agendas in education and more broadly, and at the same time recognize the structural inequalities of the current societal gender order, and of the gender regime within educational systems. Thus a relational conception of gender is assumed and the notion that a focus on boys in schooling of necessity requires a turning away from a concern with the education of girls, is vehemently rejected. We therefore deny the argument that feminist inspired policies for girls in schooling have achieved their goals, while not denying that some limited gains have been made. We do not accept the backlash argument that there is now a 'gender imbalance' with girls outperforming boys, nor the argument that the future is female because of the growth of service sector jobs requiring well-developed communication skills. Rather, we believe the backlash elements of the current call for boys' policies in schooling place the gains for girls, and indeed the whole feminist project in schooling, precariously balanced and under threat. At the same time we acknowledge that those 'toxic' aspects of hegemonic masculinity are danger-ous to boys themselves, as well as to other boys practising different, some-times, marginalized or subordinated masculinities, and to many girls and women. This danger is evident, for example, in the suicide rates for young men, in their risk taking behaviours and in the road toll, in their use of vio-lence and in sexual and other forms of harassment of girls and other boys, including homophobia.[5] In acknowledging the problems with such mas-culinities, however, we are eschewing a competing victims' syndrome (Cox 1996) and rejecting the claim that feminism in schooling has achieved its goals and now it is time for the boys to have a go. We argue instead that a goal of more equal gender relations requires, *inter alia*, a policy and practice focus in education on both boys and girls. We recognize, of course, that post-Keynesian welfare state social disinvestment also fans resentment and the likelihood of such a competing victims' syndrome as the mode for making pressure group claims. In these times of social disinvestment, gender equity (for women) can often be seen as a luxury (Blackmore 1997a: 85).

Pro-feminism requires some brief explication (see Douglas 1994; Connell 1995: 220–4; Flood 1997a; Messner 1997; see also Chapter 2), particularly in relation to the balance between focusing upon the costs of masculinity and support for feminism, and also regarding the question of which femi-nism pro-feminist men ought to be pro. The former tension has been evident in masculinity politics since the mid-1970s, in fact since the presence of feminisms forced men to take a stance in relation to it (Seidler 1994). A focus on men's pain without a structural analysis of inequalities in the societal gender order can easily slip into the self-absorbed seeking of deep essentialist masculinity through therapy, as proposed by mythopoets such as Robert Bly in his bestseller, *Iron John* (1991), and satirized in Hughes's observation that these men 'are off in the woods, affirming their manhood by sniffing one another's armpits and listening to third-rate poets rant about the moist, hairy satyr that lives inside each one of them' (Hughes 1993: 5). Kimmel and Kaufman (1995: 27) have argued that men need to participate more in practices of nurturing and care than running around in the forests together in their underpants: 'We need more Ironing Johns, not more Iron Johns', a sentiment with which we concur. In his most recent book, *Man Enough* (1997), Seidler seeks to take a compromise position which recog-nizes gendered power differentials while at the same time working to redefine masculinities (1997: 3), a position that he argues the *Achilles Heel* project in England took from the early 1970s. Other pro-feminists have recognized the need to understand 'men's pain' and the costs of dominant forms of masculinity (e.g. Kaufman 1994; McLean 1996; Flood 1997b) in an attempt to deal with and counter the worst anti-feminist elements of men's rights and angry white male politics.[6]

The tension between reconstructing masculinities and pro-feminism has been manifest in pro-feminist men's groups. The National Organization for Men Against Sexism (NOMAS), founded in the USA in the early 1980s, supports a pro-feminist and gay affirmative politics, as has done the Men Against Sexual Assault (MASA) group in Australia. Both have sought to change the gender order, humanize men and counter violence against women. The extent to which an organized men's movement is central to effective pro-feminist politics has been debated within the literature (e.g. Connell 1995; Messner 1997; Seidler 1997). Connell argues against the need for a men's movement, while also noting the difficulties of a pro-feminist politics which simply structures itself as the 'men's-auxiliary-to-the-women's movement' (1995: 220). Additionally, while rightfully recognizing the differences among and between men, Connell has noted the idiosyncratic difficulties of a pro-feminist politics which asks men as a whole to exit from their positions of power and give up their 'patriarchal dividend', that is, the benefits they gain from the current gender order. (As an aside, it is often very difficult to see certain men, say some Aboriginal men in the Australian context, or Black underclass men in the UK or USA, as beneficiaries of this dividend.) He also notes the difficulties that this entails for a united men's politics because pro-feminism means men working against men's privilege: 'How can a politics (pro-feminism) whose main theme is anger towards men serve to mobilise men broadly?' (Connell 1995: 221). Instead, he argues for coalition politics of progressive groups, practising a (utopian?) masculinity politics which is 'a politics beyond interests, a politics of pure possibility' (Connell 1995: 243). Messner (1997: 102) in his survey of the *Politics of Masculinities* quotes Kimmel as supporting the counter position – arguing the need for a progressive men's movement. Messner himself supports Connell's stance and suggests 'that pro-feminist activism among men is best accomplished not through a "men's movement" but in schools, in political parties, in labour unions and professional organizations, in workplaces, in families, and through supportive alliances with feminist and other progressive organisations that are working for social justice' (Messner 1997: 102). Having said that, we acknowledge Seidler's point that such an approach can lead to the neglect of the feminist insight that the personal is also the political (Seidler 1997: 4) and hence reinforce the 'cultural homophobia' which suggests that the emotional is feminine (Seidler 1997: 8) and that men need not provide emotional support for other men.

There are a small number of male teachers in schools who adopt the stance suggested by Connell and Messner, the one also adopted throughout this book. Hence we accept Messner's position that in rejecting current manifestations of hegemonic masculinity we might be better placed to work towards a society in which there are more equal gender relations. Our version of pro-feminist politics is thus located within a social justice framework, while acknowledging the contested and historically situated meaning of that concept, as well as the need to cater for difference. Writing in the USA, Messner (1997: 103 ff.) suggests that multiracial feminism might serve as one model for the type of coalition politics Connell has called for. One of *the* contemporary political projects is concerned with working together equality and difference (cf. Fraser 1995; Young 1997). Later in this introductory chapter we consider pro-feminism in relation to feminisms of equality and those of difference. Some of the essays in Kimmel's (1995) edited collection, *The Politics of Manhood*, which cover the debate between profeminist and mythopoetic men's movements, also indicate that there is some possibility for coalitions between pro-feminist men and at least some within the mythopoetic movement.[7]

Contexts of the book

Many of us had the experience at school and elsewhere of learning a new word in vocabulary exercises and then discovering it everywhere we read, almost as if our learning of the word brought its greater use into being. In researching this book, we have had a similar experience: the question of men and feminisms appears to be everywhere, throughout popular culture and the media, as well as the texts of high culture and theory. The same can be said of a perception of masculinity as 'under siege, on the defensive and under reconstruction' (Kenway 1995). And again in relation to men, boys, feminisms and schooling. There has been a 'discursive explosion' (Bordo 1997: 146) about these matters throughout western culture and in a Foucauldian sense, such discourses are both repressive and productive.

For instance, many of the novels we have read recently seem to deal with a politics of masculinity one way or another. Think of Pat Barker's trilogy about the First World War – *Regeneration* (1991), *The Eye in the Door* (1993) and *The Ghost Road* (1995) – which is historicist in the sense that contemporary issues to do with masculinity politics are played out and analysed in an earlier time. Interestingly, tender and caring relations between men are established in the context of the destructive collapse of the social arrangement under conditions of total war; as Barker the author puts it: 'One of the paradoxes of war – one of the many – was that this most brutal of conflicts should set up a relationship between officers and men that was . . . domestic, [c]aring' (1991: 107). Throughout the trilogy, there is also the hint of an intimate relationship between specific masculinities and sexuality in the life of one of the key protagonists, the bisexual working-class officer, Prior. Think of the social theorist and proto politician, David D'Anger, one of the central characters in Margaret Drabble's *The Witch of Exmoor* (1996), who thinks of himself as the 'New Millennial Black British Man' (1996: 21), practising a hybrid, post-colonial masculinity. Again, T. Coraghessan Boyle's American novel, *The Tortilla Curtain* (1995), is concerned with gender role reversals, as well as race politics linked to the globalization of the economy, and the paradoxical pursuit of the American dream by an illegal Mexican migrant couple in Los Angeles who practise traditional gender relations, while the 'successful' American couple with whose lives theirs interconnects, and to which they aspire, practise otherwise; he a sensitive new age man, a journalist on an environmental magazine and responsible for childcare and domestic duties and she a high flying realtor. In almost a backlash fashion, Fay Weldon's quirky novel, *Big Women* (1997b), deals with feminism (in publishing) and also its effect upon men – 'men are people too' – including the often tense and non-communicative generational relations between fathers and sons, wrought by changes in masculinity which have resulted from feminist critiques. Pursuing this men as the new victims line a little further, in an article in the *Guardian Weekly* newspaper on 21 December 1997, Weldon asked if feminism had perhaps gone too far, because boys and men were now in a sorry state, while girl power was triumphant. The Spice Girls as the triumph of feminism!

Contemporary films are also replete with concerns about masculinities, and their relationships with feminisms. The British hit film, *The Full Monty* (1997), is the most recent and one of the best informed in a sociological sense; it deals with the impact of globalization upon working-class men and their masculinities as traditional labour markets have been destroyed and replaced by an entrepreneurial culture which demands a performative self, but not the performative self of all, as indicated by the creation of long-term unemployed and an underclass. The film's screenwriter, Simon Beaufoy, has been quoted as saying the film's success has obscured 'the sadness at its heart: the disenfranchisement of working-class men' (Barber 1998: 23). The Kevin Kline comedy, *In and Out* (1997), has a wonderful scene where the chief protagonist, who is going through an awakening in respect of his (homo)sexuality, practises walking and gesturing on the advice of a 'how to' cassette about 'doing' hegemonic masculinity which demands a particular disciplining of the body. The Michael Douglas character in the 'anti-feminist, proto-resentment' film, *Disclosure* (1994), is 'the great twentieth-century suburban middle-class male victim, flattened and spread out against the surface of a narcotic screen' (McCarthy 1998: 85). Bordo (1997), in her analysis of this screen version of Michael Crichton's best-selling novel, rejects the producer's claim this is 'just a movie, not a polemic', and in contrast notes that 'both the novel and the film read like a litany from the white male hell of contemporary gender politics' (Bordo 1997: 141). As she also argues, pursuit of the question of whether or not a woman can harass a man requires consideration of the structural inequalities, including power, between men and women. The analysis in *Disclosure*, as with much of mythopoetic and men's rights argument, eschews such structural analysis. Instead, they operate from the stance of 'presumptive equality'. A number of contemporary television programmes play on the rise of the 'new laddism' in response to feminism; the British series, *Men Behaving Badly*, is the archetype here. Angry white males have been all over the US media and films since the 1980s. Think of the Michael Douglas angry white male character in *Falling Down* (1992), or the film *In the Company of Men* (1997), which as one critic put it, seems to confirm Germaine Greer's observation in *The Female Eunuch* (1970) that 'Women have very little idea of how much men hate them' (Slattery 1998: 5). We would add, 'some men'.

In quite a different mode, the films of Canadian film maker David Cronenberg ponder the boundaries between old and emergent forms of masculinity and between masculinity and femininity. For instance, *M. Butterfly* (1993) depicts a French diplomat in Beijing who falls in love with a Chinese opera singer to whom he discloses state secrets only to eventually discover 'she' is a 'he', while characters in the controversial *Crash* (1996) transgress the boundaries of hetero- and homosexuality. As Ramsay (1996: 84–5) notes, 'In his films male characters do not colonise, withstand, or overcome the body, the feminine, the irrational, or the unconscious: They collapse into them'.

Current affairs programmes regularly take up the 'What about the boys?' issues in relation to schooling. For example, in October 1995 the BBC's highly rated current affairs programme, *Panorama*, ran a programme entitled *Men Aren't Working*, which contrasted the negative school and post-school experiences of a group of young men with the more positive performances of their female counterparts (see Heath 1999). This programme essentialized males and females, failing to ask which males and which females this phenomenon related to. The influential Australian television current affairs programme, *Four Corners*, ran a much discussed programme entitled *What about the Boys?* in July 1994, which, *inter alia*, articulated the concerns of some feminist mothers with their sons' schooling and which sat in an intertextual relationship with the O'Doherty Inquiry into boys' education in New South Wales.

Newspapers and magazines throughout the western world have been full of articles about the reconstitution and defence of masculinities under dual pressures from feminism and changing labour markets – all amplified by the contemporary condition of uncertainty (Giddens 1994). For example, 'Men must help men, for crying out loud' (*The Australian*, 1 May 1995), 'Why masculinity is for losers' (*Observer*, 29 October 1995), 'Catch Eastwood to study men; academic interest in what it means to be masculine may be turning into a new campus rite of passage in the US' (*Straits Times* (Singapore),

30 November 1996), 'Altered states: the "feminisation of America" is a paradox. It is a triumph of the feminist movement – and a sign of anti-feminist backlash' (*Courier-Mail,* 11 January 1997), 'New women old men' (*Sydney Morning Herald,* 25 January 1997), 'Bourbon, bullets and beer: the blokes' book that kisses PC goodbye' (*The Australian,* 15 July 1997), 'Secret men's business: far from being absent in the cultural world, manhood is everywhere' (*The Australian,* 4 March 1998), 'Law to make men share housework' (*Courier-Mail,* 3 April 1998), 'What's the snag for 90s men: misogynist predator or feminist victim?' (*Weekend Australian,* 4–5 April 1998), 'The descent of men' (*Weekend Australian,* 13–14 June 1998).

With the increasing globalization of culture, many of these articles have been syndicated in various newspapers across the world. Perhaps the best case in point here is an article which first appeared in *The Economist* in the UK on 28 September 1996, entitled 'Tomorrow's second sex', which appropriates de Beauvoir's characterization of women in her feminist classic *The Second Sex* (1952), to refer to the likely future status of men. This article has been syndicated across a huge range of newspapers in many countries and precipitated much debate in men's movement circles. The opening of the article basically summarizes its argument; it suggests that boys are doing worse than girls at school, women dominate jobs that are growing (see Weiner *et al.* 1997 for a critique here), men will not try to do women's work, 'joblessness reduces the attractiveness of men as marriage partners', and without marriage and work men become lawless. In summary, the article suggests that men 'are failing at school, at work and in families' and that this cannot totally be explained by economic changes, rather 'male behaviour and instincts' are involved (*The Economist* 1996: 23). There is much one could say about this article and its arguments, but suffice to say here that the data on male/female school performance, as noted earlier in this introduction and as deconstructed in some detail in Chapter 4, are much more complex than this article suggests. While more women are entering the workforce, male/female wage differentials remain substantial even with the same qualifications, the labour market continues to be heavily gender segmented with women concentrated in sales and service, and career progression between males and females remains disparate and unequal. Apparent male 'lawlessness', and we would add imprisonment rates, can be linked to the economic depredations of globalization which have produced an underclass (Bauman 1997) and 'jobless ghettoes' (Wilson 1997), and a widening gap between the rich and the poor who have become more numerous. We would also reject the essentialist biological reductionism of *The Economist* article with respect to those behaviours which are described as instinctual.

One could draw up a long list of newspaper articles from around the world which also deal with the boys' question in education and the related issue to do with the reduction in numbers of male teachers and the pitfalls they supposedly face. A brief selection of mainly Australian articles will be provided here to give something of the flavour. Concerning boys: 'The trouble with boys' (*Sydney Morning Herald*, 19 August 1995), 'Suspensions from school: boys top the class' (*Sydney Morning Herald,* 27 July 1996), 'How to keep the beast out of the boy' (*The Australian*, 23 May 1997), 'Closed book boys: chapter and verse' (*Courier-Mail*, 4 October 1996), 'Nobody loves us, everybody hates us . . . why today's teenage boys have become pariahs' (*Sydney Morning Herald*, 22 November 1997), 'Boys to men' (*San Francisco Chronicle*, 22 March 1998). The last article quite presciently observed:

> It struck me that the girls I see around school have the latitude to play sports, wear makeup, be tough or soft, smart or silly. They've benefited from a women's movement that has allowed them a wider range of roles. Yet the boys seem stuck in 1950, clinging to stereotypes of the Marlboro Man and James Bond.
>
> (Ryan 1998: 4)

Concerning male teachers: 'Classrooms need men' (*Courier-Mail*, 26 October 1995), 'Men wanted: must be good role models' (*Courier-Mail*, 14 March 1996), 'Men, young turning from teaching, principals told' (*Courier-Mail*, 5 October 1996), 'Men wanted as teachers' (*Sunday Mail*, 13 October 1996), 'It's Goodbye Mr Chips – guys give our schools a miss' (*Sunday Mail*, 12 January 1997), 'Sex traps for men teachers' (*Sunday Mail*, 26 January 1997). These articles contribute to some sort of panic about the low numbers of male teachers, while also documenting the 'sex traps' which keep men out of teaching, particularly in the early childhood domain. This lack is often linked to the prevalence of single parent families (usually headed by a woman). For example, the Queensland Minister for Education was reported as saying: 'In today's society, we've got boys who will never have a male teacher in their school life and, at the same time, don't have a male at home' (*Courier-Mail*, 14 March 1996). The US bestseller, by David Blankenhorn, *Fatherless America: Confronting Our Most Urgent Social Problem* (1996), also articulates a similar, but more strident concern about single female headed families.

We mention all of this because we accept the position that cultural representations of all sorts are both 'productive and generative', not merely mimetic in mode (McCarthy 1998: 87). And as Foucault would have it, discourses are both repressive and productive. McCarthy (1998: 87) notes, 'In this sense, popular culture – the world of film noir and the B movie, of tabloids and the mainstream press – constitutes a relentless pulp mill of social fiction of transmuted and transposed power'. All these cultural forms, he suggests, fulfil 'a certain bardic function, singing back to society lullabies about what a large cross section and hegemonic part of it "already knows" ' (1998: 83), reinforcing their beliefs and working against attempts to alter social patterns of gender relations.

This bardic function is perhaps nowhere more obvious than with the 'backlash blockbusters' (Mills 1997: 11) – a range of books throughout a number of countries which have become bestsellers and which articulate the need for men to seek their true (essentialist) masculinity and which are to varying extents either more or less antagonistic to feminism. Farrell's *The Myth of Male Power* (1993) is probably the most egregious of these, particularly given the transmogrification from his earlier pro-feminist stance. Bly's *Iron John* (1991) is another of these bestsellers and, despite its North American cultural flavour of therapeutic self-help, has been widely influential beyond those shores. Bly's neo-Jungian account of masculinity seeks to reinstate men's traditional role of initiating boys through various rites of passage towards manhood. There is some echo of this position in the contemporary call for more male teachers, particularly in primary schools. The more pertinent questions are which sorts of males providing which sorts of role models, and a recognition that the homosociality of all male environments can reinforce sexist behaviour rather than ameliorate it. Consider here for a moment the culture of all male senior management, football clubs, all boys' schools, male university colleges. Interestingly, Seidler's *Man Enough* (1997), written from a pro-feminist position and rejecting Bly's essentialism and neo-Jungian stance, none the less accepts Bly's call for new ways for boys to become new sorts of men, while also accepting that there is a crisis of masculinities in western societies.

In Australia, the books of psychologist Steve Biddulph – *Manhood: A Book about Setting Men Free* (1994) and *Raising Boys* (1997) – have been extremely successful in a small market, also indicating their bardic function in respect of contemporary confusions and defensiveness about masculinities. Biddulph's *Manhood* echoes some of the essentialist posturings of Bly's arguments when he speaks of the need for men to retrieve the 'repressed memory' of the masculinity of Cro-Magnon man who was 'wise, tough, skilful, nurturing, courageous and in touch with the forces of the universe' (Biddulph 1994: 166). Rob and Pam Gilbert (1998: 34) have described this seeking after a psychic essentialism in prehistorical man as a 'cross between the primitivism of *Planet of the Apes* and the anachronism of *The Flintstones*'. We have found that it is Biddulph's work which Australian teachers who are interested in boys' issues in school have read; this is explicable, given the lack of material in the domain. In Biddulph's favour is that he problematizes masculinity, even if in an essentialist fashion, and he also recognizes the need for feminism. The somewhat more reactionary views of Farrell are articulated by those males in the teaching profession who take an ugly stance on feminist reforms. However, a more common stance is for teachers, including male school administrators, to argue that feminism has succeeded with girls in schools: women and girls have remade themselves since the mid-1970s, there is now a pressing need for men and boys to remake themselves (as one school principal explained to one of us in a recent conversation) and thus there is a requirement now for boys' policies. In this context, the backlash blockbusters appear to offer some 'easy' solutions to very busy educators whose work has been intensified through the performative culture of restructuring and who often require 'quick fixes' on the run, as it were. And more theoretically sophisticated and practical accounts such as Salisbury and Jackson's pro-feminist book, *Challenging Macho Values: Practical Ways of Working with Adolescent Boys* (1996), do not make the bestseller lists anyway, probably for the same reasons that Biddulph's do. Further, some excellent and sophisticated feminist accounts (e.g. Walby 1997) also appear to overstate the case concerning girls catching up with and outperforming boys in education. As we shall demonstrate in Chapter 4, we need to disaggregate the achievement data here – which girls and which boys are we talking about? – as well as consider the importance of the insights of feminisms of difference in terms of the valorization of masculinist school subjects.

Of course, there have been instructive and populist accounts of backlash written from a feminist perspective which have been successful sellers, for example, Faludi's *Backlash: The Undeclared War Against Women* (1991) and French's *The War Against Women* (1992). However, in the contemporary political context they perhaps speak more to the converted, and French's account is exceedingly pessimistic about any gains for women which have resulted from the second wave of the women's movement.

These usages of backlash, particularly Faludi's, have been equated with post-feminism (Brooks 1997: 2) and turn on a particular reading of 'post' as implying 'after'. In contrast, Brooks (1997) argues that post-feminism can refer to positive developments within feminism, with 'post' here being read as critical engagement with second wave feminism and a challenge to any universalist assumptions about the character of women's oppression implicit in such feminism. In contrast, the former usage deals with the backlash against formal legislative gains for women in the west, which clearly inhibit further steps towards substantive equality between men and women. The latter, Brooks's account of post-feminism, seeks an engagement between feminism and other contemporary 'post' theories, namely poststructuralism, postmodernism and postcolonialism, an anti-essentialist politics of difference within a feminism pursuing both equality and difference. This has complicated feminist politics and (as discussed below) precipitated questions about which feminism pro-feminist men ought to be pro. This situation has also probably weakened the strength of the opposition to backlash as defined by Faludi and complicated the politics around desired feminist policies and practices generally and specifically in education (cf. Yates 1993). We do not want to slip into the trap here of blaming feminisms for backlash; clearly backlash in Faludi's terms is about attempted reclamation by men of their social power which they had not really lost anyway. Women in society and girls in schools have made small gains, which have been overread as indicating the end of the male dominated gender order as we know it. However, in the Australian educational policy context, there is probably a way in which the 'uneasy alliance' between economic rationalism and gender reforms (Henry and Taylor 1993) narrowed the policy focus to getting more girls into maths and science and that some gains for middle-class girls in that respect have been read as indicative of the success of the feminist reform project in schooling.

Perhaps the strongest backlash in contemporary politics is the claim by some men that they are now a disadvantaged group requiring earmarked state policies, at the same time as there has been an attack upon the very notion of group disadvantage when applied to women, ethnic minorities and so on. This fits within the broader context of what McCarthy (1998) has called the contemporary politics of resentment and is perhaps best exemplified in the emergence of a white, working-class male militia movement in the USA, which wrought its worst in the horrific Oklahoma bombing. However, it is evident elsewhere in the rise of new racisms and in the emergence of an anti-feminist men's movement. It is also manifest in the most pungent anti-feminist elements, usually associated with men's rights, of the 'What about the boys?' refrain in education.

The rise of backlash politics must be seen in the context of the depredations of a globalized economy, the social disinvestment of post-Keynesianism and contemporary 'manufactured uncertainties', the problems created by human interventions in both the social and natural worlds (Giddens 1994). Wark (1997) has argued that the confluence of what he calls 'social rationalism' (a society which rewards only those with the right credentials irrespective of ascribed features to do with gender and race) with economic rationalism (which ensures a bleak employment future for many) together form the backdrop to the politics of resentment and backlashes of various types, for example, emergent backlash national chauvinisms and new racisms, and anti-feminism. Additionally, feminism in all its various forms has challenged men. As Kimmel (1996b) has suggested, since the early 1970s feminism has changed very considerably the expectations and experiences of women. Women have demanded equality with men in all spheres of life or alternatively their reconstitution to better meet the needs of all. Those changes have affected, as well as challenged, men in different ways. At the broadest level, Kimmel observes, feminism has ensured the widespread recognition of gender as a central organizer of social life. That recognition has also 'granted' men a gender; no longer are men, or rather European middle-class men, the silent voice of theory and progress, but rather their interested and partisan positionality in contemporary political and social debates has been laid bare by this recognition, as has the very construction of the selective tradition of history.[8] The male voice is yet another standpoint, but one infused with power. Simone de Beauvoir in *The Second Sex* showed how the equation of male experience with human experience *per se* 'othered' women and feminists have challenged the practice of regarding women as other. As Bordo (1997: 192–3) puts it: 'As cultural critics, feminist theorists have produced powerful challenges: to dominant conceptions of human nature and political affiliation, to norms of scientific, philosophical, and moral reason, to ideals of spirituality, to prevailing disciplinary identities and boundaries, and to established historical narratives'.

Kimmel also argues that feminism has been an important element in the vastly increased participation of women in the paid workforce. Other factors have been at play here too, including changes in contraceptive and reproductive technologies and changes in the structure of the economy and labour markets. This change has also affected work opportunities for men, as well as relationships between men and women within the workplace. A confluence of factors has ensured widespread insecurity regarding jobs, while the move to more service oriented economies in 'western', 'postindustrial' societies in the context of globalization, has witnessed the collapse of many traditional working-class male jobs, a scenario which was the focus of *The Full Monty*. Middle-class men have also been challenged to some degree by 'career women'. Writing about the US situation Kimmel and Kaufman (1995) have noted:

> Although . . . economic, political and social changes have affected all different groups of men in radically different ways, perhaps the hardest hit *psychologically* were middle-class, straight, white men from their late twenties through their forties. For these were the men who not only inherited a prescription for manhood that included economic autonomy, public patriarchy, and the frontier safety valve, they were also men who believed themselves entitled to the power that attended upon the successful demonstration of masculinity.
>
> (Kimmel and Kaufman 1995: 18, original emphasis)

Feminism has also led to a greater demand by women that men take a fairer share of domestic labour and childcare. In their Australian research, Bittman and Pixley (1997) show how a vast majority of men accept that there ought to be equal participation by both sexes in domestic labour and childcare, but that the actual reality is a far cry from that commitment, with women still bearing the greatest burden of all aspects of domestic labour. They thus speak of this aspect of male/female relationships within the home as one of 'pseudomutuality' (Bittman and Pixley 1997: 81), where the acknowledgement of the ideal of mutual responsibility for domestic labour does not translate into practice. None the less, there has been some challenge to men here, if more at the level of ideology than practice.

The final change wrought by feminism, according to Kimmel, is the demand by women for reconstituted intimate and sexual relationships with their partners, as well as women's reconstitution of their own sexuality and sexual pleasures. Giddens in *The Transformation of Intimacy* (1992) has written about this latter change in some detail, documenting the emergence of what he calls 'plastic sexuality' and 'pure relationships', as sexual experience has been emancipated from reproduction and potentially from the 'rule of the phallus' (Giddens 1992: 2) in conditions of greater male/female equality in intimate relations. Women's demands for the equalization of relationships inherent in the transformation of intimacy also have potential implications, Giddens argues (1992: ch. 10, 'Intimacy as democracy'), for public forms of democracy and the organization of the economy. (In contrast, Bauman (1997: 147) suggests that such transformations of sexuality are both an 'instrument' and 'consequence' of 'privatisation' and 'marketisation' of society dependent on the perpetual creation of new desires.) Now, one might be able to debate the extent to which this women (and feminist) driven transformation or even revolution, as Giddens suggests it is, has actually occurred in sexual relations, but there is clearly veracity in the observation that some changes have occurred in these respects. These also provide a challenge to men.

Thus Kimmel (1996a, b) and others are suggesting that there are both structural and individual, public and private, challenges to the various forms of dominant or hegemonic masculinity. As already noted, the British film hit, *The Full Monty*, deals with many of these challenges to contemporary masculinities in a humorous, telling and analytical, yet perhaps depressing fashion. The resonances of the film with contemporary audiences – its bardic function – is indicative of the efficacy of Kimmel's observations regarding changes, or more aptly demands for changes by women, and their impact upon men, set against the 'manufactured uncertainties', as Giddens (1994) has called them, of the contemporary postmodern world and rapidly globalizing economy. Issues concerning men and feminism generally, and more specifically men and feminist reforms in schooling, are thus also framed by a melange of political, economic and cultural changes contingent upon globalization and related challenges to the modernist political project. (The assumption that human interventions in the social and natural world would necessarily be a good thing and lead to progress.) These changes provide some pointers as to desirable goals for gender reform in schools, which focuses on both boys and girls in a relational rather than zero-sum fashion, and considers the role for men in such reforms; these ideas are taken up in Chapters 5 and 6. Considerations of how men have engaged with feminist reforms in schooling are now related to issues about boys' schooling. Mills (1998a: 149) quotes a gender equity policy officer working in the State Education Department in Queensland who indicates that all the queries that she is now getting from schools in respect of gender equity are to do with boys. Recently, one of us interviewed a large number of school principals in Queensland as part of a research project on restructuring and asked a question about gender equity. About half those interviewed, when talking about what was happening in their schools, read 'gender' simply to mean issues around the education of boys, an indicator of the sea-change we are talking about here.

In the next section we address the difficulties for men in attempting to produce coherent theoretical and practical responses to feminist critiques of men and masculinities. More specifically, we focus on pro-feminist and men's rights stances in relation to the important debate between feminisms of equality and difference. Neither position is found to be capable of meeting the challenge of bringing together the ideal of social equality with the pressing need to positively acknowledge difference. While feminists have been beset with much the same difficulties, they are compounded for men by their privileged position in analyses of social power.

Feminisms of equality and difference

The theoretical and practical implications of the debate between feminists of equality and feminists of difference play themselves out in curious ways in the context of masculinity politics. The complexities of this debate find little purchase in the essentialist and avowedly apolitical and economically naive mythopoetic position, as well as in the supposedly atheoretical and equally, though differently, essentialist biblically oriented position of right wing Christian groups, such as the Promise Keepers in the USA. However, two of the more self-consciously politically active strands of the men's movement, pro-feminist and men's rights, do engage this debate, though in quite different forms. For instance, the liberal humanist rhetoric of those sections of the men's rights position that is not explicitly conservative and anti-feminist would seem to imply some theoretical sympathy with feminists of equality and their struggle to gain the same opportunities that men have in the public sphere. On the other hand, one might expect the development of the pro-feminist position, from its initial acceptance of radical feminism in the 1970s, to ally itself with contemporary feminists of difference in their pursuit of a genuine subjectivity for women based on a cultural expression of femininity that has privilege and respect analogous to that of the masculine, on whose values the public realm is currently premised. However, these alignments have limited validity, the situation being complicated by the men's rights penchant for the notion of difference and the specificity of men's experience, and pro-feminists' difficulty in coming to terms with these notions and subsequently relying on the social construction of gender in order to justify its call for men to change in line with feminist critiques of masculinity.

The fundamental aim of the liberal humanist philosophy of feminists of equality and men's rights is to provide equal access to social power to all members of a community. For feminists this implies a social structure which is sexually neutral and within which it is in principle possible for equality to exist. Claims are therefore made for the right to equal opportunity in areas such as education, the workplace, the judicial and political systems. Demands motivated by more specifically women-centred concerns such as maternity leave are also cast in sex-neutral terms, which consequently include the rights of men to paternity leave. However, issues such as parental leave also raise the dilemma of how to incorporate women's traditional responsibilities in the private sphere into public life. Within the terms of liberal philosophy two options present themselves: either men enter the private sphere and share responsibility for domestic labour and childcare to overcome the problem for women of the 'double-shift' (Bittman and Pixley 1997), or domestic labour and childcare must themselves enter the public realm and be placed on the market. Given the majority of men's reluctance to adopt the former strategy and the economic reality of double income families, it is not surprising that childcare centres have proliferated since the late 1970s – representing the public commodification of a formerly private sphere activity. The marketing of the body and its needs and desires could also be interpreted as instances of the increasing tendency for traditionally private concerns to become commodities in the public sphere. In a similar way concerns over issues such as domestic violence, sexual harassment and relationship breakdowns have entered the judicial realm. This has fuelled a response from men's rights groups who have sponsored strong political action for reform to divorce laws, child custody and maintenance provisions which attempt to address a perceived bias against men in family law issues, as well as counter-charges of the physical abuse and sexual harassment of men by women. What we see, then, is the playing out of tensions previously confined to the private sphere in the public realm as women have gained more access to its institutions and procedures.

However, the liberal strategy of equality of access to public resources has also exposed some of the anomalies of this approach. For instance, the use of the 'battered wife syndrome' in cases where a woman has killed her male partner after years of chronic physical abuse involves the acknowledgement that women's ability to defend themselves might not be fairly assessed under a humanist judicial system which does not easily recognize difference. Sexual difference can therefore be a mediating factor even in situations where liberal humanist principles are supposedly utmost; or put in another way, a recognition of sexual difference (at least) may be necessary if the principles of liberal humanism are to be put into practice. But given that many of the inequalities that feminists struggle against are based on conservative notions of sexual difference and sex-appropriate social roles for men and women, it is not surprising that the notion of sexual difference has been tainted with charges of 'essentialism' and/or 'biologism'. Instead the more fluent notion of gender difference and the concomitant distinction between sex and gender that has been a central element to feminist theory since the early 1970s has provided the theoretical justification for the strategies of social reform and re-education which have carried the liberal feminist agenda. While pro-feminist men have accepted the theoretical basis of the sex/gender distinction and supported feminist reforms, men's rights groups have argued that the power expressed through the private and public spheres are different but complementary, and stressed that what women lose in the public they make up for in the private realm (with men in the reciprocal case).

> What you need to understand is that since feminism denies the existence of complementary role behaviour that was functional and had aspects that were mutually beneficial to both sexes, they are then able to construct a social model whereby a ruling gender autonomously oppressed a subservient gender. It is this view that is played out in our legislatures and courts.
>
> (National Coalition of Free Men (NCFM) homepage 1997:
> 'Organisational history')

The reliance on sex-role theory by men's rights authors enables oppression to be interpreted as the result of over-rigid sex-role requirements which affect both men and women, hence the assertion that men need to be freed 'from the notion that as a class they *oppress* women any more than women as a class *oppress* them, or than society in general *oppresses* both sexes through stereotyping' (NCFM homepage 1997: 'Philosophy'). The liberal humanism of the men's rights perspective seems, therefore, to adopt a position that men and women are 'equal but different', with equality and difference being distributed across the public/private distinction in a manner which implies that one receives no more social privilege or priority than the other. However, sex-role theory has been consistently criticized for more than a decade on a number of fronts. Most pertinent to the current discussion is the criticism that it evades and blurs the reality that social power is not equally distributed among the private and public spheres, and that it is therefore invalid to assert that women are no more oppressed than men. For instance Carrigan *et al.* (1985: 581) argue that the 'sex role literature fairly systematically evades the facts of men's *resistance* to change in the distribution of power, in the sexual division of labour, and in masculinity itself', implying that it is in men's interests to resist women's push into the public realm in order to retain their privileged status in that sphere of social life. So even though a liberal humanist ethic pervades the rhetoric of both men's rights and feminists of equality, there is a divergence in their theoretical perspectives which pivots around their respective definitions of social power: men's rights arguing that power is complementary and distributed across the private and public realms; and feminists arguing that social power rests predominantly in the public sphere and therefore seeking equal access to that power for women. In terms of the often used metaphor of the 'social body' which is used to describe societal structures, we find the sex-neutral social body of feminists of equality opposed to the sexed social body of the men's rights position. This same distinction is found between the two broad feminist categories of equality and difference, though certainly not in a way which would give succour to either feminists or men's rights groups.

The tensions between these two feminisms can be characterized by questions as to whether it is possible and/or even desirable for women to occupy the public sphere on equal terms with men. For instance, Gatens (1996) argues that the structure of the public sphere has evolved under the assumption that its participants have male bodies, due in part to the fact that it has been historically a predominantly male preserve.

> Specifically, it is a sphere that does not concern itself with reproduction but with production. It does not concern itself with (private) domestic labour but with (social) wage labour. That is to say that liberal society assumes that its citizens continue to be what they were historically, namely male heads of households who have at their disposal the services of an unpaid domestic worker/mother/wife.
>
> (Gatens 1996: 64)

In being defined in opposition to the traditionally female private sphere, the public realm offers women who seek equality within it the opportunity to at best become equal to men, thereby either denying their own corporeal specificity or being forced to juggle their private and public responsibilities. According to Gatens, this situation does not take into account 'the specific powers and capacities that women have developed in their historical and cultural context' (1996: 64) that are not esteemed in a public realm constituted in terms of the powers and capacities of men, but which must be acknowledged if the present and future enhancement of women's lives are to be appropriately founded. While these arguments may seem to concur with the men's rights position, the lines of agreement are superficial and the occasional appropriation of them by men's rights advocates are based on misunderstandings and/or ignorance of their deeper import. For feminists of difference, social power rests in the public sphere – a masculine domain inhabited and defined by men in opposition to the feminine private sphere and in the absence of women. For men's rights advocates, social power is distributed across the private and public spheres in a complementary fashion, and so even though women have a right to equal access to the traditionally masculine public realm, they cannot claim to be any more oppressed than men, or more to the point oppressed *by* men, as both social spheres have their own privileges and disadvantages – different but equal in their complementary relation to one another.

The charges of essentialism and/or biologism which accompany the recognition by feminists of difference of the different powers and capacities of male and female bodies are the result of interpreting the notion of sexual difference through the theoretical frame of the sex/gender distinction. While there are feminists who do argue that there are essential differences between men and women which should be affirmed and celebrated, the sex/gender distinction inevitably associates any reference to women's corporeal specificity with an understanding of the body as a biological given, tracking the dualistic conceptions of mind/body and culture/nature.[9] A choice must therefore be made as to which side of the dualism will be given priority: the mind and culture, or the body and nature. For feminists of equality, it is mind and culture that are prioritized in accordance with liberal humanist principles that posit a universal conception of human nature which denies any meaningful significance to the notion of sexual difference. Gender as a social and cultural construction which overlays the mute body (as identified with sex) assumes that the body is passive and neutral in relation to the formation of consciousness which is itself conceived as a 'blank slate' upon which are imprinted cultural mores as socially constructed. Along with the assertion of conscious individual agency, this theoretical position justifies the 'degendering' strategy of attempting to alter the cultural and historical specificity of our experience as sexed (or in this case gendered) beings, by consciously changing the material practices which are thought to influence the construction of gender.

Masculinity and femininity are consequently viewed as rather arbitrary sets of behaviours which have no essential connection with the male and female bodies which act them out. Gender is therefore an artifice over a generic human subjectivity which pre-exists its social and cultural contexts. It is this conception of subjectivity that feminists of difference (such as Gatens) object to, arguing that subjectivity emerges within a network of historically and culturally specific social forces which cannot be abstracted from the bodies they work through. In seeking to theorize outside of the strictures of the mind/body and culture/nature dichotomies, the body is understood not as part of an immutable nature and external to culture, or as 'taken up' by culture, but as *lived in culture*. The body is therefore accorded a history which takes into account the relations between bodies and their situations. For instance, Gatens argues that factors such as 'diet, environment and the typical activities of a body may vary historically and create its capacities, its desires and its actual material form' (1996: 68). So the body of a female Olympic athlete may in fact have more in common in terms of its actual form and capacities with the body of a male peer than that of another woman whose life is lived solely as a mother/wife/domestic worker: here the biological commonality of female bodies cannot account for their individual specificities. This allows us to think beyond the strict dichotomy of male and female bodies towards a recognition of a multiplicity of bodies expressing a multiplicity of differences, and therefore beyond the dualistic configuration of sexual difference that marks patriarchal social relations. In granting bodies a history, it is therefore possible to acknowledge the traditional associations between the public sphere and the male body and the private sphere and the female body, without positing an arbitrary connection between the male domination of sociopolitical power and the evolution of the public realm, or resorting to essentialist explanations. It also enables the recognition that it is not merely masculinity that has been valorized in our culture, but the inherence of those powers and capacities that have been traditionally associated with masculinity in the male body. As Gatens (1996) observes:

> The problem is not the socialisation of women to femininity and men to masculinity but the place of these behaviours in the network of social meaning and the valorising of one (the male) over the other (the female). Such valorisation is at the core of the representation of relations of sexual difference as relations of superiority and inferiority.
> (Gatens 1996: 15)

This helps us to understand that there is more involved in attempting to reformulate social relations than simply advocating women's access to the public sphere, as female embodiment will remain a barrier to women's full and equal participation in sociopolitical life as currently constituted.

The liberal humanist position of feminists of equality fails to offer a framework which recognizes this situation, based as it is on the assumption of an underlying universal human subjectivity. Difference (whether it be sexual, racial or whatever) is interpreted as an artifice that acts as an obstacle to the recognition of a common humanity which exists outside of the effects of history and culture – a strangely essentialist side-effect which rather than being capable of accepting diversity must always slide back into a unitary conception of the sameness of the one human body. This entails a singular logic which reduces difference from a multiplicity to one privileged term and its other, or lack – a situation Luce Irigaray has termed the 'economy of the Same'. The privileged term within patriarchal social structures is always the masculine, and so femininity is defined in terms of what it lacks in relation to masculinity rather than affirmed for itself. In this context we can understand the notion of 'complementarity', as used by men's rights supporters, as a hierarchical relation within which the private sphere identification with the feminine is a complement *to*, rather than *with*, the masculine public realm, wherein sociopolitical power rests. It is possible for men's rights to consistently hold such a position only as long as they adhere to the framework of sex-role theory which is unable to deal with either the inequities inherent in the expression of social power, or conceptions of the body other than as the mute biological basis for the expression of socially prescribed sex-specific stereotypes. However, the men's rights account of sexual difference is often inconsistent, commonly using the terms sex and gender in uncritically analogous ways in conjunction with notions of stereotypes and social conditioning, as well as falling back on essentialist notions such as 'male energy' in order to justify and affirm men's traditional behaviours in the face of feminist criticisms. It is not possible, therefore, to accurately characterize the men's rights position beyond its use of sex-role theory in a theoretically untidy alliance with confused notions of sexual difference which tends to psychologize sociological problems of social inequities, and a tendency to espouse liberal humanist principles of equality which are undermined by the lack of a coherent macropolitical framework and a casual flirtation with sexual difference.

While the self-definition of the pro-feminist position denotes its support of the general feminist goal of reshaping patriarchal social relations, it does not give any indication as to which particular formulation of that goal it supports. However, this decision is to some extent made for it by the limitations imposed by the theoretical options taken up, as well as the need to maintain a 'male positive' stance which accepts feminist critiques of men and masculinity, while leaving a space beyond guilt and recrimination for men to actively work to change the structure of sexual relations. In adopting notions of the construction of gender within the general framework of the sex/gender distinction, pro-feminists are able to criticize men's oppressive practices, but leave open possibilities for social and personal change by placing the blame on the construction of masculinity and its association with power and dominance. This avoids essentialist accounts of the social and political relations between men and women by asserting the mutability of social relations, an important aspect of the pro-feminist position, given that an assertion of sexual difference is often equated with men's inability to change.

However, given that the theoretical framework of pro-feminists as presented here is largely an adaptation from the liberal humanist stance of feminists of equality, the same criticisms of that position from feminists of difference apply. While the more liberal-identified pro-feminists may be comfortable with the assumption of a sex-neutral social structure within which equality between the sexes is in principle possible, the more radical elements of pro-feminism are concerned to support feminist arguments which assert that the public sphere as currently constituted is inherently masculine and oppressive to its 'others'. As discussed above, such an assertion is untenable unless the corporeal specificity of female and male bodies and their respective identifications with the private and public spheres are acknowledged. Typically, pro-feminist frameworks continue to utilize the distinction between materiality and ideology to make sense of the distinction between men and masculinity. Hearn and Collinson (1994) provide a good example:

> One powerful way is to see men as existing and persisting in the material bases of society, in relation to particular social relations of production and reproduction; in comparison, masculinities exist and persist as ideology, often in their surface form in terms of elements of production and reproduction.
>
> (Hearn and Collinson 1994: 104)

Connell's attempts at devising a systematic social theory of gender with an emphasis on the sexual politics of masculinity (or more accurately masculinities) at least acknowledges this challenge by recognizing the relation between difference and dominance and in introducing the notion of 'body-reflexive practice' (see for instance Connell 1987, 1995). However, his theory is ultimately hampered by the same structural commitments: its reliance on the notion of gender, the primacy of consciousness and its ability to alter social practices, and a sharp culture/nature distinction intended to foreclose on the possibility of biological determinism. 'Body-reflexive practice' is concerned with how the body is 'taken up' by culture, how it is 'addressed by social processes and drawn into history' (Connell 1995: 64), rather than with the historical and cultural specificity of bodies and how their powers and capacities have provided the basis for the expression and maintenance of patriarchal social structures. Even though Connell gestures towards difference and calls for the re-embodiment of men as part of a strategy of degendering, whose aim is what he refers to as 'gender multiculturalism', the body remains sex-neutral and cannot carry the task assigned to it. It would seem, then, that the differences which pro-feminists such as Connell are keen to acknowledge cannot be accommodated within a theoretical framework committed to the sex/gender distinction, tied as it is to the singular logic of the masculine 'economy of the Same', which constructs difference as a deficit.[10]

However, the model supplied by feminists of difference cannot be straightforwardly adopted either: where feminists are concerned with creating a space within which women and femininity can have their own voice, pro-feminists seek to dismantle the universality of the masculine subject – socially and personally – so that there is room for such a space to exist. Other theoretical options therefore need to be explored by pro-feminists, and the possibilities offered by poststructuralism seem promising. Poststructuralist theory attempts to think beyond the monological pronouncements of the modernist tradition from which liberal humanist notion of the sex/gender distinction stems in order to posit a *positive* difference – one that can speak for itself. However, this approach too can fail to recognize the importance of the body if it takes as its focus 'the fluidity of identity' or 'mobile subjectivities' at the level of cultural scripts, again dismissing the stubborn and irreducible role that bodies play in the formation of identities and subjectivities (Gutterman 1994: 234). Difference must therefore be seen to be embodied, speaking for the specificity of a body or collective of bodies. The theoretical strategies of poststructuralism seek to dismantle identities and universalist notions such as truth and justice, even as they recognize the necessity of both, adopting a pragmatic rather than ontological approach to such structures (e.g. Yeatman 1994). There has been concern among feminists and advocates of other oppressed groups that such strategies also spell the dismantling of emancipatory politics, given the latter's reliance on a common identity from which to make claims for social justice. However, it is possible to reconfigure notions such as social justice in a manner capable of operating across a multiplicity of domains, and feminists such as Butler, Gallop, Spivak and Yeatman have argued, in different ways, in favour of the pragmatic approach offered by poststructuralism: Butler (1990: 148) from the position that the foundationalist frame of identity politics has the paradoxical effect of constraining the subjects it seeks to liberate; Gallop (1982: xii) arguing that identity must be continually assumed *and* called into question; Spivak (1992) maintaining that a persistently critical stance must be held in tandem with the strategic use of essentialism (cf. Fuss (1989: xi) who argues the question ought not to be 'is this essentialist?' but rather 'what motivates its deployment?'); and Yeatman (1994) arguing a similar position concerning universalism:

> If universalism does not reside in what is, or even in what could be, but lies instead in a political, contestatory space that opens up in relation to existing wrongs and those who contest them in the name of equality, it is clear that this has radical implications for the nature of political vision.
>
> (Yeatman 1994: ix)

These theoretical arrangements seem to offer useful possibilities for a pro-feminist politics which seeks to recognize difference, while simultaneously wishing to question the legitimacy of the hegemonic structures which have been founded upon a masculine politics of domination – attempting to work together a politics of difference with a politics of equality.

The book and its contents

This chapter has introduced the pro-feminist approach of this book, as well as its contents, which deal with contemporary masculinity politics, structural backlash and the implications for men and women working in educational systems, the contemporary concern for boys' achievements in schooling, and emerging programmes for boys in schooling and the role of men. All of these issues, along with consideration of how men have engaged with feminism in schooling, are contextualized against an increasingly globalized economy, a more parsimonious post-Keynesian state, pervasive insecurity generally and in respect of jobs and careers – conditions which provide fertile grounds for resentment and backlash.

More specifically, Chapter 2 examines men's responses to feminist reforms and criticisms of men and masculinity by providing an overview of contemporary masculinity politics using four categories: pro-feminist, men's rights, mythopoetic and conservative. In the broadest sense, the first of these may be seen to be progressive and supportive of feminisms, while the other three may be described as 'recuperative' or seeking to regain, defend or maintain more traditional modes of masculinity and manhood. This is followed by a brief discussion of feminist responses to contemporary masculinity politics, which are often suspicious of the 'men's movement' in general, though responsive towards those elements of it that have supported women in their struggle for more equitable social relations. What then are or should be the political implications of feminisms for men? The next section of the chapter attempts an answer to this question by acknowledging that no single and definitive response is possible or desirable due to the diversity of feminist positions and the complexity of the issues involved. The most constructive approach may therefore be to seek a multiplicity of alliances with women across a broad spectrum of issues, which disperses the solidarity of men in a manner antithetical to the broad men's movement aim of rebuilding a community of men. Finally, the situation in schools is surveyed with respect to how these issues have been played out in the context of the 'What about the boys?' debate and some consideration given to the stance of men in schools in regard to feminist reform agendas.

Chapter 3, 'Structural backlash and the emergent emotional economy in restructured educational systems', considers the ways in which the restructuring of educational systems, as one element of the restructuring of the state, has reinstated a new gender segmentation within those systems. The policy producing centre has become more male oriented, while those who deliver the new policies – teachers as state professionals – are even more likely to be women than was the case before the restructuring. This is not to suggest that educational systems were not always heavily gender segmented prior to the recent changes, but rather to argue that in conditions of formal equality between the sexes, restructuring has reinstated new forms of, and a more heavily, gender segmented workforce within education. At the centre, where system-wide education policy is produced, the new performative, managerialist state has demanded a new more masculinist entrepreneurial form of management (Whitehead 1999), with similar pressures upon school principals, who now have to be 'bilingual', speaking both new managerialist and old professional discourses (Gewirtz *et al.* 1995). This has reduced the attractiveness of such positions to some women because of their resistance to managerialism. Accompanying the restructuring has been a new emotional economy which devolves a lot of stress down the line, which is then borne on the backs of women teachers, who because of the very nature, as well as discursive construction, of teaching as a job, results in work intensification. This requires emotional labour (Hochschild 1983) which hides the gap between the felt emotions in such situations and those demanded by the new performative culture – impression management – as the self becomes commodified in the need to be seen to perform (Blackmore 1997b). Across the educational system at all levels, women carry the burden of much of the emotional fall-out which accompanies continual restructuring, and which is central to the emotional labour resultant from the reculturing which is inherent in restructuring. What is different from the previous situation is that structural backlash has occurred simultaneously with the move to formal equality for women through the enactment of equal employment opportunity, anti-discrimination legislation and the like. As Yeatman (1990) perceptively observed, the new managerialism was the Trojan Horse which ensured that managerialist requirements took precedence over the political demands of the feminist reform agenda and which better met the demands of market liberal ideology which required a less expansive state both in policy and funding terms.

In Chapter 4 we document and analyse the data on male/female performance in schooling and we demonstrate that the media representations of such a comparison as indicating that all girls are now out performing all boys is false and fails to recognize differences among girls and among boys. The evidence seems to suggest that girls do much better as a whole on standardized literacy tests (in primary school) than boys, but this is probably not news anyway, and that there are clear differences and more complexities if one begins to consider the intersection of social class with gender, race with gender and so on. With respect to standardized numeracy testing (in primary schools), there appears to be very little difference between male and female performance as a whole, yet there is much less female participation in maths subjects in upper secondary schools than is the case for boys – the latter fact not much remarked upon these days. In secondary school performance, some middle-class girls appear to be challenging the dominance of their middle-class male counterparts in high status subjects. However, curriculum choice is still heavily gender segmented (as is teaching), with girls choosing a broader range of subjects at the post-compulsory levels than boys. The picture is thus much more complex and differentiated than that usually represented by the media. However, the chapter notes the 'bardic function' served by such media representations and the way in which the poor performance of working-class boys is often utilized to maintain the argument about all girls succeeding in schooling and all boys failing, which is a long way from the actuality. The narrower range of extra-curricular activities of boys, when compared with girls, is noted. This chapter also considers the question of appropriate goals of gender reform in schooling, goals which take account of both boys and girls within gender relations.

Chapter 5 addresses the manner in which the 'What about the boys?' debate has been taken up in a practical manner in schools. Prior to the controversy which emerged in the early 1990s over boys' perceived academic underachievement in school, an issue taken up in detail in Chapter 4, profeminist men had during the previous decade been developing and facilitating programmes for boys to complement the feminist-inspired focus on girls in schooling. These programmes were often concerned with issues such as the construction of masculinity, homophobia, violence against women, and sexual harassment, and sought to respond positively and constructively to feminist criticisms of men and masculinity. In contrast to the pro-feminist approach of working with boys in schools within a gender equity framework, anxiety over boys' underachievement has provided a forum for the recuperative strands of contemporary masculinity politics to advocate separate boys' strategies, arguing that boys' interests will not be served within a policy framework that has evolved through a feminist concern for girls that characterizes masculinity as pathological and boys as a 'toxic problem' for girls. The differences between these two approaches are examined in more detail, first in relation to the role played by sport and physical education in the reproduction and/or reconstruction of masculinities, and second with respect to specific programmes for boys in schools via a discussion of a typical pro-feminist programme, a recuperative response to it, and the type of strategies the latter advocate. Some brief consideration is also given to the desirable position of male teachers in such pro-feminist programmes.

Chapter 6, the conclusion to this book, draws the argument presented throughout to a close, while also hoping to open up further discussion, debate, theorizing and research agendas. As argued throughout, men have had to, either to a lesser or greater extent, engage with feminisms since the 1970s. Such responses stretch from the pro-feminist through to the more reactionary and recuperative men's rights stance. Men have engaged with feminism in schooling across a similar spectrum. The rise of a concern with boys' issues has reframed men's responses to feminist reforms in potentially reactionary ways which seek to constitute both boys and men as the new disadvantaged. However, as with all discourses, the 'What about the boys?' refrain can be reclaimed towards the goal of establishing gender equity policies and practices within a social justice framework which work towards more equal gender relations and a more socially just gender order (Mills and Lingard 1997). This will require men to engage with feminism in education in different pro-feminist ways, acknowledging both feminisms of difference and those of equality. These issues are taken up in the concluding chapter and considered in the light of a 'Boys in Education' programme being implemented in a high school in a provincial city in Queensland, Australia.

Notes

1 We acknowledge our debt to Stronach and MacLure (1997) here where they utilize 'engagement' to refer to a relationship between educational research and postmodernism. They state: 'Engagement is a doubled kind of opening – it can be a commencement of war, or an announcement of marriage' (1997: 10).
2 There are a number of things we need to say about pro-feminist and pro-feminism. Brod (1998) has discussed whether or not there ought to be a hyphen in these terms and suggests that this is more than an orthographic debate. As Brod notes, pro-feminist came into use to describe men who supported feminism because these men believed that only women could be feminists and for men to

call themselves feminists was simply another example of male appropriation. However, Brod (1998: 207) argues that the hyphen in both pro-feminist and pro-feminism leaves men too distanced from feminism. We support the hyphenated usage mainly for orthographic and historical reasons. There are other debates here: bell hooks (1984: 17–31) argues a distinction between feminism and feminist. We understand how pro-feminism encourages a reading which is indicative of support for the theoretical or political project of feminism(s). Pro-feminist appears to be acknowledging support for particular feminist women. We acknowledge this distinction, but have used pro-feminist as a descriptor of men who support feminism, among whom we count ourselves, while also pointing out that we are supportive of feminist women who are working for gender justice in educational systems and schools. Both Vicki Crowley and Deb Hayes alerted us to these debates.

3 Yates (1997: 338) provides a nice encapsulation of the dominant contemporary story about the successes of feminism in schooling for girls in relation to retention and numbers doing non-traditional subjects, and the supposed need now to focus on boys because of their 'retention rates, learning difficulties, delinquency, suicide rates and general self-esteem'. This story is reproduced at the top of Chapter 4.

4 For a sophisticated analysis of the shortcomings of this definition of backlash see the essays in the Roman and Eyre's (1997) edited collection, *Dangerous Territories: Struggles for Difference and Equality*. See the essay by Jill Blackmore in that collection for a good account and analysis of anti-feminist backlashes in Australian higher education. Blackmore also documents the media creation of a generational conflict between feminists as another element of and supplementing backlash. In Australia, Helen Garner's bestselling *The First Stone* (1995), a 'fictionalized' account about an actual sexual harassment case at Ormond College, Melbourne University, where she criticizes the young women involved for going to the police about sexual harassment, played into this generational conflict, as well as being a backlash account of sorts against feminism. For a sustained critique of Garner's work, see the edited collection by Mead (1997) *Bodyjamming: Sexual Harassment, Feminism and Public Life*. Julie McLeod (1998) has written an interesting essay review of the Roman and Eyre volume in which she is critical (both theoretically and politically) of the concept of 'backlash' because of its oversimplified action/reaction account of history and because it fails to acknowledge differences among women. She is also critical of the idea that there is one single coherent backlash.

5 We acknowledge here that suicide among young men (and also among young women) is often about sexuality. Schools ought to play a role in working against homophobia and supporting different sexualities. (See Epstein and Johnson (1998) to understand the ways schools currently work in relation to sexualities and the way they might work otherwise.) Sedgwick (1993: 1), writing about the situation in the USA, notes the horrendous situation whereby gay and lesbian teenagers are two to three times more likely to attempt suicide than other teenagers and that up to 30 per cent of teenage suicide victims are likely to be gay or lesbian.

6 The concept of men's pain requires some focused theorizing. See the work of Flood (1997a, b, c).

7 For an account of the arguments of that book, and Kimmel's pro-feminist history, *Manhood in America* (1996a), and a consideration of their relevance to contemporary debates about masculinity and schooling, see Mills and Lingard (1997).

8 Sandra Harding's work on the *Racial Economy of Science* (1994) and on the question of whether or not 'science is multicultural' has been very important in opening up these issues – *Is Science Multicultural?* (1998).

9 See, for instance, Daly's *Gyn/Ecology* (1978: 109–12). There also exists a curious parallel in the mythopoetic readings of sexual difference produced by both women and men in their respective honouring of the 'eternal essence' of femininity and masculinity.

10 For a fuller discussion of this issue see Douglas (1996).

2 Contemporary masculinity politics

I will define as 'masculinity politics' those mobilizations and struggles where the meaning of masculine gender is at issue, and, with it, men's position in gender relations. In such politics masculinity is made a principal theme, not taken for granted as background.

(Bob Connell 1995: 205)

Introduction

A feature article in a Brisbane (Australia) newspaper (*Courier-Mail* 11 January 1997: 27) bewailed the 'feminization of America' as the beginning of men's 'new role as the second sex', appropriating de Beauvoir as had the much published *Economist* article referred to in Chapter 1. According to the *Courier-Mail* article, due to the efforts of feminism women are now 'the sex *primus interpares*, first among equals, in politics, business and the media', inasmuch as they are targeted by all three because of their propensity to change allegiances more than men who are more conservative and loyal, apparently making women a much sought after group by those interested in pursuing swinging voters and consumers. Whereas Hillary Clinton is quoted as suggesting that the term 'feminization' might better be rephrased as 'maturing of politics' or the 'humanization of society', the article argues that women's 'obsession with safety and security' elicits a new 'soft focus' from marketing strategists in which 'hazy emotional appeals' replace 'hard, rational arguments', leading to an over-regulated and 'wishy-washy' society in which the manly virtues of self-responsibility and risk-taking are abrogated. It is not that men have not been concerned with issues such as caring for their wives and children and elderly people, rather that the traditional 'collaborative effort of male providing and female nurturing' is being subverted by the 'collectivization of womanly wiles', leading to a situation in which 'society might increasingly appear to men as a cynical rip-off'. Add to this a concern that 'women might be better suited to the information-age economy' due to their superior communication skills, and we have a scenario where 'the modern world might be one in which men quite naturally under-perform women' – hence the fear of men becoming the second sex.

This *Courier-Mail* article is significant to the issues to be discussed in this chapter in a number of ways: it gives voice to the belief that feminism has succeeded to the point that it is now men who are disadvantaged; it illustrates that men are genuinely feeling marginalized and confused with contemporary social, cultural and economic developments; it displays men's willingness to blame women for their perceived predicaments; and it demonstrates men's generally poor understanding or ignorance of contemporary feminist analysis. On this latter point it is interesting to note the article's spurious appropriation of 'difference feminism' (specifically that of Carol Gilligan) to support its claims. What this situation points to is the difficulty involved in developing a coherent theoretical framework within which women and men may work together towards the political aims of a more 'gender-just' society. The issue is not simply that feminism might not speak adequately for men, but more importantly that macro-scale analyses such as those arguing for women's oppression as a 'class' cast too coarse a theoretical net to satisfactorily capture the complexity and inconsistencies of the micropolitics of the everyday, face-to-face interactions of many people. These anomalies as they present themselves to students, teachers, parents and school administrators make it difficult to successfully hold the line from a macropolitical perspective through to policy initiatives and eventual implementation in schools. And while more fine-grained analyses of gender relations such as those offered under the rubric of poststructuralism may more effectively capture these complexities and inconsistencies (see Brooks 1997; McLeod 1998), they have the disadvantage of requiring more complicated political positions which the state may find too awkward to deal with, rendering political action at the community level susceptible to being out of step with the broader policy frameworks. It is with these issues in mind that this chapter sets out to outline men's responses to feminist inspired reforms since the late 1960s.

Men's responses to feminisms

Throughout western societies there is a widespread reassessment of the role of men and the constitution of masculinity. In Australia, New Zealand, Europe, Scandinavia, North America and South Africa, this reassessment has been most visible through the work of academics, political activists, men's groups, therapists and writers, and spans a range of positions from what might be termed the recuperative (attempting to recapture men's traditional social roles) to the progressive (looking forward to the constitution of a new diversity of masculine expressions and more equal gender relations). Most attempts at specifying these positions tend to converge on broadly similar categories. For instance, Connell (1995) distinguishes between masculinity therapy, the defence of hegemonic masculinity, gay liberation and exit politics; Throop (1996) mentions the mythopoetic, feminist men, fathers' rights, men's rights and Christian men's movements;

Clatterbaugh (1997) identifies conservative, pro-feminist, men's rights, mythopoetic, socialist, gay men, African American men, and the evangelical Christian perspectives; while Messner (1997), utilizing the three reference points of institutionalized privileges, the costs of masculinity and differences among men, speaks of the Promise Keepers, the mythopoetic men's movement, men's liberation, men's rights activists, pro-feminist men of both radical and socialist persuasions, and racialized masculinity politics. Drawing from each of these categorizations, the following discussion on men's responses to feminisms will proceed under the following headings: men's rights, pro-feminism, masculinity therapy, and conservative.[1] This grouping unfortunately omits as a distinct category the perspective provided by gay men, the most significant and radical response to conventional masculinity of all the categories chosen. However, given that the discussion here is focused specifically on men's responses to feminisms, we attempt to encapsulate the diversity of gay men's responses in these four categories. It should also be stressed that as with any categorization, the four perspectives presented here do not accurately represent the complexity of the blurring and crossovers that occur between them.

Men's rights

> Sexism is discounting the female experience of powerlessness; the new sexism is discounting the male experience of powerlessness.
>
> (Farrell 1993: 196)

Emerging from the 'Men's Liberation' movement in the early 1970s, men's rights groups tend to adopt a liberal humanist perspective which posits a symmetry between men's and women's social positions predicated on the belief in a post-feminist era – hence their concern with sexism against men and with the anti-male character of contemporary western societies. However, some elements of the men's rights position are far more conservative than liberal, and represent an overtly anti-feminist agenda that seeks a return to traditional roles for men and women. These views are expressed in American journals such as *The Backlash!* and *Liberator*. An informative caricature of the more liberal components of the men's rights perspective can be drawn through a brief sketch of Warren Farrell's political trajectory. Farrell served on the board of directors of the National Organization for Women (NOW) in the USA for three years in the mid-1970s, and since 1990 has been on the board of the National Congress of Men and Children (NCMC). Initially viewing the feminism of the 1960s and early 1970s as 'a voice for human rights' (Williamson 1985: 322), Farrell now perceives feminism as pursuing the interests of women alone. The evolution of his views can also be guessed at through the titles of his books: *The Liberated*

Man (1975), *Why Men Are the Way They Are: The Male–Female Dynamic* (1986) and *The Myth of Male Power: Why Men are the Disposable Sex* (1993). We see here a move away from an alignment with feminism in the early 1970s to a position critical of feminists who argue that women are oppressed by men, yet still somewhat accepting of feminist perspectives deemed egalitarian or liberal.

Carrigan *et al.* (1985: 580) in a review of 'books about men' found that much of the 'men's movement' literature of the 1970s believed that men stood to gain from women's liberation through opportunities to overcome over-rigid sex role requirements from which oppression, both women's and men's, derived. We see here a theoretical reliance on sex-role theory which is still prominent in men's rights rhetoric, though often considerably influenced by a recourse to sociobiology as expressed through references to men's 'nature' or genetic/hormonal predispositions. As a result, analyses of the relations of power that exist between men and women tend to be individualized, arguing that social power is equally distributed between men and women (or even that women have more power than men), and denying that the public sphere dominance of political and economic structures that men enjoy gives them any advantage over the power that women yield in the private sphere. Any references to problems such as violence against women and gays, which are explained by pro-feminists as a result of power differentials, are placed in the context of claims that men and women assault each other at equal rates and that violence is not only endemic, but also socially sanctioned in arenas such as war.

The 'psychologizing' of these issues led to the early men's liberation literature interpreting feminist critiques as a desire for women to break free from restrictive sex-roles, a situation supposedly analogous to that of men in that both sexes were assumed to be oppressed in a similar fashion – the culprit being outmoded and suffocating sex-roles. It was argued that what was needed was a modernizing of masculinity, and possibly even a move towards the utopia of androgyny. Networks of men's consciousness-raising groups were formed in the UK, USA and to a lesser extent Australia, and were comprised largely of heterosexual white middle-class professional men responding to emotional fallout from confronting feminist critiques (often from close friends, wives and lovers) of men and masculinity. From these groups germinated the perspectives of pro-feminist, men's rights and masculinity therapy, and despite their subsequent divergence towards the late 1970s as major differences in approaches emerged, all have continued to advocate the benefits from men learning to relate more closely to one another and (to varying degrees) of overcoming rigid and restrictive masculine norms.

The contemporary men's rights perspective concerns itself with a range of issues which seem to be organized around the premise that men are subject to expectations which discriminate against them psychologically, socially and legally. Such issues include fathers' rights and associated law reforms related to divorce and child custody and maintenance arrangements, circumcision, men's health, and opposition to feminist-inspired legislative reforms, such as those designed to address sexual harassment and affirmative action. While not feminist in its approach, the more liberal elements of the men's rights position cannot be classified as explicitly anti-feminist either. However the more conservative sections of men's rights certainly are, blaming feminists (or 'feminazis') for most of the ills these men claim as their own. For instance Clatterbaugh (1997: 72) cites a *Seattle Times* article which quotes the editor of *Backlash!* as advising women to 'Get over it! Because the real victims today are men!' (Houtz 1995). In general, though, men's rights operates within a framework which fits easily into existing economic and political structures, providing a challenge to traditional notions of masculinity and femininity without a thoroughgoing critique of the social organization within which they are defined and lived out.

A number of texts have informed and influenced the direction of men's rights politics: Herb Goldberg's *The Hazards of Being Male: Surviving the Myth of Masculine Privilege* (1976) and *The New Male* (1979); Warren Farrell's *Why Men Are the Way They Are* (1986) and *The Myth of Male Power* (1993); an edited collection entitled *Men Freeing Men: Exploding the Myth of the Traditional Male* (Baumli 1985); while the more recent *Fatherless America* (Blankenhorn 1996) seems to have struck a significant chord within men's rights circles. The general position put forward in this literature argues that in conforming to traditional masculine expectations men block their emotions, thereby distancing themselves from other men and ruining positive father–son relationships, are ignorant and negligent of their physiological and psychological needs, become violent towards women and other men, and lose their spontaneity and playfulness through the harness of work and responsibility. There is an emphasis placed on building a community of men and coming to terms with why men act as they do rather than condemning them for their deeds, often explaining their behaviour as 'hardwired' (for example men's sexual arousal and aggressiveness). Many feminist arguments are rejected as being sexist, counterproductive to social change, and derided for perpetuating negative images of men. For instance, the notions of male privilege and power are rejected on the grounds of men's lower life expectancy, their higher rates of disease, suicide, incarceration, accidents, alcoholism and drug abuse.

> By what perverse logic can the male continue to imagine himself 'top dog'? Emotionally repressed, out of touch with his body, alienated and isolated from other men, terrorized by the fear of failure, afraid to ask for help, thrown out at a moment's notice . . . when all he knew was how to work . . . The male has become an artist in the creation of many hidden ways of killing himself.
>
> (Goldberg 1976: 181–2)

In fact men's rights advocates in the late 1990s commonly cast society as anti-male in that there is supposedly little left that is 'male affirming' after thirty years of women's empowerment and men's cultural degradation and legal, social and economic disempowerment. A central theme of Farrell's *The Myth of Male Power* is men's 'disposability', pointing to high rates of workplace fatalities, denial of access to children after divorce, and military obligations. However, there is the belief that both men and women suffer in analogous ways from limiting sex roles – hence the maxim: 'For every women's issue there is a men's issue because of the historic nature of our complementary roles' (NCFM homepage 1997, 'History'). But none the less it is also argued that women have been more successful than men in overcoming their imposed limitations and so it is now men, more so than women, who need to be 'liberated' from their 'provider role'. There is therefore a refusal to blame men as a class for either women's predicaments or for social ills in general. While conservative elements of the men's rights position overtly describe themselves as a 'backlash' to feminism, their more liberal counterpart's self-proclaimed commitment to 'the true equality of both sexes and to the liberation of both sexes from their traditional roles' (Clatterbaugh 1997: 89) make it problematic to describe the men's rights position in general as nothing more than a backlash against feminism.

Pro-feminism

> Many of us have lost male friends over our antisexist politics – for the simple and terribly complex reason that we just could not abide a friend's sexism any more. There seem to be two untenable options: affiliation and assimilation with men, just falling in with men on men's terms; or separation and estrangement, self-defined isolation. Neither option seems to hold out any long-term promise or possibility; at least to my knowledge, neither really works.
>
> (Stoltenberg 1988: 190)

As mentioned above, pro-feminist and men's rights perspectives originated in the men's liberation movement of the early 1970s. Although the trajectories of both groupings have been coloured by feminist debates, it is pro-feminist men who have responded most directly and favourably to feminist critiques of patriarchal social structures and masculinity. Where men's rights groups have remained wedded to sex-role theory and notions of hardwiring, pro-feminists have taken a broader perspective and accepted the dimensions of power that feminists argue operate at social and personal levels in relations between men and women, masculine and feminine. While both perspectives perceive their positions to be 'anti-sexist', pro-feminism does not view sexism as a symmetrical relation as do men's rights advocates, arguing instead that the fundamental social inequities between men and women prohibit such a correspondence. Men's political role is therefore to work towards a 'gender-just' society via a feminist informed personal and collective redefinition of masculinity.

The differences which emerged among men's groups in the mid-1970s in the UK and USA led to the formation of self-defined groups of 'men against sexism' whose members were largely from radical middle-class milieux with allegiances to the political left and personal relationships with feminist women. Segal (1990: 284–5) reports that around this time in the UK there were between 20 and 30 such groups exploring ways to live which were less oppressive to women and gay men by being sensitive to their experiences and needs. There was a tendency for these groups to see themselves as a 'men's auxiliary to the women's movement', becoming involved in childcare, providing crèches at women's events, supporting feminist demands for abortion rights, reading feminist literature, holding discussions in the presence of feminist monitors, and working alongside rape crisis centres and women's shelters in attempting to change the behaviour of violent men. These groups were also critical of the more mainstream men's movement, arguing that their self-absorption led to a political complacency which ignored issues of race and class and failed to confront patriarchy. There was a tension in pro-feminist groups, however, over how to balance the dual agendas of personal and broader political change – of how to rid individual men of their sexism while also working collectively in an attempt to dismantle patriarchal social structures. Seidler (1991) reflects this tension in recounting his own experiences at this time as part of the editorial collective of the London-based anti-sexist men's magazine, *Achilles Heel*.

> As men we often felt guilty for being oppressive to women. We were offered the idea that we could deal with this guilt if we struggled hard against sexism or put all our energies into supporting the women's movement.
>
> (Seidler 1991: 19)

Seidler expresses here the general tendency of the time to regard masculinity as essentially oppressive to women, which left little room for the exploration and redefining of different forms of masculinity. One option which did seem politically appropriate was the alternative offered by gay liberation. Seidler recalls that in the London men's conference of 1975, 'there was a strong challenge from gay men arguing that men should make the political choice to be gay, since otherwise we were colluding in supporting the oppressive norm of heterosexuality' (Seidler 1991: 19). While pro-feminist groups are explicitly 'gay and bi-affirmative' in the sense of calling for an end to homophobia and all forms of discrimination based on sexual orientation, most of their members at this time were (and remain today) heterosexual. However, a combination of the radical feminist argument that heterosexual sex was oppressive to women and the gay assertion that mainstream heterosexual masculinity contributed to the oppression of sexual minorities led many men to experiment with the arrangements of their sexual/personal lives. Closer emotional and physical intimacy with men and open relationships with their female partners were seen as politically positive developments. However, many of these experiments failed due to the overestimation of the transformational power of conscious and rational decisions, and the concomitant underestimation of the depth of libidinal and emotional investments men had in their more traditional patterns of relationships.

A similar scene was played out in the USA and is well represented by an edited collection of essays, *A Book of Readings for Men Against Sexism* (Snodgrass 1977).[2] In a brief analysis of these essays, Carrigan *et al.* (1985: 575–6) point to: their acceptance of radical feminism as a theoretical basis and with it the totalizing logic that all men are misogynists and oppress women; the guilt that runs through the essays; the authors' admissions of past and present sexism; and a tendency towards effeminism.[3] The first Men and Masculinity Conference in the USA took place in 1975; these annual gatherings led to the formation of a national organization whose aim would be to 'provide for positive alternative masculine roles which are non-oppressive, and to oppose sexism' (National Organization for Changing Men (NOCM) in Clatterbaugh 1997: 43). Initially called the National Men's Organization, and then the National Organization for Changing Men, the National Organization for Men Against Sexism (NOMAS) constitutes the largest and best organized pro-feminist men's network internationally, and from 1979 published the magazine *Changing Men: Issues in Gender, Sex and Politics* (initially *M. Gentle Men for Gender Justice*).

NOMAS defines itself as 'an activist organisation supporting positive changes for men under the principles of pro-feminism, gay and bi-affirmative, anti-racist and working to change the qualities of men's lives' (NOMAS homepage 1997: 'Statement of Principles'). These principles provide a framework for pro-feminist groups generally. For instance in the early 1990s the Australian network of pro-feminist groups, Men Against Sexual Assault (MASA), adopted what were then the three principles of NOMAS: pro-feminist, gay affirmative and male positive, as did the Australian pro-feminist quarterly magazine *XY: Men, Sex, Politics*. The principle of gay and bi-affirmative expresses a commitment to addressing homophobia and heterocentrism, as well as an acknowledgement of the contribution gay activists and theorists have made and continue to make to the redefinition of masculinities and the relations between them. Carrigan *et al.* (1985: 589) remark in their review of the genre 'books about men' that the sophistication of gay critiques of masculinity far surpassed other contributions, bringing to the fore the plurality of masculinities and arguing that sexuality was just as, if not more, important as gender as a category for social analyses. Gay liberation had an early association with radical feminism as both challenged the dominance of hegemonic masculinity and heterosexuality; however, the alliance faded as both radical feminism and gay liberation pursued issues that were not always compatible, though of more immediate concern to their respective constituencies (Connell 1995: 217–18). More recently, though, some gays and lesbians have forged affiliations politically through their responses to the HIV/AIDS issue, theoretically through their contributions to queer theory (see Sedgwick 1990, 1993), and culturally in working together to organize events such as the Sydney Gay and Lesbian Mardi Gras. While gay men's challenge to pro-feminist heterosexual men has always been taken seriously, at least at the level of rhetoric, pro-feminist groups remain predominantly heterosexual, a reflection of the degree to which the political agendas of gay and straight pro-feminist men remain somewhat divergent. None the less, queer theory has made us aware of the 'enduring incoherence' (Sedgwick 1993: xii) of both gender and sexuality, and gay, bi and straight pro-feminist men do work together in addressing issues such as men's physical and sexual violence towards women, children and other men, including hate crimes against gays.[4] Organizations such as Men Overcoming Violence (MOVE) and the Oakland Men's Project in the USA, the White Ribbon Campaign in Canada, and MASA in Australia (Pease 1997) actively encourage men to accept responsibility for their violence and work to end it. There is always, however, a difficult line to tread between maintaining a critical stance towards masculinity as informed by feminisms, and the goal of enhancing men's lives which seems to demand in practice an acknowledgement of 'men's pain' – a central concern of masculinity therapy and men's rights perspectives.

A common theoretical solution to this problem among pro-feminist writers is the notion of 'men's contradictory experience of power' which Kaufman (1994: 142), for example, describes as a 'strange combination of power and powerlessness, privilege and pain'. The social power and privilege that accrue to men in general is accompanied by an alienation from their emotional selves and the people around them. In times and places where masculine social power goes largely unchallenged, the privileges that flow from its practice outweigh the existence of personal alienation to the extent that it does not become an issue for men. However, the impact of economic restructuring and feminism has shifted the balance of men's experience of social power towards a keener sense of their personal alienation.

> Men's alienation is our ignorance of our emotions, feelings, needs, and of our potential for human connection and nurturance. Our alienation also results from our distance from women and our distance and isolation from other men . . . Our alienation increases the lonely pursuit of power and emphasizes our belief that power requires an ability to be detached and distant.
>
> (Kaufman 1994: 150)

Masculinity itself is interpreted as a form of alienation then, which implies some concept of self to be alienated from. Given Kaufman's reliance on the sex/gender distinction and the construction of gender framework, it is not surprising that an asocial and ahistorical subject makes its presence felt. This presence is clear in pro-feminist arguments that assert the need for men to redefine their masculinity in order to express their 'true selves' or 'inner natures'. This theoretical position enables the positing of power relations between men and women and among men themselves as a source of gendered oppression, as well as allowing a notion of masculinity as fundamentally hierarchical and structured by relations of power. However, while this approach does enable men's power and pain to be explained within a common framework, it does not allow for a meaningful consideration of the corporeality of men's pain *and pleasure* as this is experienced through the bodily expression of social power; nor can it if any credence is to be given to the criticisms of the sex/gender distinction from feminists of difference, such as Gatens (1996), which were discussed in Chapter 1. The powers and capacities of men's bodies have developed through men's domination of social power, and though certainly not immutable, it is important not to ignore the pleasure as well as the pain that men experience through the expression of social power. Pointing out the costs of power does not automatically negate the benefits, and it will not be easy to convince men in general that the enactment of traditionally feminine pleasures, which at present are not as privileged as the masculine, will provide them with the same pleasures they have already. So while the pro-feminist perspective is more deeply concerned with developing a thoroughgoing theoretical framework within which to work than other responses to feminisms, it is left with the dilemma of which feminist theory to align itself with, and how to combine a macropolitical perspective with the need to appeal to individual men whose experiences may not be effectively captured by such theories.

Masculinity therapy

> Is there something good, important and distinctive about the experience of maleness itself? Something that can produce energy that is not oppressive but rather creative and life giving – and recognizably male? A deep masculine that men can find in themselves and justly celebrate.
> (NCFM homepage 1997: 'It's Good to be a Man')

Where the pro-feminist perspective has had some difficulty in coming to terms with how to deal with 'men's pain', masculinity therapy has thrived.[5] Its appeal is related to the absence of any attempt to develop a macropolitical framework, preferring to focus on individual men and their relations to masculinity, thereby seeming to address more directly and personally those experiences of powerlessness and emptiness that many contemporary men claim as their own. What is interesting here is that even though male-centred perspectives such as men's rights and masculinity therapy argue that feminism does not speak to men's experiences, the ability of men to express dissatisfaction and concern with their situations has grown since the late 1960s, coinciding with the advent of this most recent wave of feminist activity and gay activism. So while 'mainstream' men may complain that their social position has been eroded by these and other cultural shifts, it seems to have also given them the opportunity and facility to voice their concerns – an opening previously denied by the strictures of traditional masculine expectations.

As with the two perspectives discussed above, masculinity therapy developed from the early men's liberation groups as a distinct concern emerged for the men involved to explore their 'inner lives'. Initially motivated by a desire to confront their individualized sexism as a way of transforming broader relations between men and women – the personal is the political – the intervening years have witnessed an increasing number of men becoming solely concerned with the personal, ignoring the political dimensions of masculinity. (In contrast, Seidler (1997) suggests that pro-feminists have a tendency to ignore the politics of the personal while emphasizing structural politics.) The masculinity therapy scene is now dominated by co-counselling, twelve-step and recovery groups, as well as a range of activities influenced by the mythopoetic movement which has spread from the USA to other western countries. Therapists, counsellors and 'men's leaders' facilitate a range of workshops, retreats and discussion groups for men who tend to be predominantly white, middle class and middle aged. This clientele differs from those of the pro-feminist groups such as MOVE and EMERGE (a Boston based men's counselling service for perpetrators of domestic violence), in that these men are mostly referred for counselling to address a history of violent behaviour and/or sexual abuse, often both as victims and perpetrators.

The mythopoetic movement gained prominence in the 1980s with the message spreading initially through an informal network of groups and individuals via the circulation of interviews and short essays. For example, an interview with Robert Bly conducted by Keith Thompson entitled 'What men really want', which was published in the *New Age Journal* in May 1982, proved to be extremely popular, being copied and circulated around the English speaking world. By the early 1990s mythopoetic journals such as *Wingspan* and *Journeymen* had appeared, building upon the popularity of the public lectures and publications of men such as Robert Bly (*Iron John* 1991), Sam Keen (*Fire in the Belly: On Being a Man* 1991) and John Rowan (*The Horned God* 1987).[6] Deeply concerned with 'personal growth', the theoretical framework for the masculinity therapy offered through mythopoetic circles derives from Jungian notions of archetypes that are revealed symbolically through inherited stories, myths and rituals. These archetypes represent deep and pervasive psychical patterns which extend through time and across cultures, created and maintained through an interaction between our collective unconscious and society. Masculinity and femininity, as archetypal patterns, coexist in both men and women, though the essential differences between men and women mean that they have different significance for the two sexes. All people begin life 'whole' but are wounded through life and thus lose their unity. Nevertheless, by exploring the archetypes deep within our psyches we can heal ourselves and restore our wholeness as mature men and women, though the processes of healing and the rituals involved differ for men and women and must be undertaken in single sex groupings (Clatterbaugh 1997: 96–103). For instance, Bly emphasizes the importance of a community of men and the mentoring of boys and young men by their 'elders', advocating five stages in male initiation: bonding and separation from the mother; bonding and separation from the father; the meeting with the male mentor 'who helps a man rebuild the bridge to his own greatness or essence'; apprenticeship to the Wild Man or Warrior; and 'the marriage with the Holy Woman or the Queen' (Bly 1991: 182). Here Bly argues the necessity for a boy to separate from the feminine for a time and be nurtured and initiated into manhood by other men until he has grown into an appreciation of the 'deep masculine';[7] only then is he capable of entering into a mature and balanced relationship with women.[8]

Bly (1991) argues that patriarchal social structures injure both women and men, wounding and preventing us from developing into the wholeness of our mature selves. However, he sees feminism as a mixed blessing in that it has brought about a reassertion of the feminine which has been a positive force for women and even for men to the extent that it has allowed men to explore the feminine side of their natures and thus helped them to become less violent and aggressive. On the negative side though, feminism has also tended to suppress the masculine, confusing fierceness with hostility and therefore repressing the Wild Man in men who represents their male vitality (Clatterbaugh 1997: 103–6). Bly has spoken of the contemporary 'soft male' as unhappy, lacking in energy and with no energy to offer – a swing from the 'compulsive masculinity' of the 1950s to an overemphasis on the feminine which has left men vague, indecisive, troubled and ineffective. In trying to gain strength through women they have not realized that female energy and feminine archetypes are not appropriate to men's nature, and so they must now seek to reconnect with their own male energies. However, Bly lays the blame not only on women (especially mothers), but also on older men who are failing younger males by not providing them with the guidance into manhood they require.[9]

Conservative

> When appraising the real power of the sexes, it is difficult to conceive
> of a measure less pertinent . . . than the number of male Senators and
> millionaires. Most people enjoy their real gratification . . . in the domes-
> tic and sexual areas, where female power is inevitably greatest.
>
> (Gilder 1973: 12–13)

> it is men who make the major sexual sacrifice. The man renounces his
> dream of short-term freedom and self-fulfilment in order to serve a
> woman and family for a lifetime.
>
> (Gilder 1986: 32)

While the three perspectives discussed so far all derived from the early 1970s
men's liberation movement, which was a direct response to the changes
being wrought by feminism at the time, the conservative position might be
characterized by its lack of response to feminism and its explicit anti-feminism. As defenders of the dominance of patriarchal social structures and traditional sexual relations, there is no explicit masculinity politics, but rather
a persistent call to traditional patterns of social relations in order to maintain the fabric of civilized society. The conservative agenda seeks to maintain
and restore what is (supposedly) 'natural' in human relationships – the
essential differences between men and women as imbued by their male and
female natures, and the primacy of the family as the foundation of any social
organization. The strength of the conservative strand of masculinity politics
is therefore not to be found in the cogency of its arguments, but in the familiarity, and thus the supposed inevitability, of what it promotes.[10] Rather than
being atheoretical though, conservatism operates through the medium of
'received wisdom' and commonsense propositions which carry the weight of
unreflected social experience behind them – a theoretical position in its own
right, even if inconsistently and poorly enunciated.

Curiously, the conservative position agrees with the early radical feminist
criticisms of men as innately aggressive, violent, destructive, competitive and
seeking dominance. However, where feminists might argue that masculinist
social structures need to be dismantled to enable more just and equitable
social relations, conservatives maintain that these same structures need to be
reinforced to keep men 'civilized'. In this view men's nature is socially problematic in that it has no 'agenda or civilised role inscribed in it' (Gilder 1973:
19), and so without the civilizing influence of women, along with social support to aid their efforts, men are likely to lead opportunistic and escapist
lives of crime, vice and drug addiction. Feminist reforms such as affirmative
action, reproductive rights and childcare provision weaken men's sense of
familial responsibility, and the rise in the public profile of women generally
makes the sacrifices necessary for the effective socialization of men seem
less attractive to them. It is therefore women's social responsibility, the

conservatives argue, to offer a sense of place and authority to men in exchange for their role as providers and protectors.

Incorporated within the conservative perspective is what is sometimes referred to as the 'Christian men's movement', composed of primarily evangelical and fundamentalist Christians who believe that contemporary social conditioning has led to family breakdown and male irresponsibility. Books such as Edwin Cole's *Maximised Manhood: A Guide to Family Survival* (1982), Steve Farrar's *Point Man: How a Man Can Lead a Family* (1990) and Gary Smalley and John Trent's *The Hidden Value of a Man: The Incredible Impact of a Man on his Family* (1994) assume men's natural right to social authority and give advice on how a man should lead his family in the moral chaos of contemporary society. Organizations such as the Promise Keepers in the USA provide a focus for such views through a network of Christian churches, ministries and associations (see Messner 1997: 24–35). The Promise Keepers describe themselves as 'a Christ-centred ministry dedicated to uniting men through vital relationships to become godly influences in their world', and ask their members to make seven promises:

1 Honor Jesus Christ through prayer, worship, and obedience to His Word;
2 Pursue vital relationships with a few other men, understanding that I need my brothers to help me keep my promises;
3 Spiritual, moral, ethical, and sexual purity;
4 Build strong marriages and families through love, protection, and biblical values;
5 Support the mission of my church, by honoring and praying for my pastor and by actively giving my time and resources;
6 Reach beyond any racial and denominational barriers to demonstrate the power of biblical unity;
7 Influence my world, being obedient to the Great Commandment (Mark 12: 30–31) and the Great Commission (Matthew 28: 18–20).

(Men's Issue Page 1997: 'Promise Keepers')

Messner (1997) refers to the approach of the Promise Keepers as a form of 'biblical essentialism' that prescribes the relations between males and females in such a way that they are not open to 'empirical refutation'. The support of some women for groups such as the Promise Keepers suggests that this approach holds some benefits for them, but it is important to recognize that these benefits are framed by a reinstated hierarchy of gender relations that mirrors what feminists have criticized as fundamentally patriarchal. It is interesting to note that while the pro-feminist perspective has been the most vocal in advocating racial inclusivity, it has been the Christian men's movement in the USA which has managed to attract large numbers of 'minority men' into its membership and leadership. The Million Man

March in Washington, DC on 16 October 1995 was an important demonstration of this phenomenon.

Connell (1995: 212–16) also includes within the conservative perspective what he refers to as the 'gun lobby' – a type of politics which amounts to a defence of hegemonic masculinity. In the aftermath of the massacre at Port Arthur in Tasmania, the gun lobby in Australia gained increased support in rural areas in opposition to new, more restrictive gun laws. At their many rallies, hegemonic and phallocentric forms of masculinity were everywhere apparent, along with an argument about the need for guns to protect 'their women', particularly in isolated country areas. Connell argues that the 'gun lobby' as a defence of the patriarchal order is not so much an explicit form of masculinity politics, but a general trend in politics, culture and business which enacts an agenda that exalts men's power and rigorously pursues the mores of hegemonic masculinity as it is currently constructed in the west. It is expressed through the cultural production of sporting heroes, violent video games, action movies, children's toys, comics and novels, all of which promote the bodily superiority of men and their control over technology and violence. It is also expressed through the public veneration of entrepreneurs who ride the current wave of global economic competitiveness and market forces at the expense of a sense of public responsibility and a concern for the welfare of the communities they operate within and on, as well as in the new entrepreneurial masculinity of restructured state managers (cf. Whitehead 1999).

Importantly though, it is the same men who are most affected by the expression of this conservative and instrumental masculinity – marginalized men such as those from indigenous groups, racial minorities and the working class – who are prone to adopt the more physical aspects of hegemonic masculinity, perceiving it as a route to a powerful assertion of their own identities. Here as with the Christian men's movement then, we find the conservative position more attractive and/or pertinent to a broader range of men than the other three perspectives discussed above, which are supported largely by middle-class men with the opportunities and degree of economic security necessary to consider questioning the status quo in masculinity politics, without imperilling their own social positioning. While the reasons for this situation are no doubt more complex than have been presented briefly here, it is important to realize that a large majority of men have not been influenced by the more progressive elements of masculinity politics. So while even those women who have not identified themselves with feminism have been willing to take up the options that feminism has sponsored in the public sphere, men have generally not been persuaded by pro-feminists to voluntarily share the social privilege that has been traditionally theirs. Contrary to men's rights claims that social power is distributed equally across the private/public distinction, this situation only confirms feminist arguments that real social power and privilege reside in the sociopolitical structures of the public sphere, with women desiring access to it and men resistant to sharing it.

Feminist responses to the men's movement

> Make no mistake about it: Women want a men's movement. We are literally dying for it. If you doubt that, just listen to women's desperate testimonies of hope that the men in our lives will become more nurturing toward children, more able to talk about emotions, less hooked on a spectrum of control that extends from not listening through to violence, and less repressive of their own human qualities that are called 'feminine' – and thus suppressed by cultures in which men dominate.
>
> (Steinem 1992: v)

This section was, as originally conceived, to deal briefly with women's responses to the men's movement: brief not only because of the constraints of space, but also to reflect the dearth of literature on the topic. The clarification of feminist responses was required to narrow the discussion down to women who write/speak/act as feminists, as broad a category as this is, rather than women more generally, whose response to the men's movement ranges from conservative women who support traditional patterns of sexual relations, to some women who promote men's rights (for instance one of the directors of the National Coalition of Free Men in the USA is a woman), and the many women who encourage men in their lives to engage in masculinity therapy. Feminist responses may be characterized by a far more critical and circumspect approach to the men's movement, or more commonly a simple refusal to respond at all, given their limited time and energy which seems more usefully spent on woman-centred concerns – a case of attempting to set an agenda to which men must respond, rather than the more customary practice of women being defined by and responding to some masculine norm.

Segal (1990) describes the response of many socialist feminists to the men they were working with in various political struggles in the 1970s as both supportive and mocking with respect to these men's individual and collective attempts to change themselves. Other feminists were less ambivalent, maintaining that 'men in men's groups, are men in bad company' or that the new anti-sexist men were 'worse than the old breed' (Segal 1990: 281). The dilemma here for feminists and the men who responded to feminism was whether the problem lay in individual men, for which separatism was one answer, or the patriarchal social structures that men expressed themselves through and benefited from, in which case there remained possibilities for productive political action with men. More recently some areas of feminist theory have admitted the complicity of women in these same oppressive structures, arguing that there is no 'outside' from which one might escape implication in them.[11] What varies is the investment in, and benefits gained from, a masculinist social structure, and any analysis of this involves a consideration of the complex interactions of categories such as sex, class, race and ethnicity.

The diversification of the men's movement and the proliferation of masculine styles and behaviour since the 1970s has done little to ease the ambivalence of feminists towards the men's movement. There is a general conception that the changes in men and masculinities are superficial (Segal 1990: 293) and do little more than modernize patriarchy, leaving the underlying power relations between men and women largely intact. Witness for example the rise of a new entrepreneurial masculinity among the managers of the new state structures, a topic pursued in some detail in Chapter 3. Such 1990s manifestations as 'softer' masculine styles, men exploring their 'feminine side', or 'bonding' more intimately with other men also do little to convince feminists that men are willing to challenge persistent economic and political inequities. In a collection of essays entitled *Women Respond to the Men's Movement* (Hagan 1992), there is a general fear and suspicion that much of the men's movement is concerned with blaming women for the problems men claim they are experiencing, rather than being willing to work with feminists for the broader social project of a more socially just society.[12] Steinem lists a number of characteristics that men's groups should demonstrate before earning the trust and support of feminists; these include making women feel safer, putting time and money into addressing men's violence, taking responsibility for nurturing children, and breaking down barriers that perpetuate homophobia, racism, classism and keep men at an emotional distance from women (Steinem 1992: ix). Among the contributors there is a general consensus that, not surprisingly, the pro-feminist position holds the most promise for a productive alliance with feminisms, citing activities such as school programmes in New York City which attempt to teach boys how to care for babies (Steinem 1992: viii), and attempts to confront and challenge men's violence such as the White Ribbon Campaign (Adair 1992: 64), as positive steps towards building cooperation.[13] However pro-feminist men do not escape feminist criticism either, their activities censured for focusing on areas where their efforts will be automatically recognized, rather than engaging in more difficult tasks such as confronting sexism in political parties, trade unions, professional and business organizations and public institutions such as schools and universities. It has also been pointed out that it is not such a risk for the middle-class professionals who constitute the majority of pro-feminist men and who enjoy social power to play at not having it; or to find fault with 'masculinity' or men in general, rather than confronting their own individual sexism.

Nevertheless, there has been an increasing willingness on the part of feminist theorists and activists to engage with men who are genuinely willing to work constructively *with* them on issues where a respectful cooperation between men and women is required. There is a certain inevitability about such a position, given the relational manner in which femininity and masculinity are defined and lived out – changes in women's social positions have forced men to confront issues previously unacknowledged by them, and in turn feminist-inspired reforms can extend only so far without the cooperation of men. African American feminist bell hooks has consistently argued for the inclusion of men within a broader feminist movement, maintaining that a men's movement which separates itself from such an alliance undermines the feminist struggle.

> When feminism is defined as a movement to end sexism and sexist oppression, it is clear that everyone has a role to play. Fundamentally, the struggle is not defined as a conflict between women and men. It is defined by resistance to a politic of patriarchal domination that is perpetuated and maintained by nearly everyone in our culture. Defined in this way, there is no question that men can engage fully in feminist struggle.
>
> (hooks 1992: 113)

Segments of the men's movement, such as Bly-inspired masculinity therapy, are criticized for merely being concerned with the reproduction of a type of masculinity that can be safely expressed within patriarchal boundaries. The focus on 'self-actualization' within such a context leads to the depoliticization of the struggle against sexism and sexist oppression, whereas hooks believes that feminist struggle should enhance men's search for self-actualization by enabling men to bond with women in all aspects of social life from a position of mutual respect. Any men's movement which does not seek to unlearn sexism and actively struggle against sexist oppression will merely reinstitute, in a different guise, existing patriarchal structures. In challenging the men's movement to ask of itself whose interests it serves, hooks offers men the alternative of an active involvement within a feminist movement which is neither for women only nor primarily for women's benefit, but rather a joint struggle to end patriarchy and male domination. However, any such engagement is certain to be a complex and delicate process, requiring ongoing negotiation and a commitment to common goals.

Political implications of feminisms for men

> When the majority of those people in the West (particularly in the US) who are currently organising against equal rights for women, sexual liberation, abortion rights and divorce, are women, and when some of those organising for paternal rights, access to children, paternity leave and the discussion of domestic responsibilities in workplaces and trade

unions, are men – then we see the contradictory effects of some type of fundamental gender change. We see also the emergence of new fears and tensions alongside old dreams and hopes.

(Segal 1990: 274)

If we are to discuss the political implications of feminisms for men then there must first be an honest acceptance of the challenges that feminisms provide. While the men's rights and masculinity therapy perspectives are in fact responses to feminisms, they have at best only partially accepted this challenge (which conservatives reject *a priori*), inasmuch as they seek to reply to feminist critiques of men and masculinity within existing sociopolitical structures. They therefore ignore the importance of thoroughgoing feminist critiques of patriarchal social structures – structures which if left intact will simply reproduce the current privileging of the masculine over the feminine, though possibly allowing women access to this privilege at the cost of adopting masculine codes. However, for men who do seek to genuinely respond to feminism there remains the complex political question of which feminism it is that men should respond to; precisely which group of women is it that men need to engage with given the current multiplicity of alliances which exist between men and women across all four of the perspectives discussed above? A simple and definitive answer to this question is not only impossible, but also undesirable, given our need to accept and attempt to live with the complexity of contemporary sexual relations. However, the experience of pro-feminist men seems to be the most appropriate place to at least begin to discuss the terms of the question, given their active engagement with, and acceptance of, feminist critiques of men and masculinity.

Both Bob Connell and Vic Seidler have addressed the relation of men to/with feminism throughout their work, arguing that feminism deeply challenges men at a personal level (not surprisingly they both partially define masculinity as a psychological investment in the unequal power relations of patriarchal society). For example, Connell has written of how feminism is often interpreted by men as an accusation which, if accepted, sometimes results in a paralysing and disabling guilt (1993: 72). In a similar vein, Seidler relates how men often take masculinity to be essentially oppressive to women and respond by negating their own masculinity (1990: 216). Both agree that guilt and self-denial are common responses among men who take on feminist criticism. However, such responses do not lend themselves to the project of an active and positive personal and collective change agenda, and often a resultant disillusionment feeds anti-feminist sentiments and fears that feminists are out to deny men their energy and potency. It is not uncommon for men's rights and masculinity therapy groups to be populated by men with such experiences, and this points to the failure of pro-feminist groups to deal adequately with the personal ramifications of the difficult issues that men often face when confronted with feminist criticism. A solely political focus may lead to a denial of the personal changes that need to take place to ensure that equitable relationships with women and men are being built and maintained, while a sole focus on the personal often leads to the reduction of sociological issues to psychological ones which takes the emphasis off the need for political action by men. The dilemma is therefore how to combine the personal and the political in an effective anti-sexist politics of alliance with feminisms, an issue which Seidler has examined in some detail in his most recent book, *Man Enough* (1997).

Before we can envisage such an alliance on a broad scale there must first be a breakdown of the solidarity among men which exists across age, class, race, ethnicity and sexuality. An acknowledgement of the diversity of men rather than their common claim to masculine privilege is required before productive alliances with women can begin to be forged. While many men do not experience their lives as the powerful and privileged individuals they believe feminism depicts them as, many men do still gain their sense of masculinity from at least attempting to be more powerful and privileged than women of their own social position. The promised fruits of what Connell (1995) has termed the 'patriarchal dividend' – the advantage gained by simply being a man in a society which valorizes masculine traits such as strength, competitiveness, instrumentality and rationality – is distributed very unevenly, with many men such as those who are economically disadvantaged receiving little benefit, if any, over the women in their communities. Consider, for example, the situation of male indigenous Australians, or that of Black males in the inner cities of the USA or UK. However, a lack of masculine empowerment may also lead some men to rely on physically violent forms of masculine expression in their relations with both women and men in order to express what social power they can. And most men have a sense of 'entitlement' in relation to women (Kimmel 1998).

Rather than blaming women for taking their jobs, it would seem more productive for marginalized men in such positions to join in solidarity with women in their communities with whom they have more in common, rather than to continue to strive to achieve some masculine ideal which is likely to remain elusive and which too often leads to the violent and self-destructive behaviour that tears families and communities apart (see Wilson (1997) in relation to this point in the USA). However as the quote from Segal at the beginning of this discussion suggests, the fact that women and men form alliances around opposition to feminist reforms, such as equal rights for women and abortion rights, indicates that there is no easy calculus between a politics of alliance between women and men and support for feminist reform agendas. On the other hand, the fact that men are willing to organize around issues such as curbing men's violence against women, and to support workplace reforms which seek to address the reality of family responsibilities, demonstrates that feminist concerns can be served by alliances with like-minded men. And given the current political climate of resentment as outlined in Chapter 1, it is increasingly important for feminist women and pro-feminist men to work together in order to counter a conservative backlash against a progressive feminist-inspired politics of reform.

A primary emphasis on alliances with women is certainly not in concert with the broad men's movement goal of building a positive community of men in order to overcome the contemporary 'crisis in masculinity'. None the less, it can be argued from a feminist perspective that many of the problems men claim they face arise from their determination to pursue the masculine ideal when the reality of their lives dictates that it will be denied them. This is especially pertinent given that many of the contemporary challenges facing men stem from the globalization of the economy, the collapse of work for all, reduced state welfarism, and the related and pervasive structure of feeling of insecurity. A vision of a broad feminist movement as advocated by bell hooks offers a general direction towards the creation of social relations that respect the differences between men and women of different races, sexualities, ethnicities and classes, to reiterate the most commonly used social categorizations. Messner (1997) comes to a similar conclusion in his pro-feminist analysis of masculinity politics in the USA, supporting Baca Zinn and Dill's (1996) notion of 'multiracial feminism'.

Messner (1997) argues that the work of activists and theorists who occupy positions of 'multiple marginality' such as black women and gay men of colour offers a unique perspective from which to 'integrate a critical understanding of the interrelationships between race, class, gender, and sexual systems of oppression'. From such an understanding, Messner believes, lies the potential for political alliances between gay and lesbian liberation, antiracism movements, and feminist and pro-feminist organizations. Such an approach seeks 'to take into account, simultaneously, a structural analysis of power and inequality with an appreciation of and respect for difference' (Messner 1997: 105), a working together of equality and difference which we advocated in Chapter 1, when we considered the relationships between masculinity politics and feminisms of both equality and difference. He further notes the absurdity of believing that a pro-feminism articulated and practised by 'a group made up primarily or exclusively of white, class-privileged, and heterosexual men could or would ever develop such a radically progressive standpoint' (Messner 1997: 110). This approach is also in line with Connell's (1995) image of a 'gender multiculturalism' which aims to make a multiplicity of gender symbolisms and practices available to all people through a politics of alliance between men and women. This is not to say that such a project will not be difficult, nor involve some personal and public cost to men, but the alternatives offered by other perspectives of the men's movement, other than pro-feminism, merely deal with the symptoms of the social malaise they point to, as they attempt to find solutions within the framework of the social structure which causes them. Such changes, however, do not come about solely through rational choice and conscious decisions, as the men's movement since the mid-1970s has shown. Attitudinal and behavioural patterns can be slow to change and new problems and issues are sure to emerge. Given the relational nature of men and women's social lives, what is certain is that as women alter their public and private profiles men must respond in some fashion, and it unlikely that men in general will change considerably without concerted and continued pressure to do so.[14] So rather than men being left to pick up the pieces of their (supposedly) shattered masculinity in the wake of a fabled post-feminist era, where post-feminist is read as feminism having achieved its goals rather than as an indicator of various and variegated femininities and feminisms, there is instead a continuing necessity for feminism to continue to influence the direction of women's lives if men are to be convinced of the inevitability of the need for fundamental personal and collective change. As for the question of which women (feminists) men should enter into alliances with, or which feminism men should support, one possible reply is to return to the question asked by bell hooks of the men's movement as to whose interest it serves. It seems that a politics of alliance between men and women will continue to emerge, yet develop across the political and theoretical spectrum to the extent that a multiplicity of interests will be served by it. If the feminist movement is to maintain or even expand its influence in the future, it will require the active support of progressive men if feminists and pro-feminists are to convince conservative and moderate men to at least not be obstructive in the struggle to end sexism and sexist oppression. An understanding of the structural conditions of contemporary politics of backlash and resentment, as outlined in Chapter 1, might even convince some reactionary men of the worth of such a political project.

The situation in education

The matter of men's and boys' responses to feminist reform in schooling has been dominated in recent times by the 'What about the boys?' question, an issue which is the focus of both Chapters 4 and 5. While there has been some concern about 'what to do with the boys' during the focus on girls in schooling since the late 1970s, much of this concern was expressed by feminist women, and to a lesser extent pro-feminist men, who were aware that change for the girls meant, and simultaneously required, change for the boys. In the Australian context, there was some concern expressed about the restrictive nature of male sex roles at the beginning of the engagement between second wave feminism and educational policy in the mid-1970s. This concern was soon washed away, probably for a number of reasons, including the need for feminists to strategically constitute girls as a disadvantaged category to gain funding and policies, and the rejection by senior male administrators at that time of a need to focus upon boys.[15] There was also the constant and more pragmatic dilemma of what to do with the boys, while the girls were attending various programmes which aimed, among other objectives, to broaden their post-school options. Such attention to girls was also resented by some boys and some male teachers. However, we would note that many feminist reforms in schools actually included boys within their remit, particularly as the programmes became more established (Kenway *et al.* 1997a).

It is only since the mid 1990s that a concern for boys' schooling has been canvassed more generally by men, fuelled by the perception and media representations that boys' academic performance is falling below that of girls. The high profile of this issue seems to have given empirical support and justification to the conservative and men's rights voices, who have been unhappy with the way they believe the focus on girls in schooling not only has neglected the needs of boys, but also has labelled boys and masculinity as a problem. The conservative and men's rights positions diverge however, when it comes to their analyses of the issue and proposed solutions, with the conservatives characteristically calling for a return to 'the basics' of education to restore boys' sense of self-discipline and social duty, while the men's rights advocates claim that schools are failing boys, arguing for the introduction of boys' education strategies to address the specific problems boys face in schooling. In the Australian context, *The National Policy for the Education of Girls in Australian Schools* (Schools Commission 1987) has transmogrified into *Gender Equity: A Framework for Australian Schools* (Gender Equity Taskforce 1997), with gender here a signifier that boys are now included within the policy. That we now have a gender equity policy rather than a specific boys' strategy is indicative of the (successful) struggle by feminist and pro-feminist educators and femocrats (see Chapter 3) to defend gains for girls in education.

While conservative concern has been addressed somewhat by a broad swing to the political right, men's rights advocates have had to lobby governments and education bureaucracies in order to further their agenda, which is usually at odds with that pursued by a loose alliance of feminist women and pro-feminist men. The former seek a focus on boys similar to, though separate from, the feminist-inspired focus on girls in schooling, whereas the latter pursue a concern for boys within the framework of gender equity in order to build upon the experience and expertise gained from working with girls, and to emphasize the importance of encouraging the development of equal and just relationships between boys and girls, matters considered in more detail in Chapter 5.

While the term 'men's rights' is being used here as a useful category for discussion, in the context of education, this perspective is commonly expressed via parent groups and interested men such as teachers, academics, writers and fathers who believe that boys are falling behind girls. They are therefore concerned with what they perceive to be the educational disadvantages of being a boy in our school systems. The argument for a separate boys' strategy, as opposed to their inclusion within a broader gender equity framework, reflects the belief that there are fundamental differences between boys and girls that need to be taken into account – differences that would not be addressed by a gender equity framework which has developed from the feminist-inspired focus on girls in schooling. From a feminist perspective, Kenway *et al.* (1997a) and Yates (1997) argue for a similar approach, also suggesting that the needs of boys cannot be simply read off from an understanding of the needs of girls in schooling, though arguing that such an aim must be pursued within a gender equity framework.

Rather than schools being the masculinizing institutions that a number of feminist-inspired academic studies have argued[16], the men's rights position maintains that schools are feminized and feminizing, both with respect to the preponderance of female teachers and in the passivity of the process of learning itself. Attempts to address the educational needs of boys within a framework that has grown out of a focus on girls simply exacerbates this situation, it is argued, and further disadvantages boys. Apart from the debate over the academic performance of boys in relation to girls, there is the more general concern that boys are in trouble and in need of positive and affirmative intervention in schools to help them deal with a social milieu that is purportedly increasingly hostile to men and masculinity.[17] There are therefore calls for policies and programmes to address issues affecting boys, such as their general uncommunicativeness and inability to express emotions, low self-esteem, the pressure to adopt a 'cool pose' which discourages academic achievement and participation in 'non-traditional' areas such as dance, drama, languages and social sciences, the use of aggressive and violent ways of resolving conflict, reluctance to assume 'leadership' positions, their massive over-representation as 'behaviour problem students', the lack of appropriate 'male role models' and the absence of men from active participation in boys' lives, male youth suicide and other forms of self-destructive behaviour, low literacy rates and the high percentage of boys diagnosed as suffering from learning disabilities.[18]

While many of these problems have been around for some time, what is new is the increased concern over them and the tendency to blame the failure of boys on the perceived success of the focus on girls in schooling. It is argued now that the 'girls are doing brilliantly', there is no need to continue affirmative action for them and so we must now focus our efforts on giving boys the same opportunities that girls have.[19] (We would note here the failure to disaggregate the data and indicate which boys and which girls we are talking about.) This would require the affirmation of boys and boys' culture, rather than viewing them as simply a 'toxic problem' to be overcome. Some of the problems that boys experience in schools, it is argued, stem from their natural propensity to be more active and aggressive than girls, and their behaviour becomes problematic only when judged by feminized standards and by women teachers who are unable to deal with masculine exuberance. Part of the solution must therefore be the remasculinization of schooling: for instance greater numbers of male teachers, the development of more active ways to teach boys for whom passive learning is an anathema, and the inclusion into the curriculum of more robust and masculine material that would encourage boys to read and become more involved in class discussions. (We would note the dangers here of such approaches reinforcing hegemonic forms of masculinity.) However, there are also calls for boys to be encouraged into more sensitive and caring models of manhood which would enable them to resist the enormous cultural pressure for them to conform to hegemonic versions of masculinity.[20] In summary then, from this perspective there is a need for boys to be valued and affirmed as boys, but in concert with this, there is also a need to broaden the acceptable range of masculine expression available to boys.

If some of this sounds familiar it is not surprising, as much of what is argued and proposed by the men's rights position recasts early feminist arguments with respect to girls' schooling within a framework of concern for boys (cf. Kenway *et al.* 1997b).[21] As with early feminist arguments which relied on the rather coarse analysis of social life in terms of the homogenous categories of men and women, there is a totalizing logic at work here, which ignores differences among boys, even as it valorizes the differences between boys and girls. There is also much to suggest that the men's rights perspective has an outdated and simplistic interpretation of feminism which, as was mentioned above, is reflected in its own retracing of the feminist focus on girls in schooling justified by the belief that boys are as oppressed as girls, though in a different manner. There is therefore a rejection of feminism with regard to its relevance to boys' situation, yet also an appropriation of its methodology in the formulation of responses to the problems that boys face in education. However, it seems rather counterproductive to dismiss the experience and the knowledge that feminism has gained since the mid-1970s through its engagement in education simply because it does not speak directly to the needs of boys. There certainly has been some tendency in the past for feminists in education to assume that all boys are powerful and successful and therefore without problems that need addressing; however, there is nothing to be gained by boys' advocates going over the same terrain, until experience teaches them that the actual situation is far more complex and fraught with difficulties. It seems more sensible to seek an active engagement with feminists in education in order to create a broad framework within which the issues confronting both girls and boys can be addressed in a manner which recognizes that men and women will be, or at least should be, sharing the public and private realms in the future in more equal ways. And feminists have not been opposed to attempts to change men and boys; for example, Segal (1990: 272) in *Slow Motion: Changing Masculinities,*

Changing Men noted, 'if men do not change, nothing really changes, since women still live in a world dominated by men'. In her submission to the New South Wales Inquiry into Boys' Education, Kenway (1994) observed:

> To put it simply, most feminists want boys and men to change so that they cause less problems for girls and women and themselves, so that the sexes can live alongside each other in a safe, secure, stable, respectful, harmonious way and in relationships of mutual life-enhancing respect. Feminists have long made the case that gender plays a part in all aspects of education and that to recognise this is to get a particularly useful insight into a lot of educational issues and problems.
>
> (Kenway 1994: 23)

In confronting the problems that boys experience in schooling within a gender equity framework, the important issue is not how boys are disadvantaged as distinct from girls, but how we can address the problems that both girls and boys face in learning how to balance their roles in the private and public spheres of social life. That is, we need to move beyond a zero-sum, 'battle of the sexes' construction of the issues. The emphasis should therefore be on enabling and encouraging boys and girls to accept an equal responsibility for these two aspects of their lives. A summary of this approach from a feminist perspective might run as follows.

> Women are not active in public life: – Women should have the right to choose – The quality of public life is diminished by women's absence. Men are not active in domestic life: – The quality of men's lives is diminished – Men's failure to share these responsibilities is a bar to women's participation in public life.
>
> (Daws 1995: 30)

The priority here is undoubtedly on women's access to public life, and men are taken into account only as far as is necessary in order to achieve this without enunciating how men's participation might enrich the domestic/private sphere or of the ways in which women might deter or obstruct them.[22] It is this type of approach which the men's rights position in the boys' education debate fears – that boys will be addressed only in relation to the needs of girls. This context is seen as hostile to the needs of boys, as it is believed that they are cast solely as problems and in need of reconstruction. In response, boys' advocates reject the sense of guilt and responsibility that comes with what they refer to as the 'sins of the father' syndrome, and argue that boys should change only in response to an agenda that benefits them and in a manner which puts positive value on the unique qualities of boys.[23] The rift that develops here between the feminist and men's rights positions is based on the former's (initial) negligence of diversity among boys and the real difficulties they face, given their focus on the experience of girls in schooling, and the latter's lack of a coherent macropolitical viewpoint within which to understand broad scale social inequities between men and women, as well as the cultural biases which privilege the masculine over the feminine. This is the rift within which pro-feminist men consistently find themselves in their attempt to incorporate feminist critiques of men and masculinity and to find ways of overcoming sexism and sexist oppression, while also recognizing and acknowledging the personal difficulties men and boys experience, as well as the varying experiences of different groups of boys along the axes of race, class, ethnicity and sexuality. There seems to be no ready made solution on hand and there is unlikely to be one given the complexity of the issues involved. However, the 'What about the boys?' issue does provide an opportunity for men and women to form progressive alliances which could build on cooperation and respect between the sexes instead of each pursuing their own interests. That is, the 'What about the boys?' discourse can be reclaimed for progressive ends (cf. Mills and Lingard 1997). And from the solutions currently on offer, the option of seeking the best interests of boys and girls in the context of their relations to one another within the common framework of gender equity seems to be the most appropriate alternative.

Teachers and their attitudes and values are central to such reform agendas and such reforms have emotional effects (Kenway *et al.* 1997a). Teachers in schools will take a number of stances in respect of the various masculinity politics outlined earlier and thus take varying positions in respect of feminist based reforms in schools and in respect of the boys' question. We do not have the research evidence to outline with any certainty the most common attitudes of teachers, both male and female, to such reforms (see Kenway *et al.* 1997a here). It is likely, however, that some men will take a pro-feminist stance, others will be indifferent to the whole question, conceptualizing schooling as separate from such political matters. Most perhaps will not have developed a clearly thought out position, reacting to different issues as they arise, often from a melange of political standpoints straddling the pro-feminist and recuperative divide.[24] Yet others again will take the ugly stance offered by some versions of men's rights politics, which are explicitly anti-women and anti-feminism and which seek to constitute men and boys as the new victims. Kenway *et al.* (1997a: 61) suggest, on the basis of their research, that many of the men who argue that too much is being done in schools for girls and not enough for boys, conjoin such concerns with opposition to affirmative action and equal employment opportunity reforms which seek to provide equality of career advancement for women teachers. There is some synergy between the anti-feminist backlash within society and the 'What about the boys?' issue in education. The situation is such that any call for more male teachers must be handled with caution, with the danger being that an influx of conservative and uncritical men could simply reinforce more traditional patterns of gender relations, rather than contribute to achieving more equitable gender relations through schooling. It is interesting, but perhaps not surprising, that the call for more male teachers, often from those expressing men's rights or masculinity therapy stances, is not accompanied by a call for more women in senior positions in schools and educational systems. In Chapter 3 we argue that 'structural backlash' has reduced the number of such women in the more senior decision-making positions and reinstated a more masculinist core at the centre of educational policy production. These developments also put at risk the feminist reform agenda in schooling and probably reduce the likelihood of the take-up of a pro-feminist engagement with boys within a social justice framework.

Notes

1 We understand how any such categorization tends to silence some perspectives and place too strong boundaries around the categories. Within such categorization 'masculinity therapy' and 'mythopoetic' are usually used interchangeably. Many developments within schools in relation to boys actually consist of a mixture of these discourses. In the Australian context, the 'What about the boys?' agenda in education has been driven from both mythopoetic and men's rights perspectives.

2 This edited book dealt with many of the same issues as Tolson's (1977) *The Limits of Masculinity*, which focused on the situation in the UK.

3 Connell (1995: 139–40) describes 'effeminism' as a stance associated with 'guilt, antagonism to men and complete subordination to the women's movement' which 'accepts the individualizing logic that locates the source of oppression in men's individual sexism, and offers a moral rather than practical reform'. See also 'The effeminist manifesto' by Dansky *et al.* (1977). These characteristics might be seen as necessary precursors to a more productive and less categorical analysis of masculinities and more effective pro-feminist theory and practice.

4 Vicki Crowley made us aware of the relevance of Eve Sedgwick's work to ours, particularly in relation to questions of the positionality of the author; our position as men writing about feminism compared with Sedgwick's 'straight' position writing about queer politics and theory.

5 We again acknowledge that the notion of 'men's pain' needs further theoretical and empirical consideration. See Flood (1997a, b, c).

6 While Sam Keen's *Fire in the Belly* and John Rowan's *The Horned God* both share with Bly a Jungian perspective, Rowan's work differentiates itself by being explicitly pro-feminist and arguing for an ongoing engagement with women, rather than advocating the importance of a primary bonding with men.

7 The deep or mature masculine expresses the full range of male character archetypes: for example the Wild Man, the King, the Trickster, the Lover, the Quester and the Warrior (Bly 1988: 11).

8 There is a real 'heterosexual presumption' (Epstein and Johnson 1994) in Bly's argument; furthermore Christian (1994) has demonstrated the importance of the influence of mothers in developing anti-sexist and pro-feminist men.

9 Kimmel (1995) has edited *The Politics of Manhood*, which is basically a dialogue between pro-feminist and mythopoetic men. This dialogue suggests there is some

possibility of the less strident mythopoets working with pro-feminists. Messner (1997: 108) agrees, noting: 'The men who are most likely to serve as a bridge from the terrain of antifeminist backlash to the terrain of progressive coalition building are the fragments of the mythopoetic men's movement who are currently engaged in dialogue with profeminist men'.

10 A good example is Steven Goldberg's *The Inevitability of Patriarchy* which argues that 'The hormonal renders the social inevitable' (1974: 49).

11 See for instance Gatens (1996: 43) who argues that the 'peculiar complicity of women (and men) in maintaining phallocentric culture is tied to the complex investments of both in the double(s)'. The double is explained in the following way:

> Each gender is at once the antithesis of, and the complement to, the other. Each projects (and so, predictably finds) those qualities antithetical to itself, to its 'ideal image', onto its double. Each therefore becomes the indispensible complement to the other. Each is deeply complicit in maintaining not only his or her *own* body image, but also that which it assumes: the body image *of the other*.
>
> (Gatens 1996: 36–7)

12 Some of the feminist contributors to Digby's edited collection, *Men Doing Feminism* (1998), appear to be a little more relaxed, supportive and less suspicious of pro-feminist men. See, for example, the foreword by Sandra Bartky, which we utilize in Chapter 6 of this book.

13 The White Ribbon Campaign began in Canada in 1991 in response to the mass murder of women at a Montreal institution of higher education. The campaign has now spread to other countries and aims to harness the energy and resources of men in order to end men's violence against women by breaking men's silence around the issue.

14 It is a matter of debate, however, just where these pressures to change emerge from – whether they are feminist inspired, stem from broader globalizing economic forces, or, more likely, some combination of the two as we suggest in Chapter 1.

15 We are indebted to Eleanor Ramsay for this insight.

16 See for instance Mac an Ghaill's (1994) *The Making of Men: Masculinities, Sexualities and Schooling* and Connell (1996).

17 A good example of this sentiment comes from Steve Biddulph's foreword to *Boys in Schools* (Browne and Fletcher 1995), an edited collection of essays dealing with programmes in schools which address the concern over boys in schooling.

> We have to counter the signals sent to boys (from society, the media, from some women who hate men, and some men who hate themselves) that being male is somehow intrinsically dirty, dangerous and inferior. Many boys now get this rejected feeling from all sides: overstretched or neglectful parents, stressed-out teachers, the lingerie ads, soft-porn rock videos and from girls (who, with their social powers and verbal skills, have an ability to wound – even unintentionally).
>
> (Biddulph 1995: viii–ix)

18 This list was gleaned from a discussion paper that arose from an inquiry into

boys' education by the New South Wales State Government in 1994 (O'Doherty 1994: 15–18).

19 See *The GEN*, August 1993. *The GEN* was a magazine about gender reform, funded by the federal government in Australia, and distributed to schools. It has since been abolished by the conservative Howard federal government.

20 These are all issues repeatedly raised on a boys' education discussion group on the Internet (boysed@halibut.pnc.com.au) in which the authors have participated.

21 Yates (1997) has noted this phenomenon in commenting that the frameworks and findings being used and developed by those working in the area of boys' education (cf. Browne and Fletcher 1995; West 1995) are often concerned with role models, consciousness raising and the problems with attempting to be sufficiently masculine which are directly borrowed from early feminist work on girls in schooling. Kenway *et al.* (1997a, b) have also made a similar point.

22 The suspicion of men in childcare work or early childhood teaching from many women and men seems to act as a barrier to men's greater participation in these areas. There is also little discussion of the fact that just as women's increased participation in the public sphere has altered, and will continue to alter its complexion, so will men's increased participation in the private/domestic sphere of social life change it.

23 See for instance Biddulph's foreword to Browne and Fletcher (1995).

24 For example, a recent document – *Improving the School Performance of Boys* (1997) – by Jeremy Ludowyke for the Victorian Association of State Secondary Principals, attempts to take a balanced view of 'boys' underachievement' and acknowledges that the feminist project for girls in schools still has some way to go. In the final chapter of this book we discuss a boys' strategy developed at a high school in a Queensland provincial city and show how it consists of a melange of recuperative and progressive perspectives.

3 The structural backlash and emergent emotional economy in education

> . . . backlash is not merely the product of the media. I would argue that backlash has always been here, with resistance to gender equity going underground in the 1980s only to emerge reformed and recycled in more subtle and insidious ways in the 1990s. The current media representations of backlash are, I suggest, merely an overt and public manifestation of an ongoing set of institutional processes that resist gender equity reform. Backlash is a powerful part of the discursive field surrounding feminism and feminist practices in education, and it has been made possible by a changing political and economic context.
>
> (Jill Blackmore 1997a: 77)
>
> I argue that educational restructuring has itself become a form of backlash.
>
> (Jill Blackmore 1997a: 75)

Introduction

This chapter deals with what we are going to call, in shorthand terms, 'structural backlash'. Blackmore (1997a) suggests that educational restructuring is itself a form of backlash; we agree and refer to that phenomenon as 'structural backlash'. While we consider the notion of backlash elsewhere in this book and reject a simplistic 'explain everything' usage of the concept, particularly in relation to male responses to feminist reforms in education (cf. McLeod 1998), 'structural backlash' appears to be a useful way to encapsulate the gendered results of the restructuring of educational systems as part of the broader restructuring of the state. It is within the conditions of structural backlash that men are currently engaging feminisms within those educational systems.

The *sui generis* character of educational administration has been lost as a consequence of the broad restructuring of the contemporary state. Most so-called advanced economies in the context of the post-Cold War and search for a post-Keynesian settlement have restructured their state apparatuses at national and subnational levels, in the face of the global dominance of market liberal economic ideology and the concomitant emergence of a global economy which fails to recognize national borders. There is now some disjunction between the unit of political organization – the nation, and the way the global economy works with national boundaries becoming more porous. In response, we have seen the creation of the 'competitive state' which takes as its overriding policy imperative the international competitiveness of the putatively national economy (Cerny 1990). This imperative has framed other policy domains, including education. In this post-Keynesian era, the market has also been afforded priority over the state as the chief societal steering mechanism within the nation (Pusey 1991), accompanied by a narrowing and tighter focusing of state policies and desire to reduce state expenditures. At the same time, state structures and *modus operandi* have been reconstituted. The structure has become flatter – more like a coathanger than a pyramid – with many tasks devolved to lower levels within the organization, while new relationships between the policy and strategic planning 'centre' of each department and the policy practising 'periphery' have been put in place.

These restructured state apparatuses and their ways of working have also been reconstituted under 'new public management' (Hood 1991; Clarke *et al.* 1994a; Clarke and Newman 1997) or 'corporate managerialism' (Considine 1988). Waters (1995) speaks of a global organizational ecumenism which has seen private sector organizational and administrative practices taken up in the public sectors of the advanced economies in the context of post-Keynesianism. The result has been a move away from the old hierarchical bureaucracy which gave precedence to proceduralism over outcomes through a regime of rules and which attempted to control change through increased expenditure or inputs. The new managerialism within a flatter structure, in contrast, emphasizes doing 'more with less' (efficiency) and controlling change through outputs or outcomes (effectiveness), depending on the temporal frame.

Performance indicators as proof of achievement of policy goals have become pervasive within such state structures. This stress upon performance indicators is a manifestation of what Lyotard (1984) has called 'performativity', which is endemic to the postmodern condition generally, and we would argue, also endemic to the postmodern state. Thus, as well as being 'competitive' and 'flatter' in the way described above, the state also becomes a 'performative one' having to provide measurable evidence of policy outcomes. The school-effectiveness research in the UK is one obvious educational manifestation of these cultural and political pressures (Lingard *et al.* 1998; Slee *et al.* 1998), as has been the development of performance league tables for schools in the same context. Generally, the focus is on the easily quantifiable and measurable; concern for efficiency and effectiveness takes priority over concern for truth claims. 'Does it work?' becomes a more significant question than 'Is it true?' The central, strategic arm of the state now steers through such performance measures. Performativity also sees efficiency and effectiveness take priority over equity and reframe it in the process.

Performativity has also been another element of the reduction and focusing of the remit of state policies and can be seen 'as a principle of selective closure in respect of the information overload and social complexity which confronts the contemporary state' (Yeatman 1994: 117). Such social complexity includes the democratic demands made by women for equivalent citizenship rights with men; performativity supplies a new 'meta-discourse for public policy' and subsumes and transforms 'substantive democratising claims within a managerialist-functionalistic rhetoric' (Yeatman 1994: 110). Performativity appears to grant priority to formal over substantive rationality in relation to outcomes, and as we will show, also in relation to gender equity and the standing of women. Blackmore (1997b) has argued that performativity in restructured educational systems has also been evident in pressure upon state workers (including teachers) to be seen to perform, a situation which has gendered impacts, as will be shown later in this chapter.

From the mid-1970s the most successful form of 'progressive politics' has been that of 'recognition' or identity politics, rather than the older style politics of redistribution (Fraser 1995). A stark contrast between the Keynesian settlement and the search for a post-Keynesian one has been in the role of the state and the focus of its policies: the former emphasized the redistribution of resources towards equality but tended to neglect difference, while the latter stresses recognition of difference but demonstrates lack of concern for redistribution. The result of the focus upon recognition politics was a form of social rationalization (Wark 1997) which saw merit replace seniority as the basis for appointment to senior positions within the public (and private) sector, including for women and minorities. In different countries this was manifest in a range of legislation covering matters such as equal employment opportunity, affirmative action, anti-discrimination legislation and so on. However, it is Yeatman's (1990) contention that the new managerialism, both structurally and procedurally, while stressing merit over seniority, through instantiating economic rationalism across the public sector, slowed down the agenda of social rationalization. Corporate managerialism, Yeatman argues, was the Trojan Horse, which reframed the political agenda including the demands of feminism. Feminism was never simply and only about getting more women into powerful positions in both the public and private sectors; it was also about feminist women changing the structures and cultures of those organizations once they were in senior positions.

Because the politics of recognition and social rationalization occurred at a time of growing inequality and pervasive insecurity, and a turning away by the state from a politics of redistribution, there was considerable opposition to the project of social rationalization from particular sections of society. There was also opposition to economic rationalization, but usually different groups opposed economic rationalism from those who opposed social rationalism. The exception here were the far right wing groups articulating variants of backlash national chauvinisms, such as One Nation in Australia, the neo-Nazis in Germany, Jean-Marie Le Pen in France, the working-class militia and David Duke in the USA, and so on. More common was the utilization of the right wing rhetoric of 'political correctness' to attack state interventions for social rationalization through affirmative action and equal employment opportunity legislation and the like, which attempted to establish a meritocracy, while these same critics were deadly silent about the 'economic correctness' of the dominance of market liberalism. Many complainants regarding so-called political correctness in relation to feminist engagements with the state were middle class males concerned about their declining, or at least contested, 'proprietorial role in society' (Davis 1997: 51). Kimmel and Kaufman (1995: 18) note that social and economic rationalization have affected different groups of men in different ways. They suggest, however, that 'perhaps the hardest hit *psychologically* were middle-class, straight, white men from their late twenties through their forties'. These were the men, they argue, 'who believed themselves entitled to the power that attended upon the successful demonstration of masculinity' (Kimmel and Kaufman 1995: 18). The material and political conditions conducive to backlash, along with the restructuring of the state, provided a context in which such men could seek to reclaim their supposed 'entitlements'. Both the attack on social rationalization and defence of economic rationalism have had serious gendered consequences, which at a broad level constitute the backdrop to structural backlash which is the focus of this chapter.

The matters we are talking about here were played out in different ways in different countries, reflecting their histories, cultures, political structures, change traditions, organization of social movements and so on. Thus, while economic rationalism in Australia witnessed yet another attempt at reconstituting federalism to create a single, more efficient national market, Britain, with a unitary form of government, saw an attack on the relevance of local government. The new public management in the UK saw a proliferation of statutory authorities, while in Australia such new management saw a reduction in the numbers of statutory authorities with some autonomy from the minister and bureaucracy. Or in relation to affirmative action, US developments resulted in the adoption of quota systems whereas in Australia the focus was on eliminating barriers to equal opportunity and redefining merit. Or in relation to the feminist reform project: during the Conservative years in Britain this was most effective at the local government level which was then constrained by Conservative policy developments; in Australia feminists engaged effectively with the state to see the creation of 'femocrats' who most often had responsibility for the carriage of 'recognition' and equal opportunity policies inside the state; compare with the USA where a less statist political culture apparently resulted in a feminist focus upon and within the academy with the creation of women's studies courses and degrees, and greater use of the courts to redress discrimination (cf. Eisenstein 1991, 1996). Masculinity politics in Australia has seen a demand for state interventions – particularly targeted policies and programmes for men and boys, particularly in the education and health areas, while in the USA the result has been the establishment of men's studies courses in universities and attacks upon affirmative action for women and minorities.

It is in that context that we come to what we are calling 'structural backlash' to refer to the ways in which women's advancement in the public sector (and more broadly within the society) has been slowed down by the restructuring of the state apparatus, *despite* conditions of formal equality. And it is not only the advancement of women inside the state which has been slowed down, but also the capacity (and interest) of the state in achieving feminist-inspired policy goals has been considerably weakened. This situation has resulted from a number of factors, including: the meta-policy status granted to economic restructuring and the dominance of market liberalism, the narrowing of state policy coverage and reductions in state expenditure, the priority given to efficiency and effectiveness over equity, the new culture of performativity and competitiveness, the new management culture, the new accountability relationships put in place between the policy generating 'centre' and the 'periphery' which has greater freedom to choose the approach to achieve the strategic goals and performance measures mandated by the centre, and the new emotional economies which have resulted. This structural backlash has occurred in the context of a widespread social backlash against affirmative action and equal employment legislation for women and minorities (Faludi 1991; Blackmore 1997a; Roman and Eyre 1997), resulting, for example, in Proposition 209 which dismantled affirmative action legislation in California. It has resulted in the USA, McCarthy (1998) argues, in a politics of resentment and attempts by some within the suburban middle classes to appropriate the language of the oppressed. The notion of group disadvantage and the need for positively discriminating state policies have also been criticized as part of the backlash and politics of resentment. Social rationalization is on the defensive, while economic rationalization is in the ascendancy. In that context it can be seen that even the conditions of formal equality between men and women are being contested, let alone substantive gender equality being achieved.

What this chapter will seek to demonstrate is how these changes to the state have gendered outcomes – what we are referring to as 'structural backlash' – particularly in relation to those feminist political practices (state feminisms) which have worked on and within the state (Blackmore 1999), but also within schools. State structures and processes are heavily gendered; there is gender segmentation of both a horizontal, across-department kind and vertical segmentation within departments (Connell 1990), that is, women are concentrated in certain departments and at certain levels within particular departments. In a nutshell, the argument about structural backlash is that, following restructuring, the core strategic planning and policy producing centre of the state has become more masculinist in orientation, while the periphery has become more feminized and carries the burdens of a new emotional economy. However, what is different from past historical situations is that this structural backlash inhibits opportunities for women within a framework of formal equality, a situation which has (supposedly) precipitated some generational conflict among feminists. Some younger women clearly have better career opportunities than their mothers, while they, at times, fail to recognize the contribution of the feminist political project to their improved opportunities – one element of what Walby (1997) has called 'gender polarizations'. This situation is thus similar to that documented by Bittman and Pixley (1997: ch. 6) in their research on very unequal male and female participation in domestic labour, despite the avowal of most men and women in contemporary Australia that such domestic tasks should be shared equally. Given that, despite such avowals, about 70 per cent of domestic labour is carried out by women, they speak of male/female domestic relations as ones of 'pseudomutuality'. In the context of structural backlash within the public sector, we might then speak of 'pseudoequality' to encapsulate male/female opportunities within the competitive and performative, restructured state. The condition of formal equality remains but the quest for more substantive equality for women is at best marking time or at worst going backwards. And even the conditions of formal equality are under some threat. Feminism is on the defensive. However, some would argue that masculinity is also on the defensive (Kenway 1995; Seidler 1997) in relation to feminism and changing labour markets; structural backlash works in effect as a reclamation by men, practising particular and emergent versions of hegemonic masculinity (cf. Whitehead 1999), of their 'rightful' power and authority within state administrations and policy making, including in educational systems. A central element of male power is this notion of 'entitlement' (Kimmel 1998) and structural backlash works in relation to it.

Structural backlash has also seen a new emotional economy emerge within these restructured educational systems (cf. Czarniawska 1997), changing the nature of and responsibility for 'emotional labour' (Hochschild 1983) and intensifying the work, both rational and emotional, of women at the chalk face, as principals, within middle management in schools and within the state bureaucracies in education. As well as documenting and analysing structural backlash, this chapter characterizes the concomitant changes to the emotional economy of educational systems which in this post-Keynesian era have become 'greedy organizations' always demanding more for less (Coser 1974; Blackmore 1997b) and requiring that all be seen to perform at all times as part of the new performance culture.

Giddens (1990, 1991, 1994), in a range of his writing, has spoken of the detraditionalizing character of our post-traditional social order in which traditions can no longer be taken for granted but are always subject to questioning by our 'reflexivity'.[1] Such a social order, according to Giddens, is one in which traditions have to explain themselves and thus become open to interrogation. The feminist project has been about interrogating traditional patriarchal gender relations and achieving the detraditionalization of sex-based behaviour and opportunities; the same has been the case for the feminist project inside the state, which through affirmative action, anti-discrimination and equal opportunity legislation sought to break the traditional nexus between sex and career. This chapter will argue that structural backlash has worked against detraditionalization of this kind and that, indeed, the result has been a retraditionalization of sex-based career opportunities within state structures and educational systems; the core policy producing part of the state has been retraditionalized in a masculinist fashion through entrepreneurial managerialism (Whitehead 1999), while the periphery has been retraditionalized in ways which reinforce traditional feminine norms. Further, women who make it into the core of the state do so on grounds defined by this new managerialism, which grants priority to efficiency and effectiveness over equity; without essentializing male and female management styles (Weiner 1995), this entails a detraditionalization of traditional female values of caring and nurturing. Structural backlash thus witnesses the retraditionalization of sex-based careers and opportunities; the state has been regendered. It is to a consideration of this regendering of the state that we now turn.

Regendering the state and education

The gender regime of the state

Connell (1987, 1990) has developed the concepts of 'gender order' and 'gender regime' to refer respectively to the structural patterns of gender relations within a society and within any given organization. Each describes the gendered division of power, labour and the nature of emotional attachments (cathexis) in their sphere. Connell (1990) has also described the gender regime of the contemporary state, demonstrating both horizontal and vertical gender segmentation within the divisions of power and labour within state structures, that is within and across state departments. By this he means that within public service departments there is a vertical gender segmented division of labour (and power) with women concentrated at the bottom of the hierarchy in terms of status, power, income and career opportunities. Women also dominate among 'street-level bureaucrats', those who handle the day-to-day traumas and difficulties of social policy in practice, in the human interface between policy and 'clients'. Women constitute the majority of state professionals such as teachers, nurses and social workers. At the same time, there is also a horizontal gender segmentation across the public sector with fewer women in senior levels in the 'hard-nosed' departments of treasury, finance, trade, defence and more women concentrated within the social policy domains of health, welfare and education. Women in senior positions tend to be in the service departments. Further, there are more women again in what can be called the 'voluntary state', that unpaid labour contributed by women in welfare, charity and schooling and which has probably become more significant in the post-Keynesian, post-welfare state era of social disinvestment.

The above description encapsulates the gender regime of the state with men dominating and women in subordinate positions in terms of power relations and with respect to the emotional economy. Our argument is that restructuring has strengthened these features of the gender and policy regimes of the state, resulting in what we are classifying as 'structural backlash', including a new emotional economy. At the same time as this structural backlash, policies and procedures related to recognition politics – equal employment opportunity, affirmative action, anti-discrimination and so on – were being put in place. Structural backlash, along with other developments, ensured that the emphasis was upon formal equality rather than its substantive achievement – a rational, technical approach to change which denies the significance of the cultural and the emotional.

As indicated briefly in the introduction to this chapter, the state has been restructured under pressures from globalization, (under)read simply as the inevitability of the dominance of market liberal ideology on a world scale.[2] Crook *et al.* (1992) have argued that devolution, which they dichotomize into vertical (devolving tasks down the line) and horizontal (pushing tasks to other semi-government agencies), as well as privatization and marketization (the practices of market liberalism), are part of the *disetatization* central to postmodernization. It is our argument that this restructuring has resulted in the regendering of the state and while we acknowledge that the (nation) state now works in different ways, we still believe it is important politically, while recognizing the need now for effective political mobilizations at local, national and global levels (Yeatman 1990; Appadurai 1996; Blackmore 1999; Henry *et al.* 1999). Such regendering has occurred in various ways in different political regimes. An example from Australia will illustrate this regendering and structural backlash thesis. It should be noted, however, that structural backlash will have varying nuances and inflections in different political locations within different nations, given their varying histories, cultures and political structures.

Restructuring the gender regime of the state

Turning then to a consideration of the restructuring of the Australian public sector, Pusey (1991), in an elegant study of *Economic Rationalism in*

Canberra, has shown how Labor restructured the federal public service in Australia after their 1987 election victory. He documents the strengthened hand of the three central departments of Prime Minister and Cabinet, Treasury, and Finance resulting from this restructuring, both in terms of policy effects and personnel. The government argued this was necessary to ensuring across portfolio policy coherence and the meta-policy status of economic restructuring, and for putting in place the ideology of economic rationalism – all in the context of globalization. The policies of the line and service departments such as health, social welfare and education were subsumed within this framework, that is, those departments dominated by men had more policy influence even outside their particular domains of expertise. Additionally, Pusey shows how after restructuring, youngish, male economists with experience in the central agencies, where senior women were scarce on the ground, were promoted to positions such as head and deputy head within some of these service departments. As a consequence of this restructuring, education was realigned at the federal level within the Department of Employment, Education and Training (DEET), a clear indication of the new policy regime, with the former female head replaced by a male economist with experience in Treasury. Similar restructurings occurred in the state bureaucracies with comparable effects; in the states, premiers' departments and treasuries sought tighter control over the large spending domains such as health and education. Such state structures had comparable gendered divisions of labour, power and emotional economies to those suggested for the federal structure.

Offe's (1975) observation, that there is no such thing as an administrative reform which is nothing but an administrative reform, is confirmed when one considers the gendered impact of this restructuring. More masculinist gender and policy regimes were the consequence. The state had been regendered while conditions of formal rationality remained in place; within Labor's hybrid political regime social rationalization was seen as the necessary other of economic rationalization. However, after the 1987 restructuring that hybridity became one of the subordination of the social to the economic rationalization goals (cf. E. Thompson 1991). After Labor's defeat in the 1996 federal election, the new conservative Coalition government eschewed such hybridity and pursued an unequivocal economic rationalism, as well as ushering in the return of the individual deficit subject in educational policy and rejecting the notion of group disadvantage (A. Luke 1997). In the election campaign, the Coalition sought the electoral support of those elements of the electorate supporting backlash stances; specifically, these conservative parties attempted to speak directly to disaffected white, working-class males.

In the Australian context there was another associated aspect to this regendering – what we shall call the 'ministerialization' or 'politicization' of policy making (Knight and Lingard 1997).[3] We will demonstrate such ministerialization in relation to educational policy at the national level, but such ministerialization also occurred at the state level (see Dale (1989) and Ball (1990) for similar developments in England and Wales). Ministerialization in Australia contained a number of elements, including reduction in the number of quasi independent statutory authorities, enhanced influence of ministerial advisers, the move to generic managers and contract employment, and greater policy influence of the intergovernmental council in education. Each will be considered very briefly in turn in terms of its gendered effects.

The 1987 federal public service restructuring saw a reduction in the number of statutory authorities with some autonomy from the minister and which operated in terms of professional and social agendas rather than directly party political ones. In education, the Schools Commission created in 1974 by the Whitlam Labor government, and which had policy advice and programme management functions and which was pluralist and clientist in orientation, was abolished and replaced by the Schools Council, which had only advice functions with programme functions relocated within DEET. This was about more ministerial control over educational policy. The new conservative government elected in 1996 abolished the Schools Council and have not replaced it to this point with another advisory body – an indication of ministerialization of policy as complementary to the new managerialism and the conditions of its production, rather than something reflective of party political differences. Thus in the Australian context there has been little horizontal devolution. By contrast, in the UK there was considerable horizontal devolution under the Conservatives with the creation of agencies, for example, the establishment of the Teacher Training Agency (TTA) (Mahony and Hextall 1997a), which put in place a new regime of regulation for state professionals, while also apparently absolving ministers from policy responsibility. In the Australian context, the abolition of statutory authorities reduced the voice of teachers in policy production, with gendered implications.

At the same time in Australia, ministerial advisers took on greater policy significance as ministers sought alternative policy advice to that emanating from their departments. These advisers were most often young male university graduates with appropriate political credentials and an eye on future political careers. Senior bureaucratic positions within the department were also placed on contracts with the creation of the senior executive service, as the Australian public service took a step closer towards the American model of a more directly politicized senior bureaucracy. There was also the move to generic managers away from public service heads who had professional expertise in the policy domain which was the responsibility of their department; this emphasized the technical over substantive rationality. Contract employment and generic managers together strengthened the hand of the minister *vis-à-vis* that of the bureaucracy and senior bureaucrats. Significantly too, at this time the intergovernmental council in Australian education, the Australian Education Council (AEC) (1936–93) and its successor, the Ministerial Council on Education, Employment, Training and Youth Affairs (MCEETYA), consisting of the federal and all state and territory ministers for education, took on much greater policy salience with the development of a range of national policies in schooling, which none the less remained ostensibly the policy prerogative of the states (Lingard and Porter 1997).

This ministerialization and politicization of educational policy production have very clear gendered implications, particularly given the 'patriarchal gerrymander' of electoral politics and the reduction of consultation processes with the state professional providers of services, who are mainly women. Policy making became quicker, less consultative, and more politically directed. At the same time, a highly technical and masculinist input-output equation framed the strategic policy/policy practice relationship (Blackmore 1997b). Thus we can see at work in this restructuring both the detraditionalization and retraditionalization that Giddens (1994) speaks of in relation to gender and the state. The core of policy making became more masculinist, emphasizing old style masculine economistic values, while any women who made it into that restructured core had to do so within such values. The former indicates retraditionalization at work, the latter detraditionalization. What is certain is that such regendering made the achievement of feminist goals both inside the state and within society much more difficult.

Femocrats and gendered changes to policy practice inside the state

To this point the stress has been on the structural aspect of backlash, we now turn to consider the gendered aspects of policy making agency inside the state, conceptualizing the state as a strategic terrain for policy politics. Elsewhere one of us (Lingard 1995) has written about gendered policy making inside the state in relation to the development of the *National Policy for the Education of Girls in Australian Schools* (Schools Commission 1987) and to the slow development of gender equity policies in Queensland education during the period of long conservative ascendancy in that state (1957–89). That study demonstrated the significance of intricate politics played out inside the state, by femocrats (feminist bureaucrats) in this instance, to the development of both these policies, as well as the strength of the resistance of bureaucratic structures and policy cultures to these achievements. The study was conducted at a time when Labor was in government at the federal level, and had just been elected at the state level in 1989 after thirty-two years in the political wilderness, and thus because of Labor's 'hybrid' managerialist/social justice policy regime was a (reasonably) positive time for the Australian version of state feminism. Despite that context, the femocrats interviewed for the study still indicated the difficulty of achieving their goals within state structures and this became increasingly the case as economic rationalism took stronger hold in the practices of the new managerialism. As Blackmore (1997a: 77) has noted, resistance to changes for women has always been there, but is less overt in times of strong political support for such changes, and has come to the fore again in contemporary political contexts of backlash and resentment.

'Femocrat' is an Australian neologism coined to refer to the women employed in the state bureaucracies from the mid-1970s to oversee the political machinery put in place in relation to equal opportunity, affirmative action and anti-discrimination legislation for women. Subsequently, their job descriptions were expanded to responsibility for all state policies for the so-called special needs groups, while the concept lost its pejorative overtones and was used in an even broader sense to encompass all female workers inside and outside the state for whom a commitment to feminism was a requirement of their jobs. Femocrats were the agents of social rationalization which aimed to achieve a social meritocracy which recognized and accounted for difference. There were always conflicting pressures upon femocrats, particularly in terms of the dual accountability to both the women's movement external to the state and to the bureaucratic hierarchy itself (Franzway 1986). Working with a somewhat bureaucratic binary, Summers (1986) has described pressures upon femocrats to pursue either a mandarin or missionary stance, that is align more closely with either bureaucratic or feminist norms, and the apparent inverse relationship between powerful positions within the bureaucratic hierarchy and possibilities to articulate a radical feminism. Furthermore, Sawer (1990: 24) has argued that while most male bureaucrats view all femocrats as missionaries, women outside the bureaucracy tend to view all of them as mandarins. Recuperative masculinists (see Chapter 2) were very critical of femocrats and of their control of the gender equity in the education reform agenda. This situation is indicative of the political work that femocrats had to do, the pressures upon them and of their dual and conflicting political roles in respect of changing the bureaucracy and its culture and representativeness, as well as the social change role of their policies.

Regarding policy production, Lingard's (1995) research, on femocrats working for gender equity policies in schooling, demonstrated the significance of location within the bureaucracy to the effectiveness of gender equity policies. Women who had worked within the bureaucracy on gender equity policies in Queensland during the conservative era noted the significance of their marginalized bureaucratic location to their failure or limited success in achieving their policy goals. This is a point nicely encapsulated in Grant and Tancred's (1992: 113) satirical account of the 'matriarchal state bureaucracy' where the main department is that of reproduction and where the Advisory Council on Men's Issues is an 'extremely low-ranking unit within the bureaucracy'. These observations confirm Cockburn's (1991: 232) view that getting 'the equality initiative placed in a high and secure position' is central to its effectiveness. The research also demonstrated the gendered significance of the new managerialism and restructuring, with considerations of efficiency often overriding equity ones. The femocrats interviewed indicated the directive and controlling character of the new managerialism which also manifested itself as ministerial and ministerial staffer' distrust of bureaucrats, and less consultative approaches to policy production. Furthermore, the femocrats working in education noted that restructuring at both federal and state levels disrupted feminist networks inside and outside the bureaucracy which had been central to gender equity policy gains to that point. At the time of restructuring, individuals of necessity were focusing on the need to protect their jobs and to defend gender equity programmes. The imperative of procedural precision – bureaucratic exactness – to protect their policy developments was also commented upon by these policy women. The use of that limited space between the minister's office and the bureaucracy was also utilized in the political strategizing by the femocrats; that discretionary space was somewhat reduced with the increased ministerialization of policy production, discussed above. In the domain of gender equity policies, the femocrats interviewed noted the common occurrence of symbolic policies – those that had little real support, material or otherwise, for effective implementation. However, they also commented upon the use of such symbolic policies – often a begrudging response to political pressures – as the first stage in a longer term political strategy and of the significance of a politically aware teacher constituency for the effectiveness or usefulness of such symbolic policies.

A concept to develop out of Lingard's (1995) research was that of 'policy culture'. The concept was created to refer to 'the structures and policy goals, and dominant discourses and practices within public bureaucracies which frame the possibilities for policy' (Lingard 1995: 146). Thus the federal femocrats spoke of the huge change of policy culture with the move to John Dawkins as federal Minister for Employment, Education and Training after Labor's 1987 election victory which was simultaneous with the restructuring of the federal bureaucracy referred to earlier. At the Queensland level, the femocrats talked of the change of policy culture following the Labor election victory in 1989, but also noted that residues of the older anti-equity and anti-feminism culture still remained intact. When the conservatives took office again in Queensland in 1996, one of the first actions of the new state Minister for Education was to visit the gender equity unit in the Department of Education and indicate his concern for their 'social engineering' policies – another shift in policy culture. However, some considerable opposition to this stance was articulated by teachers and other constituencies outside the department which has resulted in a less frontal attack on gender equity and social justice agendas; the stance is now more one of benign neglect.

Hochschild in *The Managed Heart* (1983: 7) developed the concept of 'emotional labour' to refer to demands in some occupations 'to induce or suppress feeling in order to sustain the outward countenance that produces the proper state of mind in others'. Emotional labour thus refers to the possible disjunction – emotive dissonance – between the emotional display rules required by certain jobs located at particular points within an organization and the actual emotions or feelings of workers (Mann 1997). Mann (1997: 5) encapsulates the meaning of emotional labour as, 'The work involved in managing emotions in the workplace by either displaying appropriate emotions or suppressing inappropriate ones'.[4] Hochschild (1983) also argues that emotional labour is part of the work requirement in jobs which are traditionally dominated by women, for example, in the service sector such as airline cabin staff and in nursing and education. With the move to a post-industrial, service oriented economy, more jobs require emotional labour. Within organizations, the emotional is the other of rationality, with organizations creating and remaking changing emotional economies across time (Czarniawska 1997). The research literature would suggest that the femocrat role, with its dual mandarin/missionary responsibilities and internal organizational and change agent requirements, makes considerable emotional labour demands upon femocrats (Franzway 1986; Lingard 1995; Eisenstein 1996; Blackmore 1997d; Ramsay 1997). Such women work to support other women in their careers and in the daily demands of their jobs, their emotional needs, represent women on committees and in other policy work, while also networking with the powerful (Blackmore 1997b: 13); at the same time always attempting to be the bureaucrat *par excellence* while also politically strategizing for change (Lingard 1995). Femocrats thus have to practise 'emotional masking', while also giving effect to 'integrative emotions' necessary to team building in organizations undergoing reculturing (Mann 1997: 6).

Femocrats have worked in state organizations undergoing cultural change which results in the remaking of the emotional economy, while at the same time also being responsible for cultural change of a different sort, which likewise involves them in heavy emotional labour. Ministerialization of policy production also enhanced pressures for the femocrats to have greater loyalty to the bureaucracy (and sometimes to their own careers) than to their constituency external to the bureaucracy and to the broader feminist project. This was another source of tension for them, again demanding emotional labour.

Now, what is the point of this discussion of the femocrat experience? It is to show how even when the political climate and culture within the bureaucracy are at least partly conducive to the feminist project, that a considerable political struggle still ensues for those entrusted with responsibility for its prosecution. For the femocrats, it was difficult working inside the bureaucracy for change and became more difficult with subsequent managerialist modifications and the meta-policy status granted to economic restructuring.

There were also roadblocks to their own career advancement, often referred to as the 'glass ceiling', which Ramsay (1995) has suggested obfuscates the fact that it is male power and culture which inhibit their advancement within the bureaucracy, as well as dominant models of management, leadership and bureaucratic behaviour (often) stressing the technical over the substantive (Blackmore 1993). Eisenstein (1996), in her study of Australian femocrats, *Inside Agitators*, has documented the (demanding and difficult) gender and sexual politics experienced by femocrats and the fragility of the sisterhood which supported them. Restructuring and the backlash made their difficult work even more difficult and moved them into a defensive policy mode. The pursuit of the feminist project by state workers has thus been disciplined by restructuring (Blackmore 1997a).

Regendering and steering at a distance

There is another important element to the restructuring of the state which carries gendered implications: there has been a changed relationship between the policy generating centre and the practice periphery, if one can utilize that inappropriate metaphor. The centre has become more focused upon setting strategic goals, policy parameters and performance mandates; the periphery has been granted greater 'freedom' to implement these frameworks. This approach to the state and policy production/policy practice relations within the policy cycle has been called 'steering at a distance' (Kickert 1991), a contradictory (oxymoronic?) form of recentralized decentralization. Given the masculinizing of policy production at the centre and the predominance of women amongst state employed professionals (e.g. teachers and nurses), steering at a distance also has gendered effects, which work their way out in the changing emotional economy of educational systems, which will be discussed more fully later in this chapter. Further, Kerfoot and Knights (1993: 671) have spoken about the 'strategic masculinity' implicit in the managerialist approach of the steering arm of the steering at a distance approach.

Clarke and Newman (1997), in writing about the restructuring of the UK public sector and the emergence of what they refer to as the 'managerial state', have commented upon the changes to bureaucracy/professional relationships which result. They speak of attempts to displace, subordinate and co-opt professional discourses to corporate goals:

> *Displacement* refers to the process by which management has super-seded bureau-professionalism in the way public services are organised as regimes. Here organisations are reshaped around a command structure which privileges the calculative framework of managerialism: how to improve efficiency and organisational performance. Complete displacement is relatively rare: the dominant relationship between

bureau-professionalism and management has been one of *subordination*. This takes the form of framing the exercise of professional judgement by the requirement that it takes account of the 'realities and responsibilities' of budgetary management . . . Where 'need' was once the product of the intersection of bureaucratic categorisation and professional judgement, it is now increasingly articulated with and *disciplined* by a managerial calculus of resources and priorities. But many areas of professional service are characterised by a rather different strategy: that of *co-option*. This refers to managerial attempts to colonise the terrain of professional discourse, constructing articulations between professional concerns and languages and those of management . . . These are strategies in the struggle between regimes. They produce new focal points of resistance, compromise and accommodation.

(Clarke and Newman 1997: 76)

These tensions between corporate goals within funding constraints and professional goals framed around meeting needs have manifested themselves in educational systems (cf. Gewirtz *et al.* 1995). Clearly, with educational restructuring professional discourses have been 'subordinated' and 'disciplined' by the managerialist fetish for efficiency and effectiveness, with gendered impacts. Within the performative state they have also been linked to new demands of emotional labour and new emotional economies both within the central bureaucracy and within schools; matters to be pursued in the following sections of this chapter. Suffice to say here that the forms of devolution accompanying steering at a distance have resulted in 'devolved stress' (Clarke and Newman 1997: 77), as those at the periphery have been granted the opportunity to self-manage the cuts to the system (cf. Ball 1994). Given the regendering which results from structural backlash, and the basic gender segmentation of the state's workforce, including the preponderance of women as state professionals, the devolution of stress has heavy implications for women.

Another significant element of the regendering of the state has been the new forms of leadership which the flatter, managerialist and performative state demands. This is a more entrepreneurial approach, one bound much less by precise and fetishized concerns for correct procedures, than by the need to achieve speedier and measurable outputs. Without essentializing women's or men's leadership styles (Weiner 1995), this is a more masculinist approach (Gewirtz *et al.* 1995: 94). Kerfoot and Knights (1993) and Whitehead (1999) argue entrepreneurial rather than paternalistic masculinity has become the dominant form – one probably less attractive to femocrats and other female administrators in education.[5] Whitehead (1999: 24) suggests that 'the chaos, uncertainty and unpredictability of contemporary organizational life privileges the competitive, aggressive and instrumental actor'. In that context, he also argues that the discourse of performativity is 'particularly seductive for men/managers' (1999: 20). Commenting on male backlash in the culture more generally, Connell (1990) has observed:

> The reassertion of a dominance-based masculinity has been much discussed in popular culture. To my mind its most interesting form is not Rambo movies but the 1980s cult of the 'entrepreneur' in business . . . Among other things, their managerial jargon is full of lurid gender terminology: thrusting entrepreneurs, opening up virgin territory, aggressive lending and so on.
>
> (Connell 1990: 614)

Mahony (1997a: 99), in writing about the effects of new managerialism upon feminist heads of department in education faculties in universities in the UK, has added to this list: 'biting the bullet, biting the cherry, screwing the opposition, shafting uneconomic departments, developing the strategy and the game plan, hitting the targets, upsetting the troops and punching through new initiatives'.

Steering at a distance is thus gendered with new core/periphery relations, with its subordination of the professional to the managerial, and its new culture of management, resulting in the replacement of a paternalistic masculinity with an entrepreneurial one (Whitehead 1999).

Regendering educational systems

The introduction to this chapter and the sections above have indicated something of the impact of the regendering of educational systems. The policy producing centre has become more masculinized with policies framed by economic restructuring and human capital concerns, with a focus upon outputs as measured by performance indicators. All of this has usually been put in place in a context at worst of expenditure cuts, or at best, of steady state funding. At the same time, the take-up of globalization as rationale for state policies has seen pervasive insecurity, a growth in inequality, a turning away from redistributive policies and a political backlash against recognition politics and policies of social rationalization as outlined in Chapter 1. Simultaneous with such developments has been the increased feminization of teaching and a managerial reconstitution of the role of school administrators. Educational systems have thus been regendered, with a hardening of the gender segmentation within the state which affirmative action policies and the like sought to soften, with teachers in the schools, a high percentage of whom are women, having to bear the brunt of stress devolved down the line and to deal with the new emotional labour demands of marketized schooling systems.[6] This is an intensification of the traditional gendered relationships within educational systems and schools where (largely) men have attempted to intervene in and reconstitute the work of teachers (largely women) (Apple 1986). The steering at a distance of this new arrangement also apparently implies greater autonomy for teachers within the processes of devolution. However, there has been a simultaneous centralizing of strategic frameworks, curriculum requirements and performance indicators. These dual and apparently contradictory pressures lead to what Blackmore (1997c: 14) has called the 'institutional schizophrenia' of self-managing organizations, 'which on the one hand encourage initiative, autonomy, and innovation at the same time that on the other, workers feel more controlled and under surveillance than ever before'.

Feminist politics and the regendered state

From the late 1980s in Australia, there was weakened political commitment to changing the bureaucracy for social ends and for the social change agenda. Structural backlash was the result of the move to the competitive and performative state and the related policy goals of internationalizing the Australian economy and narrowing and reducing the remit and influence of state policy coverage. This affected the policy work and gendered experiences of femocrats inside state structures; it affected the nature and effects of state policies relating to gender; it also regendered the relationships between state policies and their practice in schools.

Since the defeat of Labor in 1996 which had been in power since 1983, the political climate has been even less conducive to the feminist project than that of the latter stages of the federal Labor government; indeed the Howard Coalition government has been overtly anti-feminism, except in its weakest individualistic and liberal forms. The goal appears to have become one of trying to get more women into senior positions in the public (and private) sector, rather than attempting to change or confront the social order which has ensured the dominance of men in such positions: material girls in a material world. The ideal was a (very weak) version of the meritocracy which eschewed conceptions of group disadvantage and the related need for (strong) state interventions to ensure equality of opportunity. The conservative federal Coalition government has attacked the feminist state agenda in both symbolic and material terms, for example, in the abolition of gender-neutral language and in the Prime Minister's refusal to use the term 'chairperson', and in cuts to financial support for the state infrastructure for equal employment opportunity, non-discriminatory practices and the like and in long delays in appointing people to senior positions (Blackmore 1999). This government has also made childcare more expensive. The feminist project of working on and within the state has perhaps been superseded politically by the need to mobilize broader support against the government. Certainly, state feminism is on the defensive in Australia (Ramsay 1997; Blackmore 1999). This has been very clear in the way in which pressures from certain men's groups for a boys' education policy at the national level have been converted to a *Gender Equity Framework for Australian Schools* (Gender

Equity Taskforce 1997), with gender here the signifier that both boys' and girls' issues will be dealt with. Femocrat strategizing ensured the mediation of the worst features of a backlash politics in that respect.[7] Furthermore, the national advisory body on gender equity in education has been abolished on the advice of ministers and senior bureaucrats.

The policy culture within both state and federal bureaucracies in the restructured state is not conducive to achieving further feminist goals in education in a broader political context of backlash and post-feminist political developments,[8] including recuperative attempts to constitute men as the new disadvantaged. The conditions of structural backlash outlined in this chapter – the increased emphasis upon efficiency and effectiveness manifest as performativity in its various guises, the more conservative policy culture – have changed the work of femocrats so that they now operate in a more chilly climate which makes even more demands upon their emotional work, enhancing their experience of emotive dissonance, and placing them in a defensive rather than offensive position in relation to feminist reform agendas both inside and outside the state. We would argue that the femocrat experience can probably be extrapolated to that of many women working inside a changing and increasingly managerialist state. Furthermore, as shown earlier and in subsequent sections of this chapter, state restructuring changed the character of gender relations between policy production and practice in schools, affecting in a substantial way the work of teachers and school principals.

We have documented the character of structural backlash, indicating the regendering of the state policy regime which has occurred. We would also stress that this regendering has implications for resultant policy outcomes, that is, we are not only talking about the impact of structural backlash upon women's career opportunities and experiences inside state structures, but also an impact upon the type of policy outcome and the work of teachers in schools. Kenway (1990), for example, has demonstrated how the *National Policy for the Education of Girls in Australian Schools* (Schools Commission 1987) was developed under a feminist minister, but implemented under a new minister concerned to subsume educational policy as an arm of economic restructuring policy; the new federal Department of Employment, Education and Training was itself a signifier of the new policy regime. She shows how this affected the gender reform agenda in schooling. Gender equity policies thus focused on getting more girls into maths and sciences as another element in the internationalizing of the Australian economy. Getting more girls into maths and science was also something which could be adequately measured in performance indicator terms, while leaving intact a gender order which benefited men over women. Kenway (1996) along with her colleagues (Kenway *et al.* 1997a), as well as Yates (1997), have also demonstrated how that managerialist and economic rationalist (as well as liberal feminist) generated policy regime was one factor in the subsequent 'What about the boys?' backlash in Australian education. (See Chapter 4 here.)

Offe (1975) has provided an important insight in his observation that the structure, organizational arrangements and culture of bureaucracy are important mediating elements in determining what issues get onto the policy agenda, how these are dealt with and what results in terms of policy text production and policy outcomes. Structural backlash with new relations between and within departments and between systemic policy and practice had such an effect upon the feminist reform project. It also had the dual and contradictory impact of detraditionalization and retraditionalization of gendered practices within and of the state. Structural backlash has worked its way out in particular gendered ways in education with implications for women. It is to a consideration of administering and teaching in restructured educational systems that we now turn.

Administering and teaching in schools in restructured educational systems

In the context of the 'What about the boys?' debates there have been calls for more male teachers, particularly in the primary schools. For example, the Teacher Training Agency (TTA) in the UK has made a concerted attempt to recruit more men to teaching, while in Queensland, the state government also has spent money on an advertising campaign to attract more male teachers. The chief executive of the TTA, Anthea Millet, has observed:

> We really are concerned about getting more men into teaching, partly because of their position as role models. But actually also to act as advocates for the profession, because I do think men make better advocates.
>
> (Millet 1995: 2)

This is not the first time there has been a moral panic about the gender of the teaching profession. Connell (1996: 207) notes how in the 1960s in the USA there was a panic about schools destroying 'boy culture', and many of us can remember in the Australian context when lower entrance scores were accepted for men than for women to teacher education courses to ensure there were some men in teaching – positive discrimination for men by other means! Acker (1995) has noted the production of moral panics about the feminization of teaching which emerge at different historical moments and in a broad range of countries. Meadmore (1996) has also traced the articulation and rearticulation of such concerns across twentieth century Australian education where at times the desire for more male teachers worked through restrictions on the recruitment and continuing employment of women as teachers with marriage bars, ceilings on numbers of female teachers, differential entrance scores to the profession and the like.

Further, and despite the historical domination of women in the teaching profession, particularly at the primary level, educational administration remains a male domain and thus largely masculinist in orientation and in its taken-for-granted assumptions (Lingard and Limerick 1995: 3). And as indicated earlier in this chapter, structural backlash has reinforced and reinstated such a masculinist orientation – retraditionalization in Giddens's terms. Limerick (1991), for example, showed that only 17 per cent of principals in the Queensland state education department were women, while an Australian government commissioned report stated that 'women remain heavily under-represented in school leadership and promotional positions', while the 'improvement in their position is very slow' (Milligan *et al.* 1994: 45). This situation continues and we have argued throughout this chapter that the reconstitution of the role of the school administrator under restructuring pressures might very well ensure that such positions become less attractive to women in the future (cf. Grace 1995). At the same time, it appears to be the case that classroom teaching at both primary and secondary schools is becoming more feminized, but we also need to acknowledge that teaching has been highly feminized across most of the twentieth century. We also note the way in which current moral panics about paedophilia have also worked in relation to getting more males into pre-school and primary teaching. There has traditionally been some suspicion about males seeking careers in pre-school and often aspersions cast about their sexuality. The status of teaching, salary levels, career rewards, the association of teaching young children with caring and nurturing, the gender regime of educational systems have all been factors in the heavily gender segmented character of teaching as a profession and need to be considered in relation to the call for more male teachers.

In terms of the argument presented throughout this chapter, it is interesting that calls for more male teachers have come at a time of substantial restructuring, including the introduction of a performance culture, and something of a backlash against older progressive pedagogies. In literacy there have been exhaustive debates concerning effective pedagogies for working-class and minority students, as compared to those which work for middle-class students, who are more at ease with the cultural capital implicit in the provision of schooling. This debate has turned around directive and explicit teaching versus a Deweyian, child-centred progressivism, a debate between visible and invisible pedagogies. Some of the school effectiveness push also appears to encourage a return to a more transmission style of teaching, which is also supported by the outcomes focus endemic to the performance culture of restructured educational systems. There is a way in which the emphasis on performance in a narrower range of activities can also encourage narrower pedagogy and narrower goals for schooling. The parsimonious funding of educational systems as part of post-Keynesian dis-investment politics also produces what Blackmore (1997d) calls 'thin' rather than 'fat' pedagogies – pedagogies more concerned with transmission. This situation affects the work of teachers, the majority of whom are women. Some have suggested that women teachers are more likely to support child-centred approaches and that the priority of the needs of the child over those of the teacher within such approaches extends and intensifies the emotional work of these female teachers (Walkerdine 1986). Such commitments also sit in tension with the current policy press for thin pedagogies.

Smedley (1997) has argued that within these restructured schooling sys-tems women teachers are often associated negatively with a caring and nur-turant, pastoral care, 'agony aunt' approach, as Chris Woodhead, the Chief Inspector of Schools in England has put it (*Times Educational Supplement*, 14 March 1997), while 'The presence of men is taken to mean there will be discipline, order, rigour and a better working atmosphere for boys' (Smed-ley 1997: 224). We can only speculate on the relationship between the call for more male teachers and the new culture of performativity within less well funded schooling systems. However, there is a way in which current public policy discourses seek to masculinize primary teaching, as much in relation to its practices, as to the gender of the teaching profession (Smedley 1997: 223). We would argue that the performance culture might also encourage such practices. None the less, there is a blend of discourses which come together in this contemporary demand for more male teachers.

Often such calls are based on mythopoetic and men's rights arguments that boys need more male role models to support them in the 'rites of passage' from boyhood to manhood. The mythopoets want to recreate the homosocial environments of a mythologized boyhood. In their worst moments many of the mythopoets charge women – female teachers, mothers, single mothers – with being the source of many of the problems facing boys and young men today. The argument is simply that more men in the lives of boys, in both the home and the school, will improve educational and life experiences for boys. Often, the argument that many boys are raised by single mothers, and are thus socially fatherless, is also garnered to sup-port the call for more male teachers. Indeed, in *Fatherless America*, Blanken-horn (1996) has argued that the rough parity in the USA between fatherless families and those with a father present is the most urgent social problem facing the contemporary USA. Chris Woodhead has blamed both female teachers and single mothers for the failure of white working class boys in school: 'Is it that in some primary schools there are few, if any, men to act as role models for the boys? Nowadays, even the caretaker may, it seems, be a woman' (*The Times*, 6 March 1996). Similar arguments have been evident in Australia.

These calls for more male teachers usually assume something of an essen-tialist view of masculinity and eschew notions of its social construction.

They are also usually about reinforcing traditional sex roles and ensuring more security for boys as they move into manhood. The danger here is the possibility of the reinforcement of dominant or hegemonic versions of masculinity. Within this framework, few questions are asked about *which* men we ought to be encouraging into teaching. Christian (1994) has shown how important mothers have been in producing men who take a pro-feminist and anti-sexist stance, but of course this is not usually a desired goal for the mythopoets. The question perhaps ought to be more one about what teachers, either male or female, do, rather than simply a question of the gender of the teachers (Gilbert and Gilbert 1998).

There have also been progressive calls for more male teachers, arguing the need for men to demonstrate that they too can be caring and nurturing. However, Gilbert and Gilbert (1998) have suggested that research seems to suggest that in terms of modelling, the sex of the person is less important than the 'sex-appropriateness of the sex-modelled behaviour'. None the less, they argue that more male teachers would be a good thing for two reasons. First, that it would help break down the heavily gender segmented nature of educational work, and second, that the presence of more male teachers would contribute to disrupting the association between intellectual work and the effeminate, and we would add, hopefully disrupt the association between rejection of nurturing and caring behaviours and the masculine. We would suggest that the move to get more women into promotional positions needs to continue in the context of moves to recruit more male teachers and that we need to consider the motivations of those calling for more male teachers and what these male teachers will actually do in schools. Smedley (1997: 218) has also asked questions concerning the impact upon men of moving into primary schools as teachers, into 'a world characterised as feminine, as a women's workplace, with all that that signifies'. Elsewhere in this book we have argued the need for more male teachers for all the positive reasons mentioned above and in so doing vehemently reject the mythopoetic and masculinity therapy rationales for so doing. We believe that men in schools have a responsibility to work within a gender equity framework concerned for both boys and girls towards the reconstruction of toxic masculinities and a more equal gender order – issues taken up in Chapter 5. It should not only be women who are responsible for such gender work in schools. Otherwise, there is danger that women will continue to do the emotional work for men and boys (cf. Kenway 1995).

Blackmore (1996) has researched the emotional labour which women principals have to do in restructured educational systems. Writing about the implementation of the *Schools of the Future* move to self-managing schools in Victoria, at the same moment as severe cuts in educational expenditure and teacher numbers, and the embrace of market ideology, she encapsulates the emotional demands upon female principals emanating from schools' participation in student, leadership and teacher markets. She notes how the conservative government in Victoria built on previous Labor government support for women in leadership positions in schools, and supported a number of women into principals' jobs. These women were appointed because of their sharing and caring leadership styles which came under challenge in the new context of marketization and the self-managing school. And as Blackmore points out, there is a significant emotional load in easing organizations – in this case, schools – through rapid change. In a somewhat Foucauldian sense, she also talks of how the management of emotions in rapidly changing organizations is also part of the management of the self – self-surveillance. Performativity demands that all be seen to perform, including female principals, and is linked to control through self-surveillance within the new core–periphery relationships involved in steering at a distance.

In telling a story about female principals in relation to the student market, Blackmore shows how the need to keep student numbers up saw a principal break with the collegiality of her fellow principals and sell her school as different from other schools in her area. She also demonstrates how a leadership market is created in this new policy context whereby principals have to market themselves and their leadership styles as much as their schools.[9] The tension between the emotionality of teaching and questions of morality and principle are put in some jeopardy in the market 'as principals are expected to respond uncritically to its demands without regard to social, moral and political agendas' (Blackmore 1996: 344). Blackmore also documents the emergence of a new teacher labour market with the introduction of contract employment and notes its gendered implications and the impact upon female principals. With respect to this new teacher labour market, she observes:

> A new core–periphery model of the labour market is emerging with the hollowing out of middle management and devolution to self managing schools. The effect has been in Victoria of the re-masculinisation of the centre or core where financial management and policy maintain a strong steering capacity for the state, and a flexible peripheral labour market of increasingly feminised, casualised and deprofessionalised teaching force as central wages awards are replaced by individual contracts in the deregulated market.
>
> (Blackmore 1996: 345)

This is another element of structural backlash and the processes of re-traditionalization and detraditionalization; female principals are caught in a bind between their collaborative approaches to leadership and the new hierarchical relations between principals and teachers inherent in marketized self-managing schools. Blackmore speaks of the distancing and denial which some female principals utilize as strategies to cope with the (emotional) pressures upon them, and while all principals have to deal with the emotional labour inherent in restructuring schools, she suggests that 'women principals are more vulnerable to the exigencies of the market and emotions' (Blackmore 1996: 348).

Thus the new management has been combined with marketization in education. Writing about the situation in England and Wales, Gewirtz *et al.* (1995), while recognizing the localized character of educational markets, show the generalized impact of this new management/market couplet on schooling. Similar to Blackmore's argument, they suggest the focus, among other things, is now upon academic outcomes, attracting particular student/clients, appeasing and responding to middle-class parental demands, effective impression management in the marketing of the school and so on. The result is a tension between management and marketing goals on the one hand and those derived from professional cultures on the other. Gewirtz *et al.* (1995: 96) suggest that in that context headteachers as managers and educators, out of necessity, become 'bilingual', able to speak both discourses. Often this cultural tension has gendered implications, as indicated by Blackmore's (1996) research referred to above. While acknowledging that these pressures have worked out differently in secondary and primary schools, Grace (1995) suggests that such positions thus probably become less attractive to many female teachers. Interestingly, Gewirtz *et al.* also show how in the marketized schooling system of England, girls have become a more attractive client group than boys for some schools, given their different behaviours and relationships with schools. (Curiously, this appears to offer some support to the recuperative masculinists' argument that schools are currently more compatible to girls than boys.) In that context, David and her colleagues (1994) have also shown how mothers have been largely responsible for the multi-layered processes of choice of school.

An Australian study of *Women in the Teaching Profession* (Milligan *et al.* 1994), commissioned by the Schools Council, an advisory body to the previous federal Labor government on schooling, was concerned to ascertain 'the effect of recent "restructuring" in the schools sector on the position of women in the workforce' (Milligan *et al.* 1994: vii). This report documented the heavy gender segmented nature of work within educational systems, noting that: 'Men predominate in management roles; in teaching older students; in teaching of industrial arts, agriculture, and science; as gardeners and building maintenance workers' (1994: 7). In contrast, the report observed: 'Women predominate as classroom teachers and teacher aides; in teaching of young children, remedial students and students who have English as a second language; in teaching of home economics and languages; in special education; and as librarians' (1994: 7). The report also confirmed the findings of research conducted by Collins and her colleagues (1996) that policy in respect of gender matters does have a real effect. Thus, *Women in the Teaching Profession* notes the goodly percentage of women principals in South Australia where gender equity has been pursued for a long period and in a committed fashion. South Australia had twice the percentage of female principals as Queensland (Milligan *et al.* 1994: 7), for example, where there has been some resistance to gender equity policies. Concerning women's position in the school sector workforce, the report pointed out that this workforce remains heavily gender segmented, with men still predominating in management roles in the system and the schools, while the overall school workforce has become more feminized. This is also true of both primary and secondary teaching. The area where there has been some decrease in gender segmentation is that of Advanced Skills Teachers (AST), a new promotional category created in Australian teaching to offer promotion to those in the teaching workforce who wanted promotion but wished to maintain teaching as their major function. Women have fared well in relation to these positions, perhaps indicating some differential valuing of teaching and classroom work between women and men.

Women in the Teaching Profession argues, perhaps surprisingly, that there was 'no inherent contradiction between the interests of gender equity for the workforce and much of the reform agenda' (Milligan *et al.* 1994: 45). However, since that report was written the reform agenda has become more marketized and equity concerns have been largely marginalized. The report argued that the continuation of equal employment opportunity in devolved systems would increasingly depend upon the knowledge and commitments of principals. The argument throughout this chapter has been that a range of pressures has reduced the commitment of systems to such goals and limited the capacity of schools to pursue them.

Acker (1995) has provided an analysis of the literature which associates caring with teaching, particularly teaching in the primary schools.[10] The subject orientations and subcultures within secondary schools perhaps mean that this association is not as strong within these schools. Acker shows how that literature suggests an ethic of care and an emphasis upon connectedness and relationships are most often associated with women's practices and that this works in a contradictory fashion for women teachers. The work of Gilligan and Noddings has been of central importance here, yet has also been criticized for its essentialist tendencies. Given that teaching is a labour process without a product and that the boundaries of teachers' work appear almost limitless, this female ethic of care can mean that, 'Like good mothers, good teachers find that their work is never done' (Acker 1995: 122). There is thus a way in which the nature of teaching and 'women's ways' work together in a contradictory fashion to both provide female teachers with the moral high ground, but also intensify their workloads. We would argue that this contradiction has been intensified by state and educational restructuring – by what we are calling structural backlash. As indicated earlier, there are pressures within the culture of performativity within educational systems to narrow curriculum and emphasize a particular range of outcomes. Further, such changes are usually accompanied by cuts in expenditure and the introduction of contract employment and the like. The changes associated with a particular public policy adoption of globalization, along with its direct effects, have also witnessed growing social inequality, pervasive insecurity, and an associated range of social problems. Teachers are in the front line of dealing with these issues on a daily basis and they demand new forms of emotional labour. Restructured educational systems have made it more difficult for teachers to deal with these issues.[11] We next turn to a consideration of emotional labour in the new emotional economy within restructured educational systems.

Emotional economy and emotional labour in restructured educational systems

To this point an account of the greedy organizations, which result from the 'more for less' approach of state structures framed by economic rationalist ideology and new managerialism, has been provided. The way this works as structural backlash has also been documented and analysed, for example, the hardening of already heavily gender segmented educational systems and the way in which stress is devolved down the line to a largely feminized teaching profession. Utilizing the theorizing of Giddens, we have also demonstrated the detraditionalizing and retraditionalizing of gender practices that this evokes. In this context, and as indicated above, certain features of teaching as a profession – a labour process without a product (Connell 1995) and the association of teaching with caring – enhance the impact of the demands of the greedy, even voracious, organization upon teachers, particularly women (Acker 1995). Restructuring is at one level about reculturing and reculturing requires emotional labour (Mann 1997), much of which becomes the responsibility of women across all levels of educational systems, including schools. It is also, of course, the responsibility of men, but the gender segmentation of the education profession, means a differential gendered effect and structural backlash reinforces such effects.

We have already utilized Hochschild's (1983) concept of emotional labour to consider some aspects of the structural backlash. In this section, we shall focus specifically on the demands of emotional labour within restructured educational systems. However, we want to move to a somewhat more structuralist analysis here and speak of the emergent emotional economy which accompanies restructuring and which forms part of the structural backlash. In so doing, we use the concept of emotional labour in an enhanced way beyond Hochschild's original definition, which simply referred to the dissonance between actual felt emotions and the required emotional display of certain jobs, particularly those located within the service sector. Here we have accepted the revisionist organizational theories which recognize the significance of gender, sexuality and emotion in organizational and occupational/professional life (Hearn *et al.* 1989; Mills and Tancred 1992; Fineman 1993; Cheng 1996). That literature requires a rejection of a rationality/emotionality binary evidenced in old organizational analysis and in talk about remaking organizations. In such accounts, as Putnam and Mumby (1993) note:

> Rationality surfaces as the positive while emotionality is viewed as a negative. The prevalence of these dualities contributes to treating emotion as a form of labour or as a tool of exerting influence in organisational settings. In organisations, emotions are consistently devalued and marginalised while rationality is privileged as an ideal of organisational life. Moreover, the devaluing of emotions and the elevating of rationality results in a particular moral order.
>
> (Putnam and Mumby 1993: 39)

Blackmore (1996) has noted how the feminist literature on organizations gives emphasis to the emotionality of organizational life. However, she suggests that this literature tends to stress the positives of this reality and neglect the down side. As such, it fails to see how women's burden of emotional work can go unrecognized and remain invisible.

The performativity of the restructured educational system operates with a reconstituted notion of technical rationality; reconstituted in the sense that any overarching meta-epistemological stance has been eschewed. This new form is given priority in a restructuring which focuses upon specific outcomes to be achieved at lowest cost. At the same time, the actual processes and practices of restructuring, particularly the reculturing element, result in real emotional fallout. Integrative practices of emotional labour are required to 'smooth' and 'manage' the effects of these changes – the manufacturing of consent within the new structures (Gewirtz *et al.* 1995: 95). The new management texts speak of the caring, sharing and team building capacities required by new managers in this new organizational structure, features often perceived, in an essentialist fashion, to be associated with female management styles (cf. Ozga and Walker 1995; Weiner 1995). At the same time, structural backlash has meant actually fewer women in such senior management positions in education as a result of its regendering effects and contradictions between these text book ideals, new management cultures and the actual requirements of leadership positions in restructured, more market driven educational systems.

The devolution of stress down the line in achieving mandated outcomes at the lowest cost plays out in schools in different ways for those in the headship, those in middle management (e.g. heads of department) and those whose responsibility is solely teaching. As argued by Gewirtz *et al.* (1995), and already noted, within such a school context, tensions are precipitated between marketing demands and managerial imperatives and professional goals and cultures. This tension is a gendered one. Further, while recognizing that there are always tensions and conflicts within organizations, and particularly in those dealing with people, restructuring has probably generated more conflict in schools than was the case previously, when there was greater congruence between the cultures of school administrators and teachers (Gewirtz *et al.* 1995: 95), particularly in the primary schools. This situation enhances the demands of emotional labour within schools.

We also require an expanded conception of emotional labour to encapsulate what is going on here: the resultant emotional demands require more than simply managing the dissonance between felt and organizational mandated expressions of emotion and feeling. Teaching is emotional and demanding work which appears in many ways to be incommensurable with the performative culture which is seeking to discipline it in a measurable, yet vastly narrowed fashion. That incommensurability makes emotional demands. Further, given that teaching is ostensibly a labour process without a product, despite the marauding attempts of the performativity culture to make it otherwise, the demands to achieve more for less within a funding cuts culture, can also have substantial emotional effects on teachers, most of whom are women.

Performativity, as already noted, is also about being seen to perform (Blackmore 1997b, 1999). This is the impression management element of the new performative culture which also links to emotional labour. The stress is on 'externalities, upon performance, upon exteriority' (Blackmore 1997c: 15) – on being seen to perform – the simulacrum, and demands the masking of any concerns about the changes under way. Real feelings are hidden and one's self is 'sold' and 'marketed' within this performative culture of the 'no hands' form of control of restructured educational systems (Ball 1994: 54). Performativity thus demands emotional work within systems and schools. In picking up on this observation, Blackmore notes:

> Performativity of postmodern organisations exploits the pleasure of the win, and getting the job done, as well as the intimacy of social relations to achieve organisational goals. This contrasts with the modernist performance principle of the gender neutral bureaucrat, which 'embraced delayed gratification, the restraint of pleasure, work and productiveness'.
> (Blackmore 1997c: 13)

In other research on women in changing universities, Blackmore (1997d) has found different discourses operating among women located at different places within the organizational arrangement, namely, executive level, middle management (heads of department) and academics. At the executive level there was talk of collegiality, corporate culture and purposes. As well, women at this level reported their practice of regulating and disciplining their emotions and language. Those at middle management level spoke of being caught at the fulcrum between, on the one hand, system wide demands for strategic plans, corporate culture, image management, performativity and so on, and on the other, the social and professional relationships with staff members in the department which required a different form of emotional labour. Academics concerned largely with teaching and research were positioned by a discourse of 'lack of purpose, disorder, chaos, fragmentation and discord, lack of direction, a sense of loss and fear' (Blackmore 1997d: 9) and a concern for the apparent disjunction between strategic plans and corporate culture and the 'real work' of academics. While this research was conducted in universities, one can probably extrapolate to restructured schooling systems and begin to conceptualize the new emotional economy at work, including the different emotional demands at work at different points within the system and their varying effects on both men and women.

Some of the new management literature appears to argue for a new style of leadership and management more at one with approaches usually associated with female managers – sharing, caring, trust, power with rather than power over and so on. For example, the Karpin Report in Australia (Industry Task Force on Leadership and Management Skills 1995) argued the need for more female managers and changed management practices. However, on closer inspection, these new approaches are geared to greater productivity rather than achieving more gender equitable organizations or outcomes. And, as has been noted throughout this chapter, there is a new entrepreneurial managerialism associated with masculinity, emerging in the restructured state. Ozga and Williams (1995) argue that the new management discourses only bear a superficial resemblance to feminist conceptions of management. They argue that new management forms and practices in actuality are simply 'more effective management tools, producing internalised controls that serve to ensure that performance indicators and other targets are met' (Ozga and Williams 1995: 37). Some have also argued that flatter structures are more conducive to female practices (Oerton 1996). Oerton's (1996) research shows that this is not necessarily the case in the flatter organizations within the social economy. She found that there were both constraints and opportunities for resistance for both male and female workers within such organizations. However, she also confirmed that women workers' commitments to paid work were 'emotional, relational and familial in form' (Oerton 1996: 179) and that because of such orientations they were more likely 'to materially engage in their own self or collective exploitation in terms of doing more after-hours work for less remuneration than their men counterparts' (1996: 180). We have argued that devolution of tasks to schools has changed the emotional economy within schools and that similarly women carry a lot of its burden.

There is thus talk today of the need for management styles which are aware of the emotional elements of organizational change in line with what have been seen as more female approaches. Yet as demonstrated throughout, the state has been regendered so that fewer women are in management positions, or those women who are have to abide by the emergent entre-preneurial masculinism of the new managerialism. What remains is a simu-lacrum in conditions of formal equality: the disembodied need for (supposedly) female management styles without the embodiment of female managers. Much of the new demand for emotional labour is devolved down the line, resulting in a new emotional economy: the simulacrum of caring at the centre, the absent presence of women, and intensified demands for emotional labour in middle management and in teaching, borne on the backs of women. Women who now enter the hard core centre have to take on detraditionalized practices, while those still doing the teaching in the schools, in being called upon to do more emotional work, have in essence been retraditionalized. The new management, superficially at least, appears to demand a detraditionalization of masculinity, but as has been shown, in reality what we see is an emergent entrepreneurial masculinity evident in the new managerialism.

Conclusion

Ball (1994) has suggested that Conservative government reforms in English schooling during the 1980s and 1990s, including particularly the creation of markets in education, have worked in effect as a middle-class political strat-egy to ensure their continuing advantages in schooling. The restructuring of the state and of educational systems likewise could be seen in effect to work as a male strategy, working through the structural backlash and regendering described in this chapter, and through the processes of detraditionalization and retraditionalization of masculinity and femininity, to reassert or at least to attempt to defend, male dominance, within state policy production and outcomes. Conditions of formal equality for women have remained, though under challenge, so that entrepreneurial (middle-class) women pursuing their own individual careers have continued to prosper. However, the effectiveness of, and support for, feminist agendas geared to changing the gender regime and practices of the state have lost momentum, while the foray into changing the societal gender order works more now as a defen-sive rather than offensive strategy. Structural backlash, including the emer-gent emotional economy of restructured educational systems, thus can be seen as a manifestation of 'the recuperative capacity of male power within organisations' (Clarke *et al.* 1994b: 240) and male resistance to the feminist agenda (Cockburn 1991).

We would also note that change is always destabilizing and that we can thus never be certain of its outcomes. It does appear, none the less, that the move to flatter structures, when framed by all of the elements of the performative culture, has seen the emergence of a new entrepreneurial managerialism, rather than encouraged those practices usually associated with feminist conceptions of educational management (Ozga and Williams 1995), despite talk of this in some of the management literature.

In our view, men's rights and other recuperative masculinist groups have not been particularly effective as political pressure groups in education, in Australia at least. They appear to have had more direct impact in the media in raising boys' issues, which we talked about in Chapter 1. It then appears that this media constructed backlash has seen some male education ministers, policy makers and teachers take up these issues.

In the new devolved and marketized context, schools have to respond to local community pressures for specific social coverage. Top-down policy probably becomes less significant in this new context. However, we would argue strong systemic policy for gender justice both for workers within education, for students and as a policy goal becomes even more important in a devolved system. We have been arguing that the restructuring of educational systems has involved a regendering and the emergence of a new emotional economy which also has gendered effects. We have also suggested that women bear much of the brunt of emotional labour within these new structures. There is something of a paradox here, however. We know that top-down policy is something of a palimpsest, being continually reread and rewritten as it is taken up in schools in an ongoing manner. In this way, teachers have some considerable influence in policy practice and outcomes. It will be ironical indeed if more local production of policy requires responses to community pressures of a more reactionary kind and provides less space for policy as palimpsest. For it is certain that the new regendered educational system, in a political context of backlash and resentment about affirmative action policies for disadvantaged groups, will demonstrate less commitment to the feminist project, while there will probably be more media driven and local community calls for a focus on boys. We provide an example of this in the concluding chapter to this book when we analyse the boys' strategy of a high school in the Queensland provincial city of Maryborough. In Chapter 1 we talked about a political backlash at work in contemporary societies, including the rise of both a virulent anti-feminism which reads small gains for women as substantial gains and a recuperative masculinity politics which sought to constitute men as the new disadvantaged. In this chapter, we have shown how globalization has evoked the development of a competitive state and a new managerialism which has worked in effect as another form of backlash – what we have called here structural backlash.

Notes

1 Giddens (1994) speaks of the rise of fundamentalism as the 'other' of post-traditionalism. It is 'nothing other than tradition defended in the traditional way'

(1994: 6). Recuperative masculinity politics written about in Chapter 2 can be seen as an attempt to retraditionalize gender relations and the biologically deterministic arguments in respect of men and women can be seen as fundamentalist in Giddens's terms. The same is true with respect to the 'religious essentialism' of the Promise Keepers in the USA as one arm of recuperative masculinist politics. Giddens also sees the self-reflexivity which accompanies the transformation of tradition as one element in moves to devolution and bottom-up approaches in state structures and practices.

2 For a discussion of globalization and education see Chapter 4 in Taylor *et al.* (1997) and Henry *et al.* (1999) and for a discussion of links to state restructuring also see Chapter 5 in Taylor *et al.* (1997).

3 In Australia those politicians from the Party in government, who are responsible for policy across the departments of the public sector, are called 'Ministers' and hence 'ministerialization'.

4 See Court (1995) for a consideration of anger in relation to women's work as educational administrators.

5 Whitehead's work (1999) deals with further education colleges in the UK, but we believe his observations have broader applicability.

6 On the question of women and marketization of education see the special number of *Discourse* (vol. 17, no. 3, 1996) edited by Jane Kenway and Debbie Epstein, entitled 'Feminist perspectives on the marketisation of education'.

7 We see this as a preferable situation to one in which a specific boys' education policy and strategy had been formulated. As we argue throughout this book, we believe a concern for boys' issues in schooling should be framed by social justice considerations within a gender equity policy concerned for both girls and boys. Of course, the recuperative masculinists view the development of the national Gender Equity Framework as yet another manifestation of feminist control of gender policies in education and those specifically focusing on boys.

8 Post-feminist is being used here to refer to the attacks on feminism which Faludi (1991) has referred to as backlash, not in the sense used by Brooks (1997) to denote an engagement between feminism and 'post' theories such as poststructuralism and postmodernism as talked about in Chapter 1 of this book.

9 In a large research project in which one of us is involved, we found that there has been something of a change in researcher/researched relationships, whereby participation in a research project, irrespective of research findings, is utilized by some administrators as another way of selling their school in the marketplace.

10 Acker's (1995) essay, 'Gender and teachers' work', provides an excellent account of the extant literature and argues that studies of teachers' work must take account of gender.

11 In making this point, we acknowledge that restructuring has usually had as its educational goal improved student outcomes, both social and academic. However, most often there has been a wish-fulfilment built into such restructuring: devolve tasks to schools and introduce school based management and *ipso facto* this will lead to improved student outcomes. In our view, improved student outcomes can only result from changed classroom practices. The existence of professional, sharing, collegial cultures within schools is also important in this respect, as can be external systemic supports for such cultures and classroom practices. The best research on educational restructuring has acknowledged and

'discovered' this: see, for example, Newmann and Associates (1996). Thus to this point restructuring has been *done* to teachers rather than *with* them. This has been very much a top-down process and a gendered one. Effective restructuring will have to acknowledge the centrality of teachers. None of this is to suggest that teachers have been mere pawns in the processes of restructuring, but rather that the dominant discourses of restructuring have positioned them in this way (cf. Ozga and Lawn 1988; Acker 1995).

4 Deconstructing the 'What about the boys?' backlash

In Australia, the most common story about gender equity in schools (according to the media and government bodies) would go something like this: *About 20 years ago, governments became aware that girls were being disadvantaged in schooling. They developed policies and funding to improve girls' career aspirations, to make curriculum and pedagogy more 'girl-friendly', and to ensure equal spending on girls and boys. At the same time a huge amount of research and writing (academic and professional) was carried out on girls, their development and their needs. Over this period we have seen a large increase in the proportion of girls completing school as compared with boys, and their increasing success in 'non-traditional' subjects such as mathematics. Now it is time for more attention to the boys. Boys' retention rates, learning difficulties, delinquency, suicide rates and general self-esteem are all cause for concern. We don't want to take away from the girls' programs, and more needs to be done in relation to issues such as sexual harassment in schools, but there is a real dearth of good research and professional support for boys, and this is what should now occupy our urgent attention.*

(Lyn Yates 1997: 338, original italics)

Introduction

As noted in Chapter 1, since the 1980s there has been a backlash against feminism. This backlash has been spawned by the media and organized men's groups of various types, but most often men's rights groups and those supporting a mythopoetic or masculinity therapy position, and has been evident across many domains of public policy, in health for example, but is very obvious when we come to considerations of boys and schooling. It is most apparent when we read the media constructions of the 'battle of the sexes' in school performance, usually in relation to boys and literacy and to differential male/female performance in the exams at the end of secondary schooling.[1] As this chapter will demonstrate, however, the situation of male and female performance in education provides a very complex picture, one much more complicated and variegated than these media representations would suggest. For a start, the media most often work with essentialist constructions of both female and male students, arguing for example that all females are now outperforming all males in education – a patently absurd observation.

In this way it could be said that 'backlashers' have intuitively understood the political pertinence of a strategic essentialism. The actual evidence is much more nuanced, once one disaggregates the data and considers, for example, working-class girls and boys, and compares their performance with that of their middle-class counterparts. Or compares the performance of Aboriginal boys and girls in Australia with that of the total population of school students. Or does the same for working-class and middle-class African American boys and working-class and middle-class white boys in the USA and their female counterparts; or African Caribbean boys in the UK and other groups of boys and other groups of girls. Additional data are usually used in the media and educational debates asking 'What about the boys?' These are to do with differential male/female figures on suspensions and expulsions from schools, behavioural problems, placement in remedial classes, non-completion of schooling, dropping-out, suicide rates, juvenile delinquency and so on.

In a sense, it is the changes in state structures as outlined in Chapter 3, which have seen a heavy emphasis on outcomes accountability within school systems, which has precipitated the concern with boys' issues, particularly concern for boys' underachievement. Restructured school systems are now replete with performance data and it is a particular reading of these data, which have been made public, that has fuelled the media representation of the backlash against feminism in education. It is also the more readily available data which are taken up by the media; end of secondary school exam results are perhaps the best case in point. There is also the way in which a liberal feminist construction of gender equity in schools in terms of getting more girls into maths and sciences – a narrow goal for such reforms – has been a factor in the emergence of a call for boys' policies in education. This narrow definition of success for such programmes and the fact that more middle-class girls are doing maths and science and doing well, combined with the widely differential performance of varying groups of boys, has fed the backlash.

The media representations and related educational debates argue more than this differential one-dimensional male/female performance and behaviour, however. They argue an improvement in the overall academic performance of girls and a decline in the overall performance and behaviour of boys, that is, there is an implied historical element to the argument. Most often this is argumentation via assertion and clever headlines, rather than reasoning from extensive and pertinent empirical evidence. The same is true at times of readings of the relevant data within some schools. However, there is not all that much readily available historical evidence which allows us to make definitive statements about such changes and for a long time girls and boys basically participated in different curricula. There is a further element to the media argument. Often there is talk of the future as being female: emergent labour markets producing the types of jobs (or non-jobs) requiring (most often) essentialized feminine skills. This is usually linked to the growth in service sector jobs and the decline in manufacturing (see Weiner *et al.'s* (1997) critique of this position). For example, a recent article in Australia's national newspaper (*The Australian*, 19 August 1997: 5) was headed, 'Schoolboys subject to caveman curriculum', which it argued did not prepare them for emergent labour markets in the service sector. Thus, by implication, not only have things declined for boys, but also they can only get worse if there is not a concerted attempt to do something about the situation.

Foster (1994: 1) has spoken of 'presumptive equality' as the 'discursive context' underpinning these representations. By this she means that underlying the argument is the presumption that men and women, boys and girls, are symmetrical populations in so far as they are regarded as having equal but different problems and are equally disadvantaged both in society and schooling. Thus much of the media and public debate about girls' and boys' educational performances, while essentializing these categories, is silent about the broad differentials between male and female power, which, in a perhaps oversimplified shorthand, is encapsulated in the concepts of 'patriarchy' and 'patriarchal dividend', which Connell (1995) suggests most men receive from the operation of a gender order with its heavily gendered divisions of labour and power. Similarly, there is little said about the failure of improved female retention in schooling and enhanced female participation in higher education to convert into more equal post-education options in terms of career opportunities and income for women when compared with men. The evidence would suggest, for example, that girls depend more on schooling than do boys – greater retention for instance – but for a host of reasons to do with subject choice, coherence and vocational relevance of that choice, and the gendered character of labour markets and careers, do not benefit in career terms to the same extent as boys (Foster 1994; Teese *et al.* 1995; Board of Studies 1996; Weiner *et al.* 1997; Yates and Leder 1996).

In the final chapter of the book we suggest how this policy moment in education of 'What about the boys?' discourse might be reclaimed for gender justice (cf. Mills and Lingard 1997). In this chapter, we provide a reading and analysis of the available data on school performance. We will then argue the need to acknowledge a broader range of goals for gender equity in education than the liberal feminist inspired one of simply getting more girls into high status masculine dominated subjects (Martinez 1994; Yates and Leder 1996; Yates 1997). We shall also argue the need to challenge hegemonic and complicit (Connell 1995) constructions of masculinity which reduce choices and narrow the work and life options for boys, while also making life in schools difficult for many girls, some boys and some teachers. There is a continuing need for gender reforms in education for *both* girls and boys, which acknowledge unequal power and material relations between men and women and take as their long-term goal the equalizing of gender relations in education and society.

What do the data tell us?

In respect of research methodologies, we are aware of the debates around positivism and quantitative methods, as well as broader feminist debates concerning epistemology. Consider also the debates about whether or not we need a postmodern sociology or simply a sociology of postmodernism, or indeed both. We do not have the space here to consider such issues, but briefly indicate some of the difficulties with existing databases on gendered performance in school. Yates and Leder (1996), in reviewing Australian databases on gender equity and 'pathways' through education, work and family life, have noted many difficulties in utilizing such databases, as have contributors to their review. One example is the feminist debate about the classification of social class of origin, which has traditionally been done through the father's occupation. Further, we need some new categories as identities change and are more fluid in the context of a globalizing world of simultaneous homogenization and fragmentation. We are also aware that access and outcomes data do not tell us anything very much about the pro- cesses or contexts of education which contribute to these gendered patterns. Quantitative studies also deal with correlations rather than causation. We need qualitative and interpretative research on the processes of education and work to augment our understandings here. Additionally we need con- textual understandings so as to be able to interpret changes in access and outcomes; retention, for example, has different meanings and significance at different historical moments. We are cognisant, taking up Foucault's work on governmentality, that quantitative research, particularly statistical data- bases, is one way that modern states govern, manage and 'normalize' their populations. Processes of naming and classifying can work in the same way. As outlined in Chapter 3, performance indicators are one important element of the steering at a distance *modus operandi* of the contemporary state and educational systems. They are also part of the performativity of postmodern culture and contemporary forms of governmentality. And as noted earlier in this chapter, it has been a particular reading of the resultant data that has fuelled concern about boys in education. The media have played a bardic function in respect of a particular construction of such data which has spoken to the concerns of some (particularly men) working in education. Suffice to say here we believe that while we need nuanced data, we also require nuanced and careful readings of them. We need to understand the complexity of the picture of male/female differences (and similarities) in educational performance, rather than bowdlerize it. It is with such caveats in mind that we provide the data below.

Literacy and numeracy

The state systems of schooling in Australia now conduct literacy and numeracy testing at either Years 3 and 6 or, as in Queensland, Years 2 and 5 (or 6). From 1998, the Conservative Commonwealth government has 'coerced' all the states and territories to agree to national literacy testing; as a consequence national literacy benchmarks are currently being developed. There is a way in which this government has reified literacy as *the* problem in contemporary schooling and *the* cause of not only poverty but also youth unemployment; which is not to deny the significant correlations between these factors (Freebody *et al.* 1995; Orr 1994), but rather to reject the restrictive and narrowing explanations and interventions which flow from this reification and the pathologizing of individuals. As Allan Luke (1997) has noted, we are witnessing the return of the individual deficit subject in contemporary educational policy. Such an approach is manifest in the reorientation of the longest running Commonwealth equity programme – the Disadvantaged Schools Program – as a literacy programme for students in schools serving poor areas with the focus now upon individual remediation rather than whole school change (Lingard 1998). It is also of interest that this focus has developed at the same moment in policy terms in Australian education as the incorporation of boys' issues into *Gender Equity: A Framework for Australian Schools* (Gender Equity Taskforce 1996) which developed subsequent to the *National Policy for the Education of Girls in Australian Schools* (Schools Commission 1987), a general weakening of commitment to policies for girls in schooling, and of concerns about boys' literacy levels, and the more general 'What about the boys?' backlash. Some are attempting to construct boys as a disadvantaged group at the same time as we are witnessing criticism of the notion of group disadvantage and the return of the individual deficit subject in educational policy, at the same time as the structural changes to educational systems outlined in the previous chapter demand the establishment of testing regimes.

Many of the literacy and numeracy data sets collected by these state and territory systems are not readily available to the public, or to researchers for that matter. Politicians also use such data for their own political purposes. In some senses the restriction of access to such data is sensible, given the usual media (mis)representations of such data and the destructive use of league tables. However, we know that there is a particular gendered pattern to the results which is inflected by a range of other factors, such as social class, 'race' – read in the Australian context as Aboriginal or Torres Strait Islander background – and ethnicity – read in the Australian context as of non-Anglo-Saxon-Celtic origins.

The general pattern of the results on the Year 6 literacy tests in Queensland is that girls outperform boys, those from non-English speaking backgrounds do not do quite as well as those from English speaking backgrounds, students in disadvantaged schools, a surrogate measure of social class, have a much lower mean score than all other students, with Aboriginal students obtaining the lowest mean scores of any targeted populations. Girls in each of these categories tend to do better than boys in the same category. Students in rural areas do not score as well on literacy tests as those in urban areas, with rural boys performing at lower levels than the girls. This pattern is also reflected in differential performance between urban and rural Aboriginal girls and boys. The differences in the mean scores for males and females on the reading and viewing element of the Queensland literacy test, stem basically from the fact that more boys are located at the lower end of the performance scale. For writing, there is a larger proportion of boys at the lower end and a smaller proportion at the upper end. Performance on the Year 2 Literacy Net in Queensland indicates that a much higher percentage of males than females are 'caught in the net', thus requiring intervention or remediation. This pattern is duplicated for disadvantaged schools, only with greater numbers in both the male and female categories, but again with many more males than females requiring intervention. (Apropos the argument above about the return of the individual deficit subject, it is significant that such intervention or remediation is done on an individual basis, failing to take account of social class and gender factors.)

This general pattern is reproduced in other states in Australia. Thus the O'Doherty Report in New South Wales, for example, noted that, 'Boys under-perform compared with girls in literacy tests at both Year 3 and Year 6 in Government schools (as measured in Basic Skills Tests)' (O'Doherty 1994: 12). The New South Wales primary school literacy data also indicate the complex intersection of gender and social class in performance. It would seem that while girls in each socio-economic grouping do better than the boys in the same grouping, boys in higher socio-economic groups tend to do better than girls in lower socio-economic groupings and so on. Aboriginal boys perform at lower levels than Aboriginal girls, but despite some improvement in Aboriginal literacy performance over time, Aboriginal students in general do much worse as a group than the rest of the student population. (According to Gillborn (1997), comparable gender differences for general school performance are found in England for African Caribbean students.) Furthermore, many Anglo-Saxon-Celtic working-class boys do very poorly on literacy testing in New South Wales.

Sammons's (1995) reinterpretation of the *School Matters* (Mortimore *et al.* 1988) longitudinal data on primary school and secondary school performance, set against gender, ethnicity and socio-economic status, provides a similar picture for the UK. Thus at age 7 at the point of entry to 'junior school' (Year 3) there were significant differences in favour of girls over boys in reading performance. Similar findings were reported for reading results at age 10, towards the end of Year 5. Elwood (1995b) summarizes UK research by observing that for the 5–16 age group, girls have consistently outperformed boys in both reading and writing.

Wilkinson (1997), utilizing results on literacy testing conducted for the International Association for the Evaluation of Educational Achievement (IEA), has documented the pattern of reading results for New Zealand students. At age 9, girls outperformed boys in all areas of reading literacy which were tested, and, while the gap had been reduced by the age of 14, girls still did better than boys on narrative and expository reading. Additionally, students whose home language was other than English (mainly Pacific Island, 'Asian' and Indian young people) achieved well below those whose home language was English. Once again we need to consider more nuanced data: which boys and which girls are we talking about?

In the USA, Linn (1992) found a decline in male/female differences in verbal ability over the previous twenty years. Elwood (1995b) reports on other US research on vocabulary and reading which also demonstrates that male/female differences in vocabulary have declined, but that there has been a widening of the gap between female and male performance in reading comprehension. She also reports on the patterns of results on college admission tests – the American College Test-English (ACT-E) and Scholastic Aptitude Test-Verbal (SAT-V) – showing that males did better on questions drawn from the natural sciences, and females better on test items developed from the humanities. There is also a difference in male/female performance in terms of type of question. Males did better on multiple-choice tests, while females did better on organizing diverse ideas and in writing. Elwood (1995b) reports UK work which also suggests significant gender-effects of the type of task set in reading and writing tests. Performance on literacy and numeracy tests, specifically the National Assessment of Educational Progress in the USA, shows girls outperforming boys in literacy, initially being ahead in maths, but losing that maths advantage from the middle years (Sadker and Sadker 1994: 138).

In terms of numeracy testing in Queensland at Year 6 level, there is no difference in the performance of boys and girls. In New South Wales boys do better than girls in numeracy testing at both Years 3 and 6 in government schools, with the gender margin at Year 3 being very small (O'Doherty 1994: 13). Sammons's (1995: 472) research indicates that for England there was little difference in male/female performance in maths at Year 3, but that in Year 5 boys were performing less well than girls. Interestingly, Sammons and others (e.g. Scheerens 1992) on the basis of their evidence argue that home factors are more important in determining reading performance than mathematics results. Elwood (1995b) notes that research in the UK indicates smaller differences between male and female performance in primary maths with the gap widening at the secondary level. She also shows how the gap between girls' and boys' results in GCSE maths has been narrowing over time so as to be almost negligible at present. There is also a hugely differential participation rate in post-compulsory maths between girls and boys, with boys doing maths, particularly in advanced forms, in much greater numbers than girls, with girls apparently having to do very well in maths to pursue it in these years. There is also a social class dimension here with girls from higher social classes much more likely to do maths at post-compulsory levels (Teese *et al.* 1995). The continuing extent of gender segmentation of curriculum is indicated by Teese's (1995) evidence that in Melbourne, boys from working-class backgrounds still do maths in greater numbers than girls from professional ones in the post-compulsory years.

Secondary school performance: HSC results in New South Wales and GCSE and A Level in England

The 'What about the boys?' backlash in Australian education emerged in the early 1990s in New South Wales in a context of putative improved performance of girls as opposed to boys on the New South Wales Higher School Certificate (HSC), the examination at the end of secondary schooling, and in Tertiary Entrance Rank (TER) which is calculated from it. Media representations of the picture here were very important in getting this issue to the fore, as were a delicate political situation for the conservative Liberal-National Party government of the day, and the links between some in the men's movement and the influential parents' body who also ran with the issue. The outcome was an inquiry which saw the production of the O'Doherty Report (1994) which rejected the need for a specific boys' education strategy, but which argued instead for boys to be included within the existing gender equity policy. This report can be read in a number of ways. At one level, gender workers and activists both inside and outside the state structures were important in deflecting the worst possible outcomes from such an inquiry – the acceptance that the feminist project had succeeded and that boys were the new disadvantaged and there was thus a need for a boys' educational strategy. This was not the result; rather a gender equity strategy focusing on both girls and boys and their differential needs was recommended. There was also recognition of the differences among boys in attachment to school, in school subject choices, in performance, in outcomes, and in behaviours (and among girls for that matter). Men's groups of both men's rights and mythopoetic persuasions saw this outcome as a partial failure of their political interventions; while some feminists and pro-feminists saw the report as eschewing the worst possible scenario, it was none the less seen as being reasonably defensive in character – a policy for holding the line rather than advancing the feminist project in schooling.

Before actually looking at the data on HSC results and changes to them over time, it should be noted how, in the Australian federal political context, where constitutionally speaking schooling is the policy responsibility of the states and territories, this issue spread or seeped across state boundaries to

be taken up in other political jurisdictions, where there had been a less concerted campaign and where (particularly but not exclusively) conservative
politicians subsequently took up the issue. The result ultimately was the
reworking of the *National Policy for the Education of Girls in Australian
Schools* (Schools Commission 1987) and the subsequent *National Action
Plan* (Australian Education Council 1992), which resulted from the five-year
review of the former, into *Gender Equity: A Framework for Australian
Schools*, approved in early 1996 by the relevant ministerial council in education, consisting of all the educational ministers in the country. 'Gender'
was a signifier here that the remit of the policy was now to include boys. As
with O'Doherty in New South Wales, this was also a defensive document, a
good example of the truism that policies are always partial settlements
attempting to suture together as many competing political interests as possible to achieve an outcome. The disjunction between the actual policy statement and the accompanying readings published with it is a good indication
of the important work that femocrats and feminist and pro-feminist activists
did in defending the feminist project, while acknowledging the needs of boys
and the necessity to work towards the deconstruction of hegemonic masculinities in schooling.

Debate about gender differences in outcomes in high stakes secondary
examinations came onto the agenda in many 'western' countries during the
1990s. Basically the media constructed picture here was that girls were now
outperforming boys. A reading of the actual data indicates a more nuanced
picture. We need again to consider which boys and which girls – for
example, there are class-based differences in results among girls and among
boys. The O'Doherty Report observed that, 'The margin by which girls are
out-performing boys in the HSC is increasing most amongst students from
low socio-economic status backgrounds' (1994: 13). A similar point has
been made by Teese *et al.* (1995), that gender differences in educational performance decrease as one goes up the socio-economic scale and increase as
one moves down the scale, indicating that working class and Aboriginal
boys are very disadvantaged in education. However, New South Wales data
on the HSC also indicate that high socio-economic girls are outperforming
their male counterparts in high status subjects. The O'Doherty Report also
noted that for Tertiary Entrance Ranks in New South Wales girls outperformed boys among all students, as well as among those from non-English
speaking backgrounds, and among Aboriginal and Torres Strait Islander
students and the gender gap had increased across the period 1990–3 (1994:
14). Additionally, gender segmentation in relation to subject choice remains
a highly salient issue, and one which will be considered later in this chapter.

In early 1996 the Board of Studies in New South Wales set up a research
project to consider differing male/female performance in the New South
Wales Higher School Certificate and in the Tertiary Entrance Rank derived
from it. This was established in the context of very widespread coverage of

girls 'topping' more HSC subjects than boys, including a *Four Corners* current affairs TV programme on 'What about the boys?' This report (Board of Studies 1996) provides a sophisticated picture of the situation and also includes some comparative data for other states. An appendix to the report prepared for the Board by Richards and Sproats (1996) suggests that the average scores for females have been higher than for males in New South Wales for many years and, utilizing MacCann's (1995) research, notes that the disparity in average scores has increased since 1991. They indicate this pattern is repeated in Queensland and probably to a lesser extent in the Australian Capital Territory and Victoria, while no pattern was evident in South Australia or in Western Australia. These data are dealing only with average scores here for the total population of girls and boys. The Board of Studies report suggests that the hypothesis that differential average female/male results are the result of different populations of girls and boys doing the HSC is not sustainable (1996: 6). Many more girls do the HSC than boys because many more boys than girls transfer to Technical and Further Education (TAFE) at age 15. This has been presented as one explanation of the differential performance – an interesting argument given the different character of the two populations.

The data on New South Wales HSC results are also reported in the review of that assessment process conducted by McGaw (1996) carried out for the government in that state. McGaw (1996: 108) graphically represents the changes which occurred in male and female representation in the top 5 per cent of TER scores for the period, 1991–5. These are the data which the media have utilized to present a picture of all girls now outperforming all boys. In 1991, females were under-represented in the top 5 per cent of students to the extent of 5.7 per cent, while males were over-represented by the same figure. In that same year, males were also over-represented at the bottom of the TER, with females over-represented in the middle ranks. By 1995, as McGaw (1996: 108) puts it, 'the position had changed markedly', with females now over-represented in the top 5 per cent almost to the extent that males were in 1991, while males are now even more highly over-represented in the bottom range. The McGaw Report seems to suggest this might reflect the fact that from 1995 English was compulsorily included in the aggregate score for all students for the first time and that there was also a new 'breadth component', so that all students also had to include a component from mathematics-science-technology, as well as a component from humanities-social science in their aggregate scores (McGaw 1996: 108).

The McGaw Report provides further evidence that disparities between female and male results on English might be the reason for the extant gender differences on the TER. Thus, for example, in 1995 the state mean for English for females was 25 per cent higher than that for males (McGaw 1996: 109), and similar differences were reflected across metropolitan and rural statistical divisions, reflecting differential female/male results across social class groupings and urban/rural locations. On socio-economic differentials, McGaw observes that females from low socio-economic areas perform much better in English than boys living in much higher socio-economic areas. Furthermore, 38 per cent of girls were in the top 30 per cent of students in English with only 21 per cent of boys in this group (McGaw 1996: 109).

McGaw also provides interesting data on gender comparisons in relation to maths, indicating that mean scores for each group are almost indistinguishable, with boys in only fractionally greater numbers in the top 30 per cent of students than girls (31.5 per cent of males as opposed to 28.5 per cent of females) (1996: 109). There are the usual relations with socio-economic background. However, McGaw notes that in the highest socio-economic areas – on the north shore and eastern suburbs of Sydney – there is a trend for girls to outperform boys, which is not to imply that these well-off boys are not doing well. In science, McGaw shows that in 1995 the mean results for males and females were almost indistinguishable, with girls only fractionally out-representing boys in the top 30 per cent of students (31 per cent of females as opposed to 29 per cent of males). Again, McGaw notes, in some of the highest socio-economic areas there is a considerable gap in performance in favour of females (1996: 110). We would suggest that it might be this challenge to the success of middle-class boys in maths and science which is one important element in the backlash, a point to which we will return.

The pattern of results at the end of secondary schooling in Queensland is also similar to that in New South Wales with boys concentrated more at the extremes of the results continuum than girls. Allen and Bell (1996: 11) summarize the Queensland situation:

> It appears that, in Queensland in the period 1987–95, not only have relatively more girls than boys been participating in senior studies, but the patterns of participation and outcomes are also different. That is, more girls than boys are found in the middle and upper third of academic achievement while more boys than girls can be found at the lower end of academic achievement and at the extremes.
>
> (Allen and Bell 1996: 11)

Allen and Bell (1996) also make the point which has been made throughout this chapter: we need nuanced data – how do race, ethnicity and social class intersect with gender in these results? They note, for example, that girls from low socio-economic backgrounds are heavily disadvantaged in maths studies.

Elwood's (1995a, 1995b) research has provided a most useful account of male/female performance in the General Certificate of Secondary Education (GCSE) in England, Wales and Northern Ireland, entered for at age 16, and in A Levels taken at age 18, and changes in these patterns of performance over time. Elwood (1995b), developing upon work by Stobart *et al.* (1992), notes the differences in entry patterns for the GCSE between girls and boys, illustrating that while girls constitute 48.5 per cent of the 16-year-old age cohort, they make up 51 per cent of GCSE entries (Elwood 1995b: 4). She also shows that more girls than boys entered GCSE English and maths, and that overall girls received more A–C grades than did boys, with this disparity growing between 1988, when the exam was introduced, and 1994 (Elwood 1995b: 4). Because of the link now between GCSE and the national curriculum, she argues that it is probably the case that more 'lower ability' boys enter the GCSE than did so in the past. Elwood's data show that in terms of the percentage of students getting A–C grades, girls outperform boys in all subjects (including chemistry and physics), except for biology and maths, and that the disparity in maths is minimal. Elwood makes the point that, given girls constituted only 33.1 per cent of the physics entry and 39.1 per cent of the chemistry entry, these are highly selective cohorts, while girls provided 51.1 per cent of the biology entry, a more 'conscripted' population, as she puts it, which might explain the better male representation in A–C grades for this subject.

As with English in the New South Wales HSC, Elwood demonstrates that the gap in performance between girls and boys is substantially in favour of girls and shows no signs of narrowing. She also suggests that changes in the contribution of course work, as opposed to examinations, in the calculation of the score for the subject do not seem to explain this gender gap in outcomes, a finding which runs counter to the common assertion that course work modes of assessment tend to favour girls over boys. In respect of maths, the pattern also appears to be similar to that in the HSC. Elwood shows how the gap in performance in maths between girls and boys has been reducing, so that the advantage to boys is now very small – about 2 per cent more boys than girls receiving A–C grades for the subject. Her interpretation of the research also suggests that girls no longer see maths as a male domain (Elwood 1995b: 16), while boys still appear to regard English as a female domain (Martino 1995b).

However, Elwood notes another gendered feature of results in maths at GCSE: the gendered pattern of participation in the tiered entry for the subject – higher (A–D), middle (C–F) and lower (E–G). Those in the top tier either obtain a minimum grade of C or are unclassified, and those in the middle tier are able to get a maximum of a B. Elwood (1995b: 5) clearly demonstrates that a much higher percentage of girls than boys choose the middle tier (girls constituted 59 per cent of entries in 1994) and that they also dominate the C grade in the middle tier. She notes how this discourages and sometimes prohibits girls from doing higher level maths at the next stage of schooling. Further, this situation would seem to be part of a broader pattern which suggests that for a host of reasons, boys continue with maths (and sciences) in post-compulsory schooling in greater numbers than girls, with girls apparently having to be reasonably assured of success to continue with both maths and science. This is an important factor in the gendered picture of results in maths (and science for that matter) at the end of secondary schooling. A more select group of girls (both in terms of academic results and social class background) does maths (and science) than is the case for boys. Girls' subject choices are broader than boys', an issue we will return to below. This would appear to be a factor in the comparative results between girls and boys in maths (and science).

Gillborn (1997) has pointed out how 'race' and ethnicity intersect with gender and social class in terms of exam results at age 16 in the UK. He thus notes that at this point in schooling 'African Caribbean young men are frequently among the lowest achieving of all groups' (1997: 72). Gillborn also reports the findings of a national survey of performance at age 16 conducted in the mid-1980s, disaggregated for race, class, gender and ethnicity. Irrespective of gender and ethnicity, the higher the social class the better the performance across the three groups classified in the research as 'black', 'Asian' and 'white'. Further, irrespective of gender, black students were not doing as well as white students, nor as well as those of Indian, Pakistani and Bangladeshi origins. The pattern for black students according to gender is different from that of white students; with the latter, girls did better than their male counterparts in each of the three family occupational categories utilized in the research. In contrast, it is only black females from manual working-class backgrounds who outperformed their male counterparts. Black males from professional backgrounds, for example, did better than their black female counterparts. Asian males from professional backgrounds also did better than Asian girls from these backgrounds.

Elwood (1995a) has also conducted interesting research in the UK on the gendered character of performance at GCE A Levels taken at the end of secondary schooling at age 18. The most important finding of this work is that the closing of the gap in performance between girls and boys at the GCSE (that research documented above) is reversed at A Levels (Elwood 1995a: 2). Thus while boys have been behind at age 16, they do better than girls at age 18. Thus, in respect of the GCSE, Elwood states: 'What is established now in the UK is that the British examination system is not failing 16-year-old girls' (1995a: 5). However, and this is very significant, Elwood argues that the media representation of the situation in the UK has basically been that girls are now doing better than boys at all levels of schooling. As her research painstakingly demonstrates, this is not the case for A Levels, and this is the most important examination, the most important point of selection, in terms of future career options. She also considers the significance of the fact that there is much less course work in A Level aggregate scores.

Elwood (1995a) begins with a consideration of entry patterns at A Levels and changes to those patterns since the 1970s. Here she demonstrates the increases which have occurred in female entry; whereas in 1970 girls made up 38 per cent of the total, the figure was 51 per cent in 1993. Her figures show that subject choice patterns are beginning to match those at age 16, especially in biology, chemistry, physics, geography and history. The patterns for English literature, French and mathematics at A Level are vastly different from those at GCSE with a much more gender stereotyped picture. She notes that while about 300,000 girls do GCSE maths only 20,000 do A Level maths. In English literature, 200,000 males do this subject at age 16, while only 15,000 do it for A Levels (Elwood 1995a: 6).

In terms of results, Elwood considers the picture in all subjects across the period 1990–3. In all except two of the subjects males are outperforming females in terms of the percentage gaining grades A–C. She also notes how in considering gendered differences in results at A Level we must also acknowledge gender differences in enrolments. Thus, males outperform females in English literature, as they do in history and French, but do these subjects in much smaller numbers than do girls. The small and highly selective group of girls who do physics outperform the boys, though only very marginally and not to the extent that they do at GCSE. The gap between male and female grades in maths and chemistry in favour of boys is slightly larger than at GCSE. Thus Elwood (1995a: 7) observes: 'The small, highly selective groups of females in science subjects at A level are extremely able candidates but they are not doing as well as their male counterparts'.

Research on GCSE reported above has indicated that, despite widespread perceptions, course work does not account for the difference in results between males and females at GCSE. Despite this, Elwood (1995a: 10) reports finding that there is a prevalent view amongst teachers that this is the case. However, she does hypothesize that the more traditional assessment approaches at A Levels might account for the reversal of the gendered pattern of results at GCSE. What Elwood's (1995a, 1995b) work does, of course, is raise many questions to do with how we ought to define gender equity in respect of academic results. At the same time, she acknowledges the complexity of interacting factors which contribute to differences between the sexes and which require consideration in terms of amelioration.

Gender segmentation of curriculum: gender differences in retention, other behavioural and extra-curricular activities

In what has been said to this point about the patterns of differential gendered performance at school, some things have been implied about subject choice and retention and participation in terms of gender. The patterns illustrated above demonstrate the continuing gender segmentation of curriculum choice, particularly in the post-compulsory years. Thus, in reporting Elwood's work, the selectivity of the girls doing maths and physics at A Levels was noted, as was the selectivity of boys doing English literature,

French and history at this stage of schooling. The work of Teese and his colleagues (1995) in Australia has starkly demonstrated these continuing gendered patterns in Australian schooling, but also changes to them as the trend for girls to stay on to the end of secondary schooling in greater numbers than boys continues. Thus, for example, they report evidence on participation in chemistry for both girls and boys in South Australia in the post-compulsory stage across the years 1987 to 1991. The gap in participation has been reducing across that time, as is the case with physics at this level. Not all of the change can be explained in terms of the greater retention of girls than boys – some is due to the reduction in the numbers of boys doing these subjects – but despite the gains for girls, boys still do these subjects in larger numbers. In relation to the reducing numbers of boys participating in the physical sciences, Teese *et al.* also note that the post-compulsory schooling population has changed dramatically with increased retention for all young people. Echoing some of the comments by Elwood (noted above) about the complex intersection of factors involved in the gender segmentation of the curriculum, Teese *et al.* (1995) state:

> Were these subjects – especially physics – to be more gender-inclusive in terms of content, teacher expectations, pedagogical values and assessment approaches, they would grow faster because they currently attract only half as many girls as boys and because girls make greater use of school than boys.
>
> (Teese *et al.* 1995: 23)

In terms of maths at the end of secondary schooling, Teese *et al.* (1995), drawing on South Australian data, suggest that the gap between male and female participation has been reducing for 'difficult' maths, while girls continue to outnumber boys in school-assessed 'business maths'. They also argue that while girls continue to outnumber boys in the humanities and social sciences, boys are more likely to participate in those humanities and social science subjects such as geography and economics 'which place an emphasis on measurement and quantification' (Teese *et al.* 1995: 31).

In the Australian context, it is not only the gender segmentation of curriculum choice which is of relevance here, but also the width of female curriculum choice as opposed to the comparative narrowness of boys' choices. Another way of looking at this pattern is to speak of the coherence and vocational relevance of boys' choices as opposed to the more diffuse and less vocationally relevant character of girls' subject selections. With the common 'loose combination of business studies, personal development, biology, and humanities subjects' (Teese *et al.* 1995: 108) which girls most often take, there is not the 'transferability' and coherence of knowledges which characterize the most common male options of maths, sciences and technologies. In terms of outcome scores, there is also evidence to suggest that there are higher correlations between boys' common subject combinations, maths and sciences, than between those most often chosen by girls (MacCann 1993; Foster 1994), suggesting perhaps that boys' choices tap similar types of capacities. Since the mid-1970s in Australia, girls have stayed on to the end of secondary school in much greater numbers than boys, but it is not simply retention which is of significance here in terms of options for both higher education and career choices (Teese *et al.* 1995).

> Girls rely more than boys on completing school because their vocational alternatives are very limited and because their employment opportunities lie in the services sector of the economy, with limited openings in manufacturing and construction. They are thus required to make more use of school than boys.
>
> (Teese *et al.* 1995: 107)

This gender segmentation of curriculum choice also extends to extra-curricular activities. Collins *et al.* (1996) comment:

> Perhaps the most interesting questions of all explored the extent to which masculinist priorities remain embedded in the curriculum, and most particularly in what are considered appropriate things for secondary school boys to know about and be able to do. The data suggests that most boys still avoid girls' subjects, still see team sport as the major extra-curriculum, and still are taught about a future in terms of paid work and career. Similar curriculum priorities affect girls, but it appears more girls than boys at secondary school take non-traditional subjects for their sex, undertake a broad range of extra-curricular activities (including arts activities, caring activities), and learn skills for a fuller range of adult life situations. Boys, generally, are caught in a narrower stereotype of what is appropriate for them.
>
> (Collins *et al.* 1996: 87)

Social class also intersects with gender in patterns of curriculum choice, so that the higher that one goes up the socio-economic scale, the less girls are disadvantaged in terms of participation and results in maths and science, and the less boys are disadvantaged in respect of English (Teese *et al.* 1995: 109). The lower their socio-economic background, the less likely girls are to take maths and they are more likely to fail. Working-class boys are less likely to take English when it is optional and rural boys are very unlikely to study history or modern languages (Teese *et al.* 1995).

As indicated above, since 1976 girls have stayed on to the end of secondary schooling in Australia in greater numbers than boys. Indeed, boys' retention fell in Australia during the period from the mid-1970s until the early 1980s. These patterns reflect a number of factors, including the impact of the women's movement, changes in labour markets, including the collapse of the teenage labour market since the 1970s, economic fluctuations, and the greater likelihood of boys to transfer to technical and further education at the end of compulsory schooling.

Any consideration of differential retention rates between various social groups drives home the point that has been made throughout this chapter, that we must always disaggregate the data and be clear about which girls and which boys we are talking about at any moment. For example, Gardiner (1997: 51) reports data on the retention of Aboriginal girls and boys to the end of secondary schooling in Victoria for the period 1989–93. The retention for all students was 78.5 per cent, for Aboriginal females, 35.8 per cent, and for Aboriginal males, 19 per cent. Thus, while in the total student population in Victoria about four out of five students completed secondary schooling, for Aboriginal boys the figure was about one in five. Victoria has one of the lowest retention rates for Aboriginal students in the country, but in other states where retention is much higher, there are still substantial disparities in performance between the Aboriginal and non-Aboriginal student populations. In terms of academic success, Aboriginal girls tend to do better than Aboriginal boys, but Aboriginal students as a group do not do as well as the rest of the population. This is a pattern repeated for African Caribbean students in the UK (Gillborn 1997) and for most minority groups in the USA (Sadker and Sadker 1994).

There is a great deal of evidence from many educational systems that it is boys who dominate in remedial classes of all types across schooling. The intersection of educational performance with behaviour is probably evident in the research of Daniels and his colleagues (1995) conducted in Birmingham schools, which indicated that while teachers had identified about twice as many males as females requiring learning support, many more boys than this were actually receiving support. Behavioural problems appear to be greater among boys than girls. Collins *et al.* (1996) document the propensity of boys to 'muck around' in class and to participate in anti-school cultures. Boys dominate among those classified as having Attention Deficit Disorder, perhaps a category for middle-class boys having difficulties at school. Truancy is more prevalent among boys. Vandalism in schools is largely committed by boys. Suicide rates are very high among all young people, but particularly high among young males. Deaths by road accidents are also much higher for young men than young women.

Differential levels of male and female behaviours and engagement with schooling are picked up in data on suspension and exclusion. We must also be careful in reading such data because they probably also tell us some things about the practices of schools and teachers in relation to different student populations. Gillborn (1997: 78) reports on exclusion data in the UK, noting that boys are excluded more than girls in the ratio of somewhere between four and five to one. Furthermore, he reports research which shows that black students are very much more likely to be excluded than the rest of the student population.

Gardiner (1997) reports rates of arrests for young people in Victoria, disaggregated for Aboriginality and gender. Thus for the period 1993–4 he found that the arrest rates for 14–16-year-old Aboriginal males were seven times higher than for Aboriginal girls of the same age group, six times higher than the rate for non-Aboriginal males, and about twenty-three times the rate for non-Aboriginal females (Gardiner 1997: 54). A similar caveat should be entered here as the one noted above in relation to reading the statistics on school exclusions; we need to consider policing practices.

Collins and her colleagues (1996) at the Australian Council for Educational Research (ACER) have provided a wealth of very useful knowledge on the experiences of girls and boys at school and their patterns of participation in extra-curricular activities both within and without school. The *Listening to Girls* report (Australian Education Council 1991), which had been part of the five-year review of the *National Policy for the Education of Girls in Australian Schools* (Schools Commission 1987), had shown the large amount of harassment experienced by girls in school, with boys the main perpetrators. Collins *et al.* (1996) paint a broader picture of such harassment from verbal through to physical manifestations. They illustrate the substantial extent of verbal harassment experienced by girls *and* boys at both primary and secondary schools (1996: 23) – interestingly with boys experiencing more verbal harassment than girls – and also the extent of homophobic harassment of boys by boys in secondary schooling. In terms of physical sex-based harassment, Collins *et al.* (1996: 27) found that 10 per cent of students claimed that it happened often in their school with about 50 per cent saying it happened sometimes. (As an aside, Collins *et al.* also found that policy and practice can have an effect upon the extent of all forms of sex-based harassment, with the data indicating that in those state systems which have the strongest prohibitive policies in this respect students reported lower incidences of such harassment.) In line with reported research by Blackmore *et al.* (1996), Collins *et al.* found that while a small number of girls were involved in sex-based harassment of all kinds, it was predominantly boys who harassed both boys and girls. Collins *et al.* (1996) observe, regarding the gender regimes (Connell 1987) of some schools:

> It was also clear, however, that some girls took part in these harassment games constructed by boys. It did not seem to be uncommon for girls to orient their lives around the opinions of boys in the school, and to share in the derogation of those 'on the outer' when this was required to retain popularity with the right group of boys.
>
> (Collins *et al.* 1996: 29)

Collins *et al.* also report their findings that generally girls feel that boys' sports are more highly valued in school than theirs. Kenway *et al.* (1997a: 155) note the common feeling of victimhood among boys in schools when girls' sport is given a high profile and priority. Collins *et al.* report that there is more unequal access to computer usage at lunch time for girls in primary school than in secondary school. The dominance by boys of playground space and equipment is also reported in the research (1996: 36).

In terms of out of school activities, Collins *et al.* (1996) report more involvement by girls than boys in housework and child minding, with 21 per cent of boys and 8 per cent of girls at the secondary level doing no housework at all. Boys spent more time 'gardening and fixing things' than girls, and more time helping in the family business (1996: 89). At the primary level, boys spent more out of school time on sport, watching television and on computers than did girls, while the girls spent more time than boys reading for fun, on musical activities, and on other arts activities (1996: 91). By Year 10, boys had increased the time spent on team sports, while the number of girls participating in no sport had increased from 15 to 21 per cent from the primary years, while the number of boys not participating in any sport remained constant across the primary and secondary years at about 12 per cent. The gender gap in musical participation had been reduced considerably by mid-secondary schooling. At both primary and secondary school, boys watched more sport and cartoons on television than did girls, while girls were more likely to watch soaps than boys (1996: 93).

University education

During the 1980s most western societies moved towards the provision of mass higher education. This has been the reality for a longer period of time in North America, where the schooling system has also been less selective and more comprehensive in terms of both participation and curriculum, and where there have been substantial status differentials between universities and where standardized testing plays an important role in determining access. In all countries a much higher proportion of the age cohort is now studying in higher education than was the case in the past. Research for the McGaw Report in New South Wales, for example, showed that of the 1994 HSC cohort, 34.2 per cent enrolled in university in 1995 and a further 6.2 per cent in 1996, indicating that more than 40 per cent of the 1994 HSC cohort were enrolled in university by 1996 (McGaw 1996: 173).

Accompanying the transition to mass higher education, has also been a substantial change in the gendered pattern of participation. In Australia, the granting of university standing to many teacher training institutions and the transfer of nurse education from hospitals to universities have been important contributing factors in this respect. Skuja (1995: 64) reports how in Australia in 1950 only 22 per cent of university students were female. In 1987, female enrolments in higher education exceeded those of males for the first time. According to Skuja (1995) women now have higher access and retention rates and outperform males in most courses. Reflecting the secondary school situation, there is, however, a heavy gender segmentation in university study. While women dominated in numbers, they are concentrated in education, nursing, arts, humanities and social sciences. They are also under-represented in traditional male fields, such as engineering, agriculture, architecture and in some subject areas, namely computing, physics and maths (Skuja 1995: 65). Women also remain under-represented in research higher degrees, even in areas in which they dominate at the undergraduate level, and are heavily over-represented in other types of postgraduate work, particularly course work higher degrees (Skuja 1995: 65).

Skuja (1995: 66) looks at men and women in non-traditional fields of study in higher education. He defines non-traditional female fields as those with fewer than 40 per cent female enrolment and traditional female fields as those with more than 60 per cent female enrolment. He argues, using these criteria, that males are more under-represented in traditional female fields than are women in traditional male fields. This might reflect some of the changes which have occurred at secondary level in the gendered patterns of subject choice, which have been outlined above. It also probably reflects factors to do with different reward structures for those fields dominated by females and those dominated by males and historically, the gendered character of different professions.

In Australia, Aboriginal and Torres Strait Islander people now access higher education in similar numbers to their representation in the total population. However, while access rates have improved, success rates are well below those for the total student population. Women are very substantially over-represented among Aboriginal and Torres Strait Islander people studying at university, constituting more than 60 per cent of this population.

In terms of access to higher education, the changing gender inflected patterns of success on tests in the USA is interesting. Thus, while girls overall appear to get better school reports than boys throughout schooling, but with this advantage reducing from the middle years, boys strongly outperform girls on the Scholastic Aptitude Test (SAT), now Scholastic Assessment Test, which determines access to either high or low status higher education institutions (Sadker and Sadker 1994: ch. 4). (It should also be noted that average SAT scores reduced from the late 1960s into the 1990s.) Minority girls do even worse than their male counterparts on SAT (Sadker and Sadker 1994: 140). Nevertheless, females still tend to get better higher education grades than males. On this picture, Sadker and Sadker (1994: 140) comment, 'Boys looking into the SAT mirror see in it an image bigger than life. Girls see less than there is really there'.

Interpreting the data

The data traversed above indicate the complexity of the patterns of gendered performance in schooling and the need to consider always which girls and which boys we are talking about. We also must eschew a competing victims' syndrome in relation to comparisons of male and female educational performance. The broader backlash, of course, provokes such readings. As economies develop and change over time, so too do labour markets and cultures. The meaning of educational performance changes historically, set against such shifts. Thus in Australia, for example, in the mid-1970s only about 30 per cent of students in government schools stayed on to the end of secondary schooling; in the mid-1990s the figure was 80 per cent. The completion of secondary education thus has a different meaning from what it did in the 1970s. The upward credential spiral demands more competition and longer educational careers for more young people. At the same time the non-completion of schooling has more disadvantages than it did in the past (Dwyer 1996).

In terms of the data on literacy, it is not new news to those who have been involved in schooling for a lengthy period of time that boys are slower to read than girls and require more remedial intervention. Nor is it new news that it is working-class boys and working-class minority boys who most often experience such difficulties. What is different is the changed policy context surrounding such evidence. As Alloway and Gilbert (1997: 50) point out, historically little concern has been expressed over this situation, even though Connell (1996: 207) notes in the early 1960s in the USA there was a 'minor panic' about feminized schools 'destroying "boys' culture" and thus denying them their "reading rights" ' (see Sexton 1969; Austin *et al.* 1971). Indeed, from the early 1970s, more concern in policy terms was expressed with the under-representation and under-performance of girls in maths and science. More girls are now doing maths and science, particularly chemistry, at the upper secondary levels. However, these tend to be girls from high socio-economic backgrounds (Teese *et al.* 1995). Despite these small gains, there is still a heavily gender-segmented pattern to subject choice in the post-compulsory years of schooling (and on into university). It is interesting that concern over boys' literacy levels has emerged as a policy issue in this context. This does seem to be a case of Faludi's argument concerning backlash, that it 'has been set off not by women's achievement of full equality but by the increased possibility that they might win it' (Faludi 1991: 4). In the context of backlash, these data are 'over-read' to suggest all girls are achieving and all boys are failing (cf. Foster 1994).

We should also note the complexity of defining the concept of literacy and the related necessity to understand what is measured in literacy tests. Reference has also been made earlier in the chapter to the effect of test item type on male/female results. Furthermore, Gilbert (1994) and Alloway and Gilbert (1997: 50) have argued that success in school measures of literacy do not appear all that 'critical in terms of post-school options and career advancement'; yet another example of schooling working as a different 'critical filter' (Board of Studies 1996) for males and females. They also suggest that school literacies represent only one type of literacy and that it is probably the case that other constructions to do with computer and technical literacies might not see such poor performance by boys and, of course, we also need to keep the social class differences in mind here. It might be the case at the current time that we are witnessing the emergence of alternative public education systems based around computer technologies and requiring different literacies (cf. C. Luke 1996). Boys – particularly middle-class boys – might very well be ahead of the game here given the usual cultural lag of education systems.

Alloway and Gilbert (1997) argue that successful performance in early school literacy in its various forms requires a particular disciplining or policing of the body. There is a disjunction, they say, between such assumed docility and dominant constructions of masculinity. Yet (as noted earlier) remedial practices usually assume a pathological individual, rather than the influence of social practices around dominant constructions of masculinity (and femininity), and their inflection by social class, race and ethnicity.

Wilkinson (1997) points out that the reasons for differential male/female performance in literacy testing are not well understood, even though we would argue some of the research on the social construction of gender linked to the working of a particular societal gender order might point us in a useful direction (e.g. Alloway and Gilbert 1997). Wilkinson does, however, offer two more psychological explanations. First, is the 'culture hypothesis', which argues better performance by girls than boys in literacy results from the dominance of female teachers in the primary schools. There have been calls in the media in Australia, for example, for more male teachers. Indeed, in 1996 the new Conservative Minister for Education in Queensland, Australia, established a campaign to attract more males to teaching, given his acceptance of the so-called 'culture hypothesis'. Kruse (1996) has documented similar calls from within a mythopoetic framework in Denmark and Weiner *et al.* (1997) note a similar situation in the UK. Interestingly, Wilkinson's reporting on research accompanying the IEA survey in New Zealand provides some evidence against this hypothesis (see p. 101). This research indicated that differences in reading comprehension between the genders were smaller in classes taught by women than those taught by men. Wilkinson (1997) suggests that this situation reflects differences between female and male pedagogy in reading. Thus he observes:

> In New Zealand, female teachers more often assessed pupils' lower-order skills (for example, word recognition, vocabulary) than male teachers, they more often taught pupils how to read expository texts and documents, and they were somewhat less likely to view reading instruction as requiring systematic progression through graded materials. Female teachers were also more likely to have a classroom library and to have a greater number of reading materials in class.
>
> (Wilkinson 1997: 3)

Once again we see the need to establish a more complex picture.

The second psychological explanation considered by Wilkinson is the 'maturational hypothesis', which suggests that different maturational stages between boys and girls explain these early gender differences in reading performance. Wilkinson (1997: 2) notes that in the IEA study, New Zealand was only one of three countries where school began at age 5 and that in all three systems there were very substantial differences in favour of girls in terms of reading performance. A recent evaluation of the Year 2 Reading Net in Queensland has shown how many teachers believe the greater numbers of boys than girls being picked up by the net for remediation can be explained by this maturational hypothesis (A. Luke *et al.* 1997). Alternatively, this situation might be explained by teachers' propensity to accept psychological and developmental explanations for performance.

Boys' lower literacy levels than those of girls translate into poorer performance than girls in English in the upper secondary years. They also participate less in English in these years when it is not a required subject. This is of real significance, given the traditional role of subject English in relation to questions of culture(s) and what we might now call critical citizenship, though we realize the contestation in schools and policy between various constructions of subject English, stretching from a skills orientation to a critical literacy approach. Teese *et al.* (1995) have nicely encapsulated the significance of subject English (within a critical literacy, yet monocultural, mode) in the following fashion:

> There are good reasons for our social and cultural commitment to the centrality of English in the school curriculum. Its general aims are the extension of the creative and critical abilities of students and the development of oral and written communication skills. English works as a 'cultural transmitter', locating students within the framework of their own culture and developing appropriate knowledge and skills. It aims for maturity and depth of thinking together with fluency and pleasure in the use of language. Its importance in the preparation of young people for citizenship, for full participation in social and cultural life, and for adulthood more generally cannot be overstated.
>
> (Teese *et al.* 1995: 45)

The picture of male performance and participation in English indicates a real shortcoming in the education of many boys and one which needs to be redressed in some ways.

Elwood (1995b) demonstrates the complex interaction of factors to do with differential gendered patterns of performance in GCSE English and maths. Thus, she avers, we need to look at the assessment techniques and instruments used in relation to these patterns. Her work appears to indicate in terms of GCSE English that, while examiners have attempted to take account of appropriate stimulus for tasks to account for gender, this might not be the case in terms of the different tasks set and approaches to marking. Thus she suggests that 'holistic marking' of written examination scripts, which emphasizes content, organization, grammar and spelling, tends to favour girls over boys (Elwood 1995b: 13). Consequently, she implies that gender equity requires consideration of both the type of task set and the nature of the marking scheme. Furthermore, she argues that there are other relevant factors in different gendered performances across subjects, including 'the contribution of student perceptions of subjects and the experiences they bring to the subject' (1995b: 9). While the emphasis upon extended writing tasks in GCSE English might favour girls, she argues that 'boys' own devaluation of the subject' is an important compounding factor. She suggests that 'The relatively modest success of boys in English is not of great concern to them as a group, they tend to view English as less relevant both in terms of their post-compulsory education as well as their future academic and vocational aspirations' (Elwood 1995b: 17). In contrast, Elwood notes girls' increasing rejection of the view that maths is a male domain.

The implications of these findings would appear to place her position here in agreement with that of the McGaw Report in New South Wales, which suggested, on the basis of the complex patterns of differential gender performance on the HSC, which were inflected by social class and locational factors, that 'more comprehensive gender equity strategies' are required (McGaw 1996: 110).

The data on gender segmentation in the curriculum, and extra-curriculum, in both schooling and higher education, retention and participation in school and university, on behaviours at school and outside of school, tell us something about the working of dominant forms of masculinity and femininity. These hegemonic forms narrow options for both boys and girls, but it does seem as if boys are more constrained by traditional gender stereotypes. Boys, or at least those who are doing okay, tend to see their futures in terms of work and careers (Collins et al. 1996: 87). Girls' greater width of curriculum choice and extra-curricular activities, while maybe disadvantaging them in career terms, certainly seem to better prepare them for a 'fuller range of adult life situations' (Collins et al. 1996: 87). And the evidence would seem to be clear that girls' good educational performances do not convert into career advantages in the same way as they do for many boys, given the ongoing gender segmentation of labour markets, differential patterns of pay for males and females, and different career opportunities.

As Connell (1996) and others (Mac an Ghaill 1994, 1996) have noted, schools are sites of masculinizing practices and for 'doing' masculinity, and also of feminizing practices and for 'doing' femininity, for that matter. This involves the school's gender regime, including power relations, the division of labour, emotional attachments, and symbolization (Connell 1996: 213–14). Within a school's gender regime, Connell (1996: 216–17) argues there are three central vortices of masculinity formation which result in the gender segmentation across curricular and extra-curricular activities considered in the previous section. These include the construction of so-called 'boys' subjects', the practice of discipline, and sport.

Dominant and constraining constructions of masculinity also affect gender relations in school and the broader society, as reflected in harassing and dominating practices between males and females and males and males. Foster (1996) speaks of boys as 'space invaders' in discursive, material, territorial and interpersonal senses. We must be careful not to psychologize the data here. Blackmore *et al.* (1996: 209) found a tendency for teachers to regard harassment perpetrated by boys, including sexual harassment, as resulting from boys' late maturity and incapacity to deal with emotions and relations, while neglecting the patriarchal dividend and how boys benefit from hegemonic practices of masculinity, including the suppression of emotionality. As Kenway *et al.* (1997b: 34) have argued, 'it should be understood that boys are both victims and beneficiaries of their emotions'.

Implications for gender equity policies and programmes in education

McLean (1996) has noted that there is much at stake in contemporary debates around boys and education. We agree. We also accept his concerns about the possible outcomes of the contemporary debates:

> Will these new programs be part of the backlash against women, based on notions of men's 'oppression' and pitting the needs of boys against those of girls? Or will they be informed by a pro-feminist analysis, and seek to develop ways for boys to act in partnership with girls in the larger struggle for gender equity and social justice?
>
> (McLean 1996: 65–6)

This book is about attempting to promote the latter rather than the former outcome. However, the data presented above, and our reading of them, do raise a number of questions to do with the goals of programmes for girls in schooling, and indeed for gender equity approaches which consider both boys and girls. In particular, questions of the terrain across which one measures 'success' become important (Yates 1993; Kenway *et al.* 1997a). Foster (1994) has shown how early feminist interventions for girls in schooling in Australia operated upon an assumption of a 'lack' in girls in relation to participation and performance in high status masculinist subjects. She also notes how when both the participation and performance of some girls, notably those from middle-class backgrounds, improved in these respects, this was reread through the filters of 'presumptive equality' as boys' underachievement. Weiner and her colleagues (1997) have proffered a similar account of the changing discourses of gender and education in England in relation to girls' 'improvements' in respect of GCSE subject participation and results.

As Yates (1997) has observed, there is a way in which the data traversed in this chapter indicate some partial success for liberal feminist goals in schooling. More girls, particularly those from middle-class backgrounds, are now challenging the boys in high status school subjects in the high stakes exams at the end of secondary schooling. And while there is a political need to deflect the anti-feminist 'What about the boys?' backlash, there is also a need to celebrate such gains of the feminist project in schooling. However, as Kenway *et al.* (1997a) cogently argue, the feminist reformers who 'mobilised and popularised generalisations about girls' poor performance in the mathematics and science areas' perhaps made a strategic mistake, as they suggest they did, when getting more girls into 'non-traditional subjects also came to dominate the gender reform agenda', at least in the Australian context. One senior femocrat commented to one of us in the early 1990s, that the latter had so come to dominate the agenda at that stage, that it was almost as if whenever one mentioned girls one had to add 'and science and maths'. In Chapter 2 of their book, *Answering Back*, entitled 'Success', Kenway *et al.* (1997a) conclude that this construction of gender reform has been a factor in feeding the 'What about the boys?' call. They note:

We have pointed to the ways in which teachers and students reworked such logic in unanticipated ways which ultimately meant that the policy subverted its own intentions with regard to both girls and boys. Indeed, we have implied that the discourse of the under-achieving, disadvantaged boy was able to gain a stranglehold on gender reform precisely because of the dominant gender reform discourse on success for girls.

(Kenway *et al.* 1997a: 62)

This might be slightly overstating the case, but there is no doubt some veracity in the observation. None the less, the rise of organized men's groups, particularly those of anti-feminist persuasions, the broader context of backlash against feminism, and media representations of the same, also provided fertile ground for the increasing pervasiveness of a construction of boys as the new disadvantaged in schooling. Changing labour markets and growth in service sector employment, increases in female workforce participation as against declines in male participation (however, with male participation still higher than for females), more competition for tertiary places and for jobs, continuing high levels of unemployment, rapid change, and a pervasive sense of insecurity and uncertainty are also other framing elements of concerns about boys' education and the putative success of the feminist reform agenda for girls.

However, the goals of the feminist project in schooling were never this narrow (cf. Yates 1997). Feminist reforms in education began in the UK, continental Europe, North America and in Austral-Asia in the mid-1970s, coterminous with the second wave of the women's movement. In considering appropriate goals for gender equity in education and in response to the contemporary debate about gender differences in end of secondary school results, Yates and Leder (1996: 8) suggest that we should return to the starting points of the feminist project in education in the mid-1970s. They state, concerning that starting point in Australia:

> it is interesting to consider the first landmark national report in this area, the 1975 report commissioned by the Schools Commission, *Girls, School and Society*, and how it established that there was a problem of gender inequity in relation to girls in schools. Its prime data or indicator in that regard was not any particular statistical record of what was happening to girls in schools, but the data on record about women and men in Australia post school. The 'hard' data here were women's unequal earnings, power, and responsibility for unpaid work. It argued that what happened in schools (what girls and boys were taught, the careers advice they were given) did have some causal link to these outcomes, but it was not primarily establishing the case about gender inequity in schools by data about retention or about Year 12 results.
>
> (Yates and Leder 1996: 8)

The goals of gender equity in schooling need to be broadened (or reaffirmed) to include more equal gender relations in the broader society. More equal gender relations require better career opportunities for women and more commitment by men to fuller participation in domestic labour and childcare. It must be recognized that end of school results are only one element in the future career pathways and post-school experiences for girls (Yates and Leder 1996: 9); indeed, for both girls and boys, what they 'learn in school about themselves and each other and about their future, and not just what they achieve there is relevant to their pathways beyond school' (Yates and Leder 1996: 9). As Martinez (1994: 8) has asserted, the goal must be about 'educating students for gender relations based on equality, non-violence and empathy'.

The discussion so far has indicated the relationship between how we define the goals of gender equity and how we measure success in terms of these programmes. Seidler (1994: 94–5) has noted how feminism challenged a liberal rights' construction of equality and freedom. Feminist analysis demonstrated the disadvantages experienced by girls in schooling as a group. Feminist demands for equal access to education and work immediately raised questions about the definitions of education and the structure of work and how relations between the so-called private and public spheres restricted opportunities for women. Thus, for example, gender segmentation of the curriculum raises a number of dilemmas here for gender equity through education, particularly in relation to goals to do with more equal career opportunities for women and greater male participation in the domestic sphere. Somehow there needs to be a move to encourage non-gender stereotyped processes of subject choices. A problem here is that

Collins *et al.* (1996: 176) found that schools by and large were not particularly concerned about boys' narrow range of subject choice, while at the same time many were concerned to change girls' choices. Questions of the differential valuing of different school subjects are also immediately raised. We then come up against the construction of success in the public sphere, in work, which appears to demand that gender equity in schools requires more girls to do those 'masculinist' subjects and groupings of subjects most strongly linked to career success. Such an approach concedes or takes as a given a masculinist construction of subject hierarchies. The broader goal of more equal gender relations in society, including in the home, possibly requires that more boys do the collection of subject choices currently favoured by girls. Boys at present do *not* make such curriculum choices because of dominant constructions of masculinity and an 'accurate' reading of the bases of 'success' in career terms. And as long as childbearing and childrearing have a greater impact on the lives of women than on men, equal career opportunities for women will remain a chimerical desire rather than become a reality. Since the 1950s more and more women with children have participated in paid work outside the home. This phenomenon has not been accompanied by much change in terms of responsibility for domestic labour and childcare with women still carrying the bulk of the 'second shift' (Bittman and Pixley 1997). As Rowbotham (1997: 575) observes, 'Women have lived this incongruity of being expected to be in two places at once as an apparently insoluble dilemma'. Gender equity in schooling needs to take account of these dilemmas, but these very dilemmas also indicate the complex relationships between changing and resistant social arrangements and schools as sites of gender reform. Such complexity is compounded by the politics of backlash.

Gilbert and Gilbert (1998) trace three stages in the development of gender equity policies in Australian education, specifically as they relate to females. They then consider the usefulness of this conceptual frame for considering policies for boys' education. The first stage was the attempt to get more girls to access powerful bodies of knowledge, the valorized subjects in the curriculum. The second stage concerned attempts to get women's knowledge into the curriculum and to end the silences about women in many pockets of the curriculum, for example within various historical narratives. The most recent stage relates to an acceptance of the social and relational constructions of gender, including both femininity and masculinity, and the plurality and differences within such constructions. The first and second stages were framed by liberal feminism, the third by poststructuralist and postcolonial feminisms with the focus of each of these three stages still playing out at the present time. (Kenway (1990) has demonstrated how elements of the old feminist theoretical triumvirate of liberal, radical and socialist feminisms impacted differentially on the earlier stages of gender equity reform in Australia's schools up until the late 1980s.)

Now, in terms of how concerns for boys' education might be illuminated by an understanding of these three stages, Gilbert and Gilbert (1998) argue that it is difficult to convince boys that they are disadvantaged, at least in career terms, by their current dominant patterns of subject choice. This remains the situation, no matter how strongly we want to put the case that such narrow choices are inimical to broader goals for gender equity in education, as argued above. Additionally, getting boys' and males' representations into school subjects and resources has not been a problem. It is in the third domain of the social construction of gender that the Gilberts suggest there might be some useful pointers for boys' educational policies and practices. They argue:

> Boys' insertion into dominant stories of masculinity and maleness predisposes them to reject and resist literacy and humanities subjects in favour of numeracy and vocational learning; to dominate and compete in classroom and playground arenas for space, time and attention; to valorise sport and physical prowess; to devalue qualities of nurturing, caring, sharing and loving.
>
> (Gilbert and Gilbert 1998: 24)

Furthermore, social and institutional valorization of these male choices reinforces gender segmentation within education, and contributes to its perpetuation within labour markets. Along with the Gilberts then, we would argue that a consideration of the social construction of gender and a tolerance and acceptance of different practices of femininity and masculinity should be a central concern of schools committed to gender equity. Current practices of hegemonic masculinity are dangerous to some teachers, to many, many girls, and to a lot of boys. On the latter, witness the commonplace of homophobia in schools. As Collins *et al.* (1996) put it in relation to boys:

> The big challenge for schools in relation to boys is to support them to dismantle the walls they construct around themselves and others in order to feel safely 'masculine'. This includes supporting them to accept and enjoy a variety of masculinities (and femininities) in others; helping them to be happily challenged rather than threatened by a less straightforward world; and expecting, pushing and supporting them to extend themselves across the whole range of human activities and learnings, including those girls do (McLean 1995). The alternative may be that many boys continue to redraw the boundaries in ways that are constricting of their own development as well as restricting, hurtful and dangerous for other boys and girls.
>
> (Collins *et al.* 1996: 176–7)

Hegemonic constructions of masculinity need to be deconstructed. Such constructions appear to be complicit in the narrowed patterns of subject choices, extra-curricular activities, and destructive behaviours documented earlier in this chapter. It is those boys practising 'complicit' masculinities who are important in holding this 'edifice' in place and who might be a focus for change. Concerns for boys also need to be situated within a gender equity framework which concedes the reality of the current unequal gender order, and the complex and different ways of 'doing' gender, and which is positioned within a broader social justice framework (Connell 1996).

Schools need to be involved in the processes of constructing what Connell (1995) has called gender multiculturalism – a postmodern multiplicity of acceptable ways of performing gender. Several theorists have written about the emergence of hybrid new ethnicities in the context of a globalized diasporic world (e.g. Hall 1996; Bhabha 1994), while others have spoken of more fluid and emergent hybridities of sexual identity (e.g. Sedgwick 1993). In some senses, these particular postcolonial, postmodern plays of difference are cultural forms of resistance to the rational categorizations endemic to modernist techniques of governmentality. Perhaps there is a space here for resistance to dominant ways of being male and female and for the emergence of gender multiculturalism, as well as a role for schools in relation to this.

Conclusion

This chapter has outlined and interpreted the data on male and female performances in education and in so doing attempted to deconstruct the media and recuperative masculinists' constructed picture of these differences – a picture which claims that there is a crisis with boys' education. The data presented throughout this chapter indicate the situation is much more complicated than that represented in the media and in other backlash discourses. The chapter has shown that there are still clear differences in subject choices between girls and boys, with girls dominating in the humanities and social sciences and boys in the sciences, maths and technologies. In a vocational sense, this still appears to work against girls. Good schooling and educational outcomes for girls do not as readily convert into better life chances and career options as they do for boys. Girls choose a broader range of subjects than do boys and also participate in a much broader range of extra-curricular activities. There are evident disparities in educational performance among differing groups of girls and boys, with working-class and minority boys leaving school early and performing badly. This situation for these particular boys is compounded by developments in transitions between school and work, and related changes in labour markets, contingent upon the globalization of the economy. The evidence would also seem to suggest that some middle-class girls are now challenging their male counterparts in high status school subjects, a manifestation of gender convergence which Walby (1997) speaks about. We would also note that working-class girls do not benefit from schooling in the same ways as their middle-class female and male counterparts. The latter point often gets forgotten in media representations of gendered patterns of school performance. We also note how the fact that girls do about as well as boys in maths in the primary years and yet are still substantially under-represented in maths in upper secondary schooling is also often erased from contemporary debates.

It is difficult to make definitive statements about the historical claim that girls' educational performance is improving while boys' is declining. This might even be a silly way to ask the question, given the attempt throughout this chapter to stress the need to disaggregate the data; which boys and which girls are we talking about? However, it is the case in Australia that girls stay on to the end of school in greater numbers than boys and now participate in university education in greater numbers than males. It is probably the case that girls from high social class backgrounds are now challenging boys' dominance in high status academic subjects in the secondary schools. Further, with changes to labour markets, it is probably the case that those who drop out from school are probably more disadvantaged than they might have been in the past and these tend to be boys from the most disadvantaged families. (Rowbotham (1997: 551) documents how in the USA the median income for 25–34-year-old males fell considerably from the early 1970s.) This is just one manifestation of the more general point that the meanings of educational participation, retention and performance fluctuate as the broader social context changes. Thus, for example, as more students stay on to complete a secondary education or as more young people participate in higher education, the meaning and worth of such activities change.

The media representations have had a political effect with policy developments which now take account of boys in gender equity policies, programmes and practices. The Lyn Yates quote at the beginning of this chapter accurately encapsulates the now dominant, yet debatable, account of gender reform in schools. These media representations have also encouraged some teachers, mainly, but not exclusively, males, to accept reasonably uncritically that girls are now outperforming boys in schools – a manifestation of Foucault's observation that discourses, in this case media discourses, 'systematically form the objects of which they speak' (Foucault 1974: 49). State gender equity workers in Australia tell us that they are now inundated by calls from schools asking 'what to do about the boys in both academic performance and behavioural terms?' There is a way, then, in which oversimplified readings of educational performance data are played out in the media and then feed back into actual school and policy practices as *the reality* – the bardic function of the media as noted in Chapter 1. For many men in education in the late 1990s this simply feeds into their paranoid concerns about the challenges of feminisms after two decades of feminist reforms in schools. Improved performance by some girls is read in a zero-sum way: girls' gains must be at the expense of boys. There is no celebration of girls' gains, only concern about the challenge to boys. Further, as Kenway *et al.* (1997a: 52) demonstrated from their research, good academic performance by boys is naturalized and goes unremarked, while good academic performance by girls in high status masculinist subjects is 'seen as exceptional and thus remarkable' and explained as the result of hard work. In their research schools they also found that often teachers would compare the academic performances of high achieving girls with those of low achieving boys and then conclude the boys were doing badly. Collins *et al.* (1996: 176) note how teachers and principals in their research tended to construct gender issues in education in such a zero-sum way, rather than as a 'mutual benefit matter', and comment how this reflects 'how gender is untruthfully and destructively construed in popular culture'. Weiner *et al.* (1997), for example, argue that media representations of the supposed 'underachievement' of boys in the UK is predicated upon the corollary that female success *ipso facto* means male failure. Furthermore, given the evidence on boys' behaviour in schools, it is difficult for teachers to ignore the boys. As Kenway *et al.* (1997a) suggest, 'boys' failure is more noisy and noticeable' than that of girls.

None the less, there is a way in which the zero-sum reading of the changing pattern of girls' and boys' school results has some veracity. Merit rather than chromosomal make-up as the basis for selection does bite, as it were. Despite the move to mass higher education in Europe, including in the UK, and in Australia and New Zealand, and a similar situation in North America, where mass higher education has been the norm for a much longer period of time, there is still considerable so-called 'unmet demand' in many of these countries for access to university. Additionally, there has been a clear credential spiral upwards: young people now have to run faster to simply keep up and there is greater competition for places in high status courses. Thus the privilege of some well-off boys has been mildly challenged by their female counterparts. At the same time, those who leave before completing a full secondary education are more disadvantaged than they were in the past, given the changing character of labour markets. Working-class boys and minority boys from poor families are falling behind in this more competitive race. The traditional working-class masculine transitions between school, apprenticeships, and semiskilled and skilled manual jobs are less certain. Many traditional working-class jobs have disappeared in the move to the postindustrial economy. Unemployment among young black boys from poor families in Australia, the UK and North America is appallingly high. For example, Estelle Morris (1996) in the UK Labour Party consultation paper, 'Boys will be boys? Closing the gender gap', observed that in excess of 60 per cent of young black men in London were unemployed. Gillborn (1997: 66) quotes British research showing that more than half of young black men aged 16–24 in the UK were unemployed, compared with 33 per cent of Bangladeshis and 18 per cent of white males of the same age group. As Walby (1997) notes, there is also a widening gap between successful girls and their less successful counterparts.

Fine and her colleagues (1997: 52) have shown how in the USA in these 'insecure times', white working-class males still construct their identities 'as if they were wholly independent of corroding economic and social relations', refusing to see themselves located 'inside history'. They thus search for 'scapegoats' in people of colour and white women. Frank (1996: 295) has observed: 'Condensing themes of race and class along with those of gender, angry white boys are emerging as the constituency around which the Right has recommenced its battle for the soul of the nation'. In Australia, both conservative and far right wing politicians now seek the support of blue-collar males – the 'battlers' in Australian parlance – in the context of a new racism, anti-feminism and insecurity spawned by economic globalization. Thus the result is a situation of backlash and critique (perhaps too genteel a word in this context) of affirmative action programmes and the like and sustained and vehement criticisms of the success of the progressive agenda across the previous decades, often framed within attacks on so-called 'political correctness'. A case in point is the passing by referendum in California of Proposition 209, which has outlawed affirmative action for women and minorities in education, public employment and contracting in that state. Progressives are on the defensive, as witnessed, for example, in the call by US civil rights leader Jesse Jackson, at a large demonstration in San Francisco on 29 August 1997, in response to this outlawing of affirmative action in California, to 'Save the dream'. The backlash manifests itself variously in different political contexts with their varying histories, structures and cultures (cf. Rowbotham 1997). Thus in the USA there have been attacks on affirmative action legislation, in the UK structural attacks upon the progressivism of local government, and in Australia a weakening of the femocratic project inside the state. In this political context, a new 'ladism' is on the rise again, as indicated in popular television programmes, such as the British series *Men Behaving Badly*, and in some publishing successes, for example, *The Big Damn Book of Sheer Manliness* (Von Hoffman 1997) in the USA and within the media; there are many variegated forms of backlash.

It is thus not only feminism which has spawned the backlash, but also a range of factors associated with the globalization of the economy – read as the dominance of market liberal ideology – in the post-Cold War era. This new world of global capitalism has seen production processes spread across the globe with the emergence of underclasses in what were called 'first world' countries and the emergence of middle classes in 'third world' countries. There has been a simultaneous upward and downward skilling of work, with one section of the labour market demanding multiskilled and highly educated workers and those without the requisite skills being excluded from labour markets altogether. In one sense, merit has become more important than gender or ethnicity as a determinant of opportunity; the overall result is more competition for jobs with careers attached, and greater and more pervasive uncertainty. Even those who access the 'good' jobs with career prospects are in a more uncertain position. Insecurity abounds and has been a significant factor in the emergence of backlash politics, including backlash national chauvinisms and anti-feminism, as has been the almost global dominance of market liberal ideologies which encourage a weaker and less protective state, competitive individualism and rapacious social Darwinism. There is also a way in which this situation has been mobilized in conjunction with the challenges now faced by well-performing middle-class boys to create a backlash in education.

'Manufactured uncertainty' according to Giddens (1994) is the condition we all face today – the result of at least two centuries of modernist intervention in the social and natural worlds, predicated upon the assumption of unilinear progress. We are more doubtful today about many of these assumptions. And with the global dominance of market liberal ideology there is less optimism and indeed likelihood that the nation state and its politicians will take a more expansive view of the role of government. Individualism is rampant and fans opposition to progressive politics of intervention for those disadvantaged by group processes to do with race, class and gender. This reconstituted relationship between the state and the market has seen enhanced social inequality and a shifting of a range of economic and psychological costs from the public to the private domain (Rowbotham 1997: 576), with real impact on working-class men and women, but with greater impact on such women given their role in the private sphere. Thus, while 'backlash' might be an adequate concept for explaining the role of the media in suggesting the success of feminism and depicting men and boys as the new victims, there are some broader social changes going on: in labour markets, in home life, in transitions from education to work which also need to be considered (Hall 1996; Morris 1996; Fine *et al.* 1997; Mac an Ghaill and Haywood 1997; Fine *et al.* 1998; McLeod 1998).

Working-class boys face new insecurities in the transition to adulthood. Working-class girls also face insecurities – the gender polarizations that Walby (1997) talks about in relation to working-class and middle-class girls. Middle-class boys are challenged by middle-class girls, even though, given the continuing gender segmentation in post-compulsory schooling, this is a relatively small challenge. Instead of celebrating what might be seen as the gains of liberal feminism in education, or as others have argued, the broader impact of feminism (Moore 1996; Riddell 1998), we have a backlash in education and an attempt at reconstituting boys as the new disadvantaged.

Despite some positive gains, girls are still under-represented in the sciences and maths in the post-compulsory years, there is still a heavy gender segmentation of curriculum choice, and girls' school performances do not convert into positive post-school options in terms of careers and incomes as they do for boys. As Mahony (1997b) has noted, the gendered pattern of engagement with education has not changed all that much, but now in a vastly different political context, is read differently. The story is now one of the underachievement of boys, rather than the failure of girls to take up maths and science.

Kenway *et al.* (1997a) also make a number of important points in relation to the politics of backlash and the specific call for more to be done for boys in education. First, they note that what has been done for girls under the rubric of gender reform is often 'grossly exaggerated' (p. 59). Second, their research shows that often boys have been included in school-based 'equal opportunity' reforms. Third, in terms of resources spent on girls and boys, they note that in their research schools a whole range of support programmes for students 'at risk' in effect work 'unofficially as boys' programs' (p. 60), what they refer to as 'accidental gender imbalance' (p. 61). They also point out that very often, 'While boys themselves are seldom invisible, often programs for them seem to be' (p. 61). Their final point relates to the way many male teachers, who argue that too much has been done for girls and thus it is now time to focus on boys – who basically accept the media constructed backlash account and who accept the narrative outlined by Yates at the beginning of this chapter – cannot separate issues of gender in schooling from the matter of equal employment opportunity and systematic attempts 'to facilitate the advancement of women teachers'. In this way boys' issues in schooling become inextricably entwined with men's responses to feminisms.

Kenway (1996) has also attempted to show how the working out of the feminist reform agenda in schools has been a factor in precipitating the backlash against such reforms in schooling. Thus, she suggests, the media backlash is partially about the attempted reassertion of specific forms of masculinity, but she also argues that for some time now certain ways of 'doing' masculinity have been reasserted in schools in response to the feminist agenda. For example, 'oppositional' boys construct themselves as victims in response to feminist reforms in schools, arguing that such programmes 'blame and punish' boys, fail to understand the 'essential' nature of boys, and at the same time neglect boys' problems, all of which lead these boys 'to feel particularly neglected, resentful and angry' and 'to seek to rebuild male solidarity around a sense of neglected masculinity' (Kenway *et al.* 1997a: 154). Anti-feminist men in schools are also angry and bitter, while both passive and active pro-feminist men at times feel guilty and powerless, and constantly seek affirmation from feminist teachers. Kenway (1996) outlines a number of strategies utilized by men in schools in response to feminist agendas, including a divide and rule attitude to women in relation to the strength of their support for varying feminist reforms in school, the policing of femininities, a recuperation of equal opportunity discourse to constitute boys as the new victims, and the constitution of males as victims of feminism in schooling, particularly in relation to affirmative action approaches for women teachers. The danger in all of this, Kenway asserts, is the implication that in response to the anxieties felt by many boys and men in relation to feminist reform agendas, women should develop 'nurturant pedagogies' for them – a contemporary inflection on the old practice of women doing emotional labour for men. Again Kenway raises the point that, despite a gender order which demonstrably benefits men, many boys and men do not see themselves as powerful, and, of course, the return from the patriarchal dividend is very different for varying groups of boys and men. Aboriginal boys are the best case in point. There is a complex array of issues which arise here, including the mix of the emotional and rational in reform strategies, effective pedagogies and approaches for boys and girls and for different groups of girls and boys, the distinction between the academic and cultural elements of a pro-feminist gender reform agenda, and the roles of male and female teachers in these reform processes.

The impact of changes occurring at the dawn of the new millennium has been a dual one of not only spawning backlash, but also precipitating a rethinking of gender and gender relations in respect of 'work, time, the social forms of technology, the utilisation and distribution of resources and power, the role of the state, the bringing up and educating of children' (Rowbotham 1997: 576). Walby (1997) has documented the changes which have occurred in gender relations since the early 1970s. We also drew on the work of Kimmel (1996b) in Chapter 1 to provide such an account. It is both a 'best of times and the worst of times' scenario in terms of gender relations. And changes in gender relations cannot be dissociated from changes in, and reconstitution of, class structures in a globalizing world. In that context, we would observe that among men pro-feminism contests anti-feminism, while feminism in its many guises, including the 'I am not a feminist, but' position, also contests backlash. Backlash discourses have opened up opportunities for contesting the production of hegemonic masculinities through schooling, a point returned to in the final chapter of the book. The reading of the data provided in this chapter suggests a need in education to focus on the poor academic achievement of both working-class boys *and* girls, as well as a need to focus on 'minorities', while seeking to break the tight nexus between gender and curricular and extra-curricular choices. Chapter 5 outlines the sorts of programmes for boys in schools which have been developed to this point and distinguishes between those with pro-feminist and recuperative masculinist provenances, with the former rightfully, in our view, acknowledging that the feminist project in education has not yet achieved its goals, with the latter usually arguing the converse.

Note

1 The recuperative claim that boys are disadvantaged as a group *vis-à-vis* girls has also had the effect of denying differences among girls. This is particularly so in relation to the disadvantages experienced by working-class and non-English speaking background girls in education. Georgina Tsolidis brought this point to our attention.

5 Programmes for boys in schools

Boys will change when they are helped to understand themselves better, are affirmed and valued 'as they are' and are given the tools to feel safe and equal around girls.

(Steve Biddulph 1995: ix)

If we are not pursuing gender justice in the schools, then we are not offering boys a good education – though we may be offering them certain privileges. Boys' programs are appropriately located in gender equity programs when those are based on a general social justice framework.

(Bob Connell 1996: 17)

Introduction

The 'What about the boys?' debate cannot be simply characterized as a 'backlash' to the feminist-inspired focus on girls in schooling. Since the early 1980s there has been interest in developing and facilitating relevant and appropriate programmes for boys to complement the work being done with girls, and as Kenway *et al.* (1997a) suggest many programmes in schools for girls have had an element which focused upon boys. While programmes such as personal development and sex education have been part of curriculum requirements, others addressing more contentious issues such as homophobia, violence against women and sexual harassment have been more *ad hoc*, usually sponsored by individual schools and often as 'one-off' sessions within the broader framework of personal development and sex education. Some educational systems have, however, systematized policies and procedures in respect of sexual harassment. The *ad hoc*, one-off programmes usually arise from a concern for social justice, with the focus on boys presupposing their social hegemony and aiming to alter those patterns of boys' behaviours that harm and denigrate themselves and others. Even though such programmes are beginning to mature and spread as more experience is gained in the area, their existence has been somewhat overshadowed by more recent calls for programmes to address 'boys' underachievement' as a response to the performance-based educational indicators discussed in Chapter 4. The focus here is on encouraging and assisting boys to overcome socially and self-imposed limitations in a manner similar to the focus on girls in schooling. While programmes coming from a social justice perspective also endorse these goals, they are mediated by a wider concern for gender equity rather than focusing more narrowly on the needs of boys in abstraction from their social and personal relationships with girls.

This chapter discusses the tension between these two positions in the 'What about the boys?' debate with respect to how best to address the needs of boys through the medium of 'boys' programmes', that is, programmes in schools designed to address what is perceived to be the underlying cause of the problems boys face in schools. The consideration of this debate will first locate the four strands of masculinity politics outlined in Chapter 2 in relation to programmes for boys in schools, and then discuss the importance of sport and physical education as a tacit boys' programme, before examining more explicit attempts by pro-feminists and recuperative masculinists to develop what they perceive as appropriate responses to the 'What about the boys?' debate. The chapter will conclude by seeking to move beyond the divide between pro-feminists and recuperative masculinists by arguing that the important insights of both positions can be effectively incorporated into a gender equity framework, and indeed must be if we are to adequately prepare boys for a very different world to that of their fathers. Such a position would require most recuperative masculinists to rethink and change their stance in relation to feminism and reject the stance of 'presumptive equality' (Foster 1994) – witness the Steve Biddulph quote at the top of this chapter. However, we believe that many policy makers and teachers in schools need, and are probably open to, a way through and beyond the commonly constructed pro-feminist/recuperative masculinist binary. In moving beyond this divide we seek to conjoin the notions of equality and difference within a pro-feminist framework, the difficulties of which were discussed in Chapter 1.

Masculinity politics in schooling

In terms of Chapter 2's categorization of the politics of men's responses to feminisms, programmes which address boys in relation to a social justice agenda are supported by pro-feminists, while those advocating the need to address boys' underachievement are generally representative of the recuperative masculinist position as an amalgam of the related men's rights and mythopoetic categories. This is not to say that pro-feminists are unconcerned with the educational welfare of boys. However, pro-feminists argue that many of the problems that boys face are a result of the same attitudes and behaviours that impact negatively on others, and so an approach which critically appraises aspects of the construction of masculinities is essential to positively addressing the needs of all sectors of the community. The advantage here is that boys are more able to be viewed in their diversity – for instance as coming from different social classes, sexualities, racial and ethnic backgrounds – and so their needs are able to be put into a broader perspective which acknowledges these differences. In contrast, the recuperative masculinist position argues that within such a framework boys' specific needs are subsumed under the priority given to girls and minority concerns, leaving them in the role of villains who must change in order to alleviate the problems they cause. This situation, they argue, mistakenly identifies all boys as powerful, ignores the powerlessness many boys experience, and leaves them alienated from themselves and without a positive sense of their masculine identity.

While differences among boys are often alluded to, recuperative masculinists' arguments constantly refer to 'boys' and 'masculinity', whereas most pro-feminists emphasize diversity and work with a notion of a hierarchy of masculinities. This issue was taken up in Chapter 4 by arguing the need to 'disaggregate' the data on educational achievement beyond an essentialist reading which fails to acknowledge diversity among girls and among boys in relation to important factors such as class, race and ethnicity. The essentializing strategy of recuperative masculinists has led some feminists in education to accuse them of appropriating the disadvantages experienced by marginalized boys, which have been known about and discussed since the 1970s, in order to justify their call for a focus on boys in general. (That strategy is similar in some ways to that utilized by conservative politicians to attract the votes of disaffected and sometimes disenfranchised working-class males.) However regardless of the approach, recuperative or pro-feminist, there is agreement that boys are more limited in their choice of subjects, extra-curricular and out of school activities than girls, and that the more girls expand their options the more boys seem to contract their own (see Chapter 4). This situation has been explained either as a reaction to the (supposed) anti-male culture that now pervades western societies, or as a result of the constrictions imposed by the constructions of dominant masculinities defined in opposition to femininities and the activities of women and girls.

In the former case recuperative masculinists propose a 'male-repair' agenda which seeks to reaffirm masculine identities and create a sense of community among men and boys. This takes the form of a re-establishment of bonds of guidance and friendship between older men and boys in order to give boys a sense of ease and pride in their impending manhood. In schooling this translates into calls for a greater masculine presence in schools – more male teachers, more masculine literature, more active modes of learning and a greater involvement for fathers in their sons' education. Through these initiatives it is envisaged that boys will be able to define their identities positively in relation to masculine influences rather than negatively in opposition to the preponderance of female teachers and to a feminized curriculum and pedagogy. Some of these arguments also push the need for schools to provide boys with opportunities for playing out 'safe', 'risk-taking' behaviours which do not compromise the well-being of boys or of others.

Contrary to this approach, pro-feminists argue that the need to encourage the formation of socially just and equitable relations between men and women, girls and boys, is more important than attempting to organize social life around the pastoral myth of the necessity of an initiation into manhood. For pro-feminists the problems that boys face are a result of just this belief that manhood is something that must be earned, and that the alienation boys experience is a result of the supposed need for them to prove themselves in relation to the harmful standards of hegemonic masculine expressions. It is argued that the competitive and emotionally stultifying demands of hegemonic masculinity reproduce the need for unequal relations of social power and privilege amongst males themselves and more obviously between males and females. They therefore reject recuperative masculinist claims that the masculine is devalued in a contemporary culture regarded as post-feminist, in the sense that the conditions for formal equality between the sexes have already been achieved, but recognize that conditions of formal equality are being challenged and substantive equality has not been achieved, as suggested in Chapter 3. Rather, the masculine is interpreted as something that needs to be fragmented and reconstructed into a diversity of forms in a manner that Connell (1995) has referred to as 'gender multiculturalism'.

While the conservative position has more to do with the maintenance of traditional educational values than with the current debate over how best to deal with boys' 'underachievement' in schooling, its influence is by no means inconsequential. In representing an underlying masculine ideology of competitiveness, rationality, and physical and emotional strength, the conservative perspective continues to support a general framework within which education continues to operate. Almost by definition then, the conservative position provides the ground upon which debates take place, and in this sense it is possible to characterize the dominant voices in the 'What about the boys?' debate with respect to their relation to the conservative perspective. Where the pro-feminists have had a tendency to reject traditional and conservative masculine norms, seeking to redefine masculinity in a manner responsive to feminist critiques of men and masculinity, recuperative masculinists have tended to defend boys' rights to express attitudes and behaviours associated with traditional expressions of masculinity, while some have also sought space for boys to move beyond the limitations inherent in such expressions. It is useful, therefore, to explore pro-feminist and recuperative masculinists' relations to an area of schooling within which traditional masculine values have been, and continue to be, exemplified and reproduced – sport and physical education (PE).

Sport and physical education

For the boys, to accommodate the girls would mean a reduction of the virility of the game as they understand it. For the girls, participation would mean accepting that their bodies, as well as the ball, would be the target of play.

(Alloway 1995: 40)

Nowhere in schooling are the powers and capacities of bodies brought more to the fore than in sport and physical education. The general fact that male bodies tend to be larger, stronger, faster and more competitive and aggressive than female bodies seems to justify conservative beliefs in the appropriateness of traditionally defined roles for men and women, even though at different stages of development this observation is not necessarily true. The belief that women are ill suited to vigorous exercise seems to find some support in casual observations of school playgrounds. Boys tend to dominate open spaces, participating in games which often require a robust and energetic use of their bodies, while girls tend to use less space and engage in activities which do not require frequent and vigorous bodily contact. However the 'policing' of these norms brings into question their supposed 'naturalness', with less active and less physically able boys often labelled 'wimps' or 'girls', and robust and energetic girls frequently seen to be compromising their femininity by being 'butch'. While there is obviously some validity to the manner in which boys' and girls' activities are traditionally categorized, the need to defend these behavioural norms through social censure belies their ubiquity. However, not only does this generalization extrapolate from a monological characterization of men's and women's bodies that ignores the diversity within and the overlap between them, it also overlooks the way that the powers and capacities of sexed bodies are structured by the expectations and practices of particular historical and cultural patterns.

Apart from the arguments on this point from feminists of difference outlined in Chapter 1, research into 'forms of embodiment', such as that undertaken by Mauss (1973), Bourdieu (1984) and Elias (1978, 1982), has argued that the powers and capacities of bodies tend to reflect the historical and cultural settings in which they are found. Mauss's notion of 'techniques of the body' alludes to the variability in the patterning and organization of physical abilities, facial and physical gestures, comportment, body adornment and decoration. Mellor and Shilling (1997) describe these techniques of the body in the following fashion:

Techniques of the body refer to how people learn to relate to and deploy their bodies in social life. This often takes place at a pre-cognitive level, but involves practice and accomplishment, and serves to mould the body in ways which make it fit for certain activities and unfit for others. The acquisition of body techniques, then, involves the acquisition of a particular bodily history. These techniques affect the very fundamentals of social and individual life: they are implicated in how people learn to walk, talk, look and think, and differ both historically and cross-culturally.

(Mellor and Shilling 1997: 20)

Elias and Bourdieu have both dealt with the social organization of these embodied dispositions and capacities through the concept of 'habitus'. For Elias this has meant a focus on the bodily reflection or 'internalization' of social processes and structures; while for Bourdieu, an individual's habitus is a bodily mechanism forged by the conditions of their socialization that makes possible the achievement of diverse tasks, producing dispositions that are expressed through an individual's 'taste' or conscious preference for certain kinds of food, art, sport, work and so on. In building upon such research, Mellor and Shilling (1997) argue that the body is neither the determinate basis for culture nor a passive template awaiting the imprint of social forces. Rather the 'unfinishedness' of human embodiment – the relative 'openness' and malleability of the human form – necessitates culture in a manner that both limits and allows for the diversification and evolution of its capabilities. The role of sport and physical education in contemporary western cultures might therefore be interpreted as a particularly direct mechanism through which the powers and capacities of bodies designated male and female have been given differential opportunities to develop and express themselves. For instance, boys have been strongly encouraged, if not required, to be active, vigorous and even aggressive in their bodily expressions. The sports we most immediately identify as male necessitate the development of bodies capable of giving and receiving physical punishment in highly competitive environments. Even those sports that do not require excessive body contact stress aspects such as competitiveness, combativeness, and the overcoming of one's opponent. The cultural environment within which this takes place privileges those who succeed in developing and expressing the requisite abilities and attitudes, as well as reproving those who do not. For example, the familiar description of 'throwing like a girl' can be interpreted in two ways. First, if a boy 'throws like a girl' he is seen to have compromised his masculinity – the fault lying not in the too general nature of the definition of masculinity but in the boy's 'deficiencies'. Second, as a self-reinforcing expectation that girls are not capable of performing certain privileged physical acts as well as boys, and so they are not granted the opportunities to learn to 'throw like a boy'.

What is at stake here more generally is the maintenance of a strict delineation of what male and female bodies are supposedly 'naturally' capable of. This kind of policing attempts to compensate for the imperfect nature of the processes by which particular patterns of embodiment are reproduced from generation to generation by both ceding less cultural value to those boys who do not or cannot express them effectively, and denying girls an equal opportunity to develop them. However, the imperfect nature of the process also provides opportunities for its alteration, and so we have witnessed since the early 1970s an increase in opportunities for girls to participate in a wider range of physical activities that have encroached upon traditional masculine preserves. This is reflected in representations of contemporary women's bodies that are often as muscular and active as they are passive and decorative. In all likelihood this phenomenon will further increase opportunities for girls and women to develop the powers and capacities of their bodies in a manner that has been traditionally viewed as masculine. What this trend is not likely to do, however, is to question or challenge the cultural positioning of the sports and physical activities that produce these privileged forms of embodiment. So even though since the mid-1980s there has been an emergence of an overt eroticization of men's bodies in the media and advertising, as well as a degree of tolerance towards homosexuality – witness the general popularity of the Sydney Gay and Lesbian Mardi Gras – the cultural, social and economic hegemony of traditional masculine traits such as competitiveness, aggression, toughness and individualism has not been displaced by more feminine and caring concerns. In fact, as argued in Chapter 3, these masculine traits have re-emerged as more central than ever under the pressures of global economic competitiveness, and as Chapter 4 demonstrates, the gains of liberal feminism in schooling have been largely restricted to girls gaining access to the traditionally masculine domains of mathematics and science. Women's access to the public sphere has done little to subvert its traditionally masculine ethos, then, and if anything, contemporary trends in areas such as schooling and sport indicate a broadening of the influence of this ethos as more girls and women adopt its characteristics in order to gain a measure of social and economic independence.

In such a context it is not surprising that physically demanding activities such as dance and gymnastics where both women and men excel are not as esteemed as those sports which serve to provide a stage for the expression of traditional forms of hegemonic masculinity – various codes of football, for instance, which celebrate a tough, aggressive and pseudo-warlike physical demeanour. Messner and Sabo (1994) have linked the importance that such sport has assumed in consumer societies with the definition of hegemonic forms of masculinity which bind 'manliness' with violence and competitiveness and the marginalizing of the feminine. Citing ethnographies from the USA (Foley 1990), Canada (Gruneau and Whitson 1993), Australia (Walker 1988) and the UK (Robins and Cohen 1978), Connell (1996: 12) argues that high profile school sports such as football carry great significance in the cultural life of schools, engaging the school population as a whole in the 'celebration and reproduction of the dominant codes of gender'.

Taking their cue from such critiques of sport and masculinity, pro-feminists such as Salisbury and Jackson (1996) advocate the need to find a balance between cooperation and competition in school sport. They argue,

> The unresolved tension between PE and school sport, cooperation and competition are still major blockages that prevent many boys from

developing a fuller, healthier approach to their bodies. The wider concerns of PE (often emphasising a more cooperative method of playing) for the physical, psychological and social well-being of the student are often in open conflict with the more limited sports focus of heroic performance in team games.

(Salisbury and Jackson 1996: 211)

Rather than simply condemning traditional competitive team games which tend to reproduce and confirm notions of a 'muscular manliness', Salisbury and Jackson argue for a greater emphasis on cooperative games within the PE curriculum to balance the competitive nature of school sport. Through this shift in emphasis it is envisaged that PE programmes would encourage personal challenge rather than overcoming opponents, thereby catering for a wider range of boys' abilities and interests and avoiding the need for boys to 'prove their manhood' on the sports field. More specific proposals include dance (see Gard 1998), gymnastics, solo rowing, swimming, climbing, running and sailing – all of which supposedly avoid 'the humiliating, pressurizing climate of team games' (Gard 1998: 214), while offering an opportunity for boys to 'find their own comfortable level without any comparative pressure being brought to bear on them' (p. 214). Similar proposals have been made elsewhere with, for instance, Kirk and Wright (1995: 340) arguing that gymnastics and dance promote 'a broader notion of skill and body awareness than that which underpins most of the narrow motor/sports skills approaches'. A slightly different approach is outlined in Kenway *et al.* (1997a), where attempts to create a 'gender inclusive' PE programme have included boys' involvement in a traditionally female sport such as netball, with girls and boys playing together in a setting where girls' skills will often exceed those of the boys.

While recuperative masculinists would probably have no objection to broadening the range of physical activities offered to boys, there is resentment of what is perceived as the denigration of those same traditionally masculine body-contact sports that a more cooperative approach aims to decentre. The association of aggressive and highly competitive body-contact sports with a greater propensity towards sexual violence or violence in relationships or family situations (Messner and Sabo 1994) is flatly rejected, interpreted instead as a feminist-inspired hatred of what is quintessentially (and here labelled conservatively) masculine. Seen to be consistent with a broader 'feminization of society', attempts to decentre highly competitive and aggressive sports are therefore considered as an attack on boys' right to be themselves (an essentialist conception of masculinity). What is for recuperative masculinists likely to lead to further alienation from a healthy masculine expression is for pro-feminists a way to move beyond men's and boys' abusive behaviours. So the pro-feminist supported move away from conservative expressions of masculinity in sport is resisted by the recuperative masculinists' position, as here represented, on the basis of the way it further marginalizes boys' 'natural' expression of a healthy masculinity. Recuperative masculinists argue that the robust physical exuberance expressed through such activity is perceived as threatening or menacing because its foreignness is misunderstood by feminist concerns. They further argue that it is the repression of such 'natural' masculine expressions which leads to unacceptable behaviours such as sexual and physical violence, rather than the 'training' into violence that they might receive from participating in such activities. The problem, it is believed, is a lack of activities for boys through which they can celebrate and enter into a healthy expression of their masculinity; and this is exacerbated by feminist and pro-feminist attempts to further emasculate boys by marginalizing the very activities which would enable them to grow confidently into themselves as men.

The divergent positions of pro-feminist and recuperative masculinist stances in the 'What about the boys?' debate are therefore quite clearly articulated in relation to sport and physical education. While the notion of human embodiment outlined above provides some conceptual leverage with which to come to terms with the cultural and historical variance in the patterning of the powers and capacities of sexed bodies, it does not help us understand just how malleable these patterns are, or how deep they run. Pro-feminists seem to assume they are quite supple and shallow, pointing to the diversity among boys' physical abilities and the changes in girls' and women's physical accomplishments since the early 1970s. Given this plasticity, then, pro-feminists feel justified in arguing that a conscious alteration in the way we approach sport and physical education in schools will affect the way boys relate to themselves, other boys, and girls. By shifting the balance from an emphasis on overly competitive and aggressive team sports towards physical activities that foster cooperation and a sense of personal accomplishment, from the pressure of having to conform to some masculine ideal of how a man uses his body *against* other men towards the pleasure of exploring one's physicality either *with* others or alone, it is believed that boys (and girls) will be more likely to feel a sense of ease and comfort in their embodiment, rather than feel inadequate when compared with the 'chosen few'. Recuperative masculinists, on the other hand, seem to assume that the powers and capacities of male bodies, though variable, are the result of a physically ebullient and robust 'masculine energy' that finds its expression through the same competitive and aggressive team sports pro-feminists find fault in. In devaluing such sports, recuperative masculinists argue that pro-feminists and feminists alike are alienating boys from the very activities they need to develop into healthy and balanced men. So where pro-feminists see plasticity and diversity in the powers and capacities of male bodies that can only be affirmed by pluralizing allowable expressions of masculinity, recuperative masculinists find a less pliable masculine essence that needs to be acknowledged and celebrated. Not surprisingly, these differences carry over and determine what it is that pro-feminists and recuperative masculinists argue should be the aims and rationales guiding the development and implementation of specific programmes for boys in schools, and it is to these issues that the next section of this chapter is devoted.

Programmes for boys in schools

In an article addressing the 'What about the boys?' issue, Connell (1996: 3) cites four main themes which run through the debate: the alienation of boys from schools and its supposedly feminine environment which is purportedly unsympathetic to boys, resulting in boredom, failure and dropout; boys' academic failure, especially in the humanities; a growing awareness of violence and intimidation perpetrated by boys and blamed on the acting out of aggressive masculine scripts; and the hopes and anxieties attached to changes in masculinity as articulated by the contemporary 'men's movement' and academic research on gender and men. While all four of these themes are of some concern to both pro-feminist and recuperative masculinist positions, there is a divide of emphasis, with the latter focusing more on the first two issues and their concern for boys' welfare, and the former more interested in the last two themes which position boys' problems within a larger concern for social justice.

As previously stated, programmes for boys in schools sponsored by pro-feminists seemed to have gained some recognition by the early to mid-1980s. Salisbury and Jackson (1996: 5) outline the development of such programmes in the UK from the Inner London Education Authority conference *Equal Opportunities – What's in it for the Boys?*, to Trefor Lloyd's (1985) *Working With Boys*, the Sheffield Men Against Sexual Harassment's SMASH pack (originally published in 1984 and revised in 1987), Chris Meade's *The Him Book*, and through to their own outline of programmes and practices for boys from a pro-feminist perspective. Similar programmes were being developed by Men Against Sexual Assault (MASA) groups in several Australian cities from the late 1980s and by governments, for example *No Fear: A Kit Addressing Gender Based Violence* (DEET 1995), while programmes such as those developed by the Oakland Men's Project in California have been addressing issues of masculinity and violence through workshops and publications such as *Men's Work: How to Stop the Violence that Tears Our Lives Apart* and *Making the Peace* (Kivel 1992, 1996). Connell (1996) also mentions a number of papers which outline work with boys in schools in the USA (C. Thompson 1988), the UK (Reay 1990) and Germany (Kindler 1993).

Responding in general to the feminist focus on girls in schooling and the obvious need for complementary programmes for boys, pro-feminist programmes such as those mentioned above tend to be guided by similar principles and goals. Avowedly anti-sexist, they focus on an examination of the construction of masculinities with the aim of encouraging boys to take personal and collective responsibility for the emotional, sexual and physical abuse perpetrated by them, as well as highlighting the emotional fallout from adherence to restrictive masculine norms. Cast within a general framework of gender equity and social justice, pro-feminist programmes aim to complement feminist work with girls to build just and equitable social and personal relationships.

Boys-Talk: A Program for Young Men about Masculinity, Non-violence and Relationships (MASA 1996), developed by Brooke Friedman in Australia, is quite typical of pro-feminist programmes generally in its approach and structure. Developed as a resource for secondary schools, parent groups and youth services, its stated aim is to 'support young men with options as they search for their own understanding of masculinity' (1996: 6). Cast within a theoretical frame that seems to owe much to the work on gender by Connell (see e.g. 1987, 1995), it relies on notions of the social construction of gender, a plurality in the expressions of masculinities and femininities, and the existence of power relations which differentiate and sustain the differences between these expressions. Central to its concern, then, is the social power and privilege that accrues to men over women, the role this plays in the construction of masculinities, and those expressions of masculine identities which harm and oppress others – especially and most commonly girls and women. *Boys-Talk* is therefore meant to complement gender equity strategies for girls in schools, most specifically those addressing violence, sex-based harassment, improved relations between and within the sexes, and equality of educational opportunities.

While acknowledging that an effective approach to gender equity must adopt a 'whole-school' approach, *Boys-Talk* offers a series of ten topics or sessions which focus on the construction of gender, relationships, sexuality and alternatives to violence. This type of format is quite typical of pro-feminist programmes, developed as they often are around the need to fit into 'normal' school time constraints as single or double lesson sessions, or as part of specially organized whole day activities addressing gender issues (see also Mills 1998a). The rationale for formats such as this is therefore more pragmatic than pedagogical, as it is often a matter of taking whatever opportunity presents itself to raise these issues with boys, rather than having licence to approach them in a more effective and thoroughgoing manner. The emphasis on issues regarding interpersonal relationships and increasing boys' emotional expressiveness can also be explained in this way. Given the thoroughgoing feminist critique of patriarchal social relations which pro-feminist programmes commonly accept and work from, it is deemed more realistic to attempt to affect individual lives and work for change from the ground up rather than wait until broader sociopolitical structures are more amenable. The situation here reflects a tension discussed in Chapter 2 between the need for men to work towards both political and personal change. The emphasis on the personal might be interpreted as the easier option, but it does address feminist criticism of men's need to deal with their individual sexism and for men to support each other emotionally. Whatever justification or rationale be given though, it is more an issue of what can be accomplished with limited resources, and work with boys in schools has been seen as one of the more effective ways to bring about change without institutional support and little or no funding. However, since the 'What about the boys?' backlash, it appears that some schools and systems have been putting money into boys' issues. Unfortunately some schools have taken a recuperative masculinist rather than pro-feminist stance in this work, accepting the (erroneous) notion that feminist reform projects in schools have achieved their goals and that it is now time for the boys to have a turn.

The facilitation of programmes such as *Boys-Talk* is generally undertaken by men, preferably in collaboration with other men and women in order to 'model' more cooperative styles of relating for the programme participants. It is considered to be crucial for boys to realize that it is not simply women who want expressions of masculinity to be re-evaluated and altered, but that men are also interested in change and willing to accept responsibility for seeking solutions to problems such as men's violence against women. In a similar vein, it is also suggested that facilitators be familiar with the cultural specificities of the boys they are working with, and seek the support and guidance of members of local communities. This is particularly important, given that the issues addressed often challenge boys' sense of their masculine identities, and so it is necessary to ensure the relevance of the programme to the participants if the concerns raised are not to be summarily dismissed by them.

Even though pro-feminist programmes are designed specifically for boys, they are not meant to be entirely given over to an examination of boys' or men's experience in abstraction from broader gender relations. For instance, *Boys-Talk* suggests that its material, with some modification, is appropriate for work with girls as well, arguing that both boys and girls need to understand the issues and concerns of one another if more equitable relations between them are to be forged. Individual sessions can therefore be held in both single and mixed sex groupings, though it is common for concerns around sexuality and violence to be dealt with separately, at least initially, due to the different focus required for boys and girls as well as to encourage a greater freedom of expression for participants.

Given the pro-feminist predilection for degendering strategies which proceed from the assumption that gender practices can be consciously altered, it is not surprising that there is a heavy reliance on discussion based approaches in their programmes. *Boys-Talk* uses teaching strategies such as journal writing, brainstorms, activity sheets, role play exercises, value and opinion walk continuums, graffiti sheets and audiovisual materials. As an overall principle then, *Boys-Talk* promotes conversation as the 'prime tool' with which to engage programme participants. Thus,

> Conversation is recognised in the program as a primary foundation of our personal system for constituting and positioning ourselves in relation to others and the world. It is hoped that through facilitation of structured conversations the program will provide young men with opportunities to examine their personal relations and to develop critical perspectives of their beliefs and their behaviour.
>
> (MASA 1996: 26)

Other programmes also use drama (see e.g. Hocking 1983; Novogrodsky *et al.* 1992), dance and movement, though the latter two tend to be rarely utilized. This is possibly a result of a lack of expertise in these areas, the common association of dance with marginalized masculinities (Gard 1998), as well as a theoretical commitment to mind over body as demonstrated in the above mentioned reliance on conscious rational change. However, some programmes have addressed the body in less direct ways than dance and movement through initiatives such as the Hackney Downs' 'Skills for Living' course which was developed in the 1980s (see Salisbury and Jackson 1996: 223). This programme was designed to encourage boys to learn domestic skills such as cooking, cleaning, washing and ironing, childcare and shopping in order to help them become more self-sufficient.

Pro-feminist programmes such as *Boys-Talk* attract criticism from recuperative masculinists for being more concerned with feminist principles than helping boys, as well as for being too narrow and negative in their focus. For example, Vogel's (1997) review of *Boys-Talk* argues that there is 'little in the program that might help boys feel good about themselves', adding sardonically: 'Perhaps the expectation is that boys will feel good about getting a pat on the back from women?' (1997: 2). Vogel identifies poor self-esteem as one of the biggest problems facing boys, and he accuses *Boys-Talk* of containing much that would shame boys instead of helping them.

> Perhaps the tension between the stated position that masculinity accrues 'status and power that maintains male dominance and female subordination' prohibits admission that boys often do not feel good about themselves.
>
> (Vogel 1997: 2)

The programme's pro-feminist perspective is therefore at fault, according to Vogel, for reinforcing the view that girls are morally superior to boys. For instance, the portrayal of violence as a masculine characteristic rather than a human failing (an overstatement of the pro-feminist position which argues that violence is an integral to the construction of 'hegemonic' masculinity) is said to promote the belief that men are always perpetrators of violence and rarely victims. When this is coupled with the programme's emphasis on violence against women, Vogel argues that the result is a minimization of the problem of violence against males which inhibits boys from seeking help when they are victimized, particularly by women. This line of argument extends to the issue of self-violence, and probably the most cogent criticism Vogel makes against *Boys-Talk* is its failure to deal with the issue of youth suicide among boys. However, where the recuperative masculinists advocate the celebration of masculine culture to bolster boys' self-esteem in order to address this problem, pro-feminists would argue that it is the pressure brought to bear by the imperative to conform to a too narrow construction of masculinity that forces boys into such desperate action. So while both positions would agree to a limited extent that aspects of 'traditional masculinity' are harmful to boys and that a broader range of 'acceptable' expressions of masculinity would be beneficial to them, their different theoretical approaches towards what masculinity actually is and how it comes to be, prevent them from coming to any broad agreement on how best to achieve such aims.

This contrast is especially stark in respect of the issue of homophobia – a central concern of pro-feminist programmes and an issue recuperative masculinists rarely mention. The ubiquitous and often vicious intolerance towards effeminate and/or bisexual and homosexual boys is, we would speculate, more likely to drive boys to suicide than any other probable cause (an observation also applicable to lesbian girls).[1] And at a time when boys' awareness of their sexuality is burgeoning, any confusion over sexual experimentation and/or sexual preference is not dealt with kindly by the hyper-heterosexual expectations of traditional masculine norms. While recuperative masculinists' theoretical reliance on sex-role theory and biological determinism seeks to give comfort to boys in *general* in the context of a supposed 'anti-male' culture, it does little to comfort *particular* boys who do not conform to traditional expectations – those who find no easy place in the celebration of masculinity as it is dominantly expressed. This is the strength of the pro-feminist perspective, as it is able to speak to the specificity of individual boys in its emphasis on the fluid social dimensions of the construction of masculinities (and sexualities), which acknowledges and celebrates diversity rather than conformity.

In contrast to the pro-feminist position which takes as its starting point the feminist-inspired focus on girls in schooling, recuperative masculinists have argued that schools are overly feminized and therefore hostile, or at least unsympathetic, to boys. So while pro-feminist programmes have attempted to complement feminist work in schools, recuperative masculinists have argued for a focus on boys similar to what has taken place with girls since the early 1970s. In some cases this takes the form of an acceptance of feminist reforms along with a call for an acknowledgement that boys' needs are just as immediate.

Feminist thinking – that girls deserve the same opportunities as boys – has become recognised as common sense. But we are still confused about directions for boys . . . we are some way from knowing how schools might serve boys well.

What is starting to change is our complacency about boys' behaviours and attitudes. We are also beginning to recognise that we don't know much about boys. This is not the same as discovering that boys are oppressed just like girls, but it does mean noticing how poorly schools are serving boys. The recognition that boys are not 'the winners' in the contest for academic and social rewards is an important step.

(Fletcher 1995: 205–6)

In other cases there is a vehement rejection of the feminist influence in schooling, arguing that it positions masculinity as pathological and boys as 'toxic problems' for girls. For example, Blankenhorn's (1996) *Fatherless America* maintains that schools are institutions run by women in which the goal for girls is to help them achieve, while the aim for boys is to make them behave. In general though, the recuperative masculinists' perspective refuses the pro-feminist gesture of placing boys in a position which constitutes them as privileged and powerful, placing emphasis instead on a schooling system which is failing boys and girls (although the more vehement recuperative masculinist voices would contend that girls are advantaged to the detriment of boys). It is argued that the needs of boys cannot be seen clearly through the needs of girls, and that as soon as attention is placed on the effects of boys' negative behaviours such as verbal and physical harassment, the way boys get victimized cannot be seen. Attention is continually drawn by recuperative masculinists to 'female dominance' in schooling – referring to both the preponderance of women teachers and a passive (read feminine) mode of learning which works against boys' more 'robust and energetic' tendencies. When this is compounded with the pro-feminist strategy of approaching boys' needs through a gender equity framework, it is believed that the only form of acceptable masculinity for boys is that of wimp/apologist. The recuperative masculinists therefore argue that rather than addressing boys' needs, the pro-feminist strategy exacerbates their problems by further attacking their self-esteem through a constant denigration of their masculinity, leaving them unprepared to negotiate the complexity of gender relations in ways that also allow them to meet their own needs.

In line with such arguments, recuperative masculinists have called more for changes in the organization of learning than the implementation of specific programmes (although these also exist to some extent – see for instance Browne and Fletcher's (1995) *Boys and Schools* for a range of programmes framed outside of the specific gender equity focus of pro-feminists and which aim to improve boys' self-esteem, self-motivation and understanding of themselves and others). For instance, there have been numerous reports of attempting to improve boys' academic performance in humanities subjects such as English through single sex classes and using 'masculine texts' such as *Lord of the Flies*, war poems and *Macbeth*. One such attempt was undertaken at the Cotswold School, a coeducational secondary school in Leicester, England, in order to counter the 'disadvantage' that boys (supposedly) faced by being taught with girls. A newspaper report commented on this approach in the following way:

> The teenage boys were separated from the girls two years ago in GCSE English classes because teachers believed they would feel more confident writing and reading and discussing emotional topics without the presence of girls, who have traditionally had the edge in language skills.
> ('Single-sex classes raise boys' grades', *The Times*, 25 August 1996)

The experiment was reportedly a success for both the boys and the girls, with the percentage of students receiving high grades increasing by up to 50 per cent. For recuperative masculinists, this educational experiment demonstrates three important points.

> First, it acknowledges that boys generally have a slower development of language skills. Second, it takes account of the dynamic by which boys, feeling verbally outclassed by the girls in expressive subjects, often become hoonish and macho as a defence mechanism, spoiling the class for themselves and the girls. Third, by specifically targeting English, it tackles the key life skills of self-expression, self-awareness and communication – the very things men traditionally lack. These are the skills that make boys into better fathers, partners and workmates – which most girls and women long for.
> (Biddulph 1998: 3)

This is just one example of initiatives which attempt to take into account 'boys' specific learning style', and is consistent with the argument that 'We owe it to both girls and boys to recognise that teachers need to value and encourage both sexes equally but differently, because of the different learning styles they adopt' ('Let boys be boys: head[master]', *West Australian*, 10 February 1997). It is believed that schools adopt passive and therefore feminine teaching and learning practices which favour girls in as much as they are 'more docile and motivated', whereas boys' 'robust behaviour' as an expression of their preferred learning style is not only unaccounted for, but also interpreted as inappropriate and disruptive. So when feminists argue that there is already a disproportionate amount of resources dedicated to boys in the form of behaviour management programmes (Foster 1994), recuperative masculinists reply that what is needed is teaching practices appropriate to boys, rather than a disciplinary ethic which marginalizes and discourages them. There is, therefore, a perception that teachers are prejudiced against boys, not only because a majority of them are women, but as an article entitled 'Boys held back by teacher bias' in the *Electronic Telegraph* (Wednesday, 2 October 1996 Issue 497) reported, also because boys are stereotyped as

> less sensitive, less reliable and less inclined to be cooperative than girls. As a result, less was expected of boys and they were more likely to face repeated criticisms . . . [Staff] agreed that they tended to praise what they saw as female traits, such as quietness in class and neatness of work, and that the cumulative effect of criticism demotivated boys.

Just what boys' specific learning style actually is is never canvassed in any detail beyond positing it as energetic and robust (supposedly as a consequence of some biological predispositions), with strategies such as those mentioned above and more male teachers seen as important factors in addressing it. The latter initiative is a recurrent theme of recuperative masculinists' arguments, with the notion that boys need the opportunity to grow up seeing themselves 'like men' rather than 'not like women' – being able to define their masculinity positively in relation to male presence and influence rather than negatively in opposition to female ones – in common currency. Connell (1996) has pointed out that similar sentiments were expressed in the late 1960s and early 1970s (see for instance Sexton (1969) and Austin *et al.* (1971)). In a similar vein, Kimmel (1996a) has argued that the reassertion of 'traditional' forms of manliness in the USA at the beginning of the twentieth century was similar to that occurring in the contemporary situation, pointing out that both cases are responses to a perceived feminization of American culture.

> At that time, masculinists argued that changes in the nature of work, the closing of the frontier, and changes in family relations had produced a cultural degeneracy – American men and boys were becoming feminized. Men searched for homosocial preserves where they could be real men with other men (fraternal lodges, Muscular Christian revival meetings) and sought vigorous ways to demonstrate their hardy manhood (wilderness retreats, dude ranches and rodeos, health and exercise crazes, evocations of martial glory), while they also sought ways to ensure that the next generation of young boys would not grow up to be an effete elite (Boy Scouts, single-sex classrooms, a fatherhood movement).
>
> (Kimmel 1996a: 309)

The revival of many of these strategies in the 1990s suggests that the recuperative masculinist position can be justifiably characterized as an attempt to reassert masculine hegemony in the face of feminist gains. However, viewed from a different (recuperative) standpoint, the pro-feminist stance might be interpreted as selling out boys' future to a 'politically correct' ideological position which will leave unaddressed the very real problems and needs that boys have. The next and concluding section of this chapter attempts to work beyond the divide between these two positions, and suggests ways to incorporate the insights of pro-feminists and recuperative masculinists within a gender equity framework.

Beyond the divide

In seeking to move beyond a straightforward reproduction of the differences between pro-feminists' and recuperative masculinists' arguments on programmes for boys in schools, it is pointless to attempt to find some value-free terrain upon which the important insights of both positions might be brought together. Apart from the fact that such a space does not exist due to the unavoidably political nature of social relations between the sexes, the practical policy implications of the 'What about the boys?' debate in relation to programmes for boys demands a reply in terms of either separate strategies for boys and girls, as advocated by recuperative masculinists, or the pro-feminist approach of addressing the needs of boys within a gender equity framework. In accordance with the principle that we need somehow to work towards social equality through a recognition of difference, it may seem at first glance that the option of separate strategies for boys and girls selects itself. However, the recuperative masculinist 'equal but different' argument does not fare well under closer scrutiny. As was discussed in Chapter 1 in the section on the theoretical and practical relations of contemporary masculinity politics to the debate between feminisms of equality and difference, the recuperative masculinist position fails to acknowledge that the notion of 'complementarity' upon which this argument is based requires a hierarchical relation that identifies the feminine as a complement *to* rather than *with* the masculine public sphere where sociopolitical power resides. The notion of difference appealed to by recuperative masculinists is also undifferentiated within the two categories of male and female, ignoring the complexities introduced by other important social categories such as class, race, ethnicity and sexuality. (This was highlighted in Chapter 4 through an analysis of school performance data.) Whatever its other shortcomings, the pro-feminist position has the advantage of recognizing a plurality of social relations both between and within the sexes, and it can therefore take account of and work with the complexity of our sociopolitical landscape. This is essential if we are to pursue the principle of social equality through a recognition of difference. It is for this reason that programmes for boys in schools must be placed within the pro-feminist-preferred model of a broad gender equity framework as informed by notions of social justice.

The choice of this model does not exclude the possibility of learning from and incorporating the insights that recuperative masculinists have into the problems that boys face in schooling. In a broader context, pro-feminists such as Seidler (1997) and Tacey (1997) have argued that common ground needs to be found between the recognition of the general and continuing social and political inequality between men and women, and the reality that many men are experiencing difficulties in coming to terms with the changing relations between men and women, as well as the structural changes driven by the move towards global economic markets. Seidler (1997) has argued that the confusion and disorientation that many men have experienced in the face of social changes is expressed as anti-feminism and as a claim for men's rights because of men's failure to critically explore inherited forms of masculinity. However, as advocates of a critical reappraisal of masculinities, pro-feminists have failed in as much as they have not sufficiently come to terms with those aspects of men's experience that recuperative masculinists emphasize.

> We need to be able to engage critically with some of these movements, learning what draws men into their ranks. To do this we have to grasp the contradictions in men's experience and be ready to challenge feminist notions which would identify masculinity exclusively as a relationship of power. We have to be ready to listen to what men have to say about themselves so that we do not discount their feelings of anxiety, frustration and powerlessness. This needs to be part of a critical engagement with men in their relationships with diverse masculinities.
>
> (Seidler 1997: 14)

Tacey (1997) makes a similar point, though from a perspective that 'repossesses' Jungian theory for progressive social and political causes.

> We must, I believe, muddle away at getting both perspectives in our minds at the one time. Men's pain and men's power, spirituality and politics, feeling and reason: the claims of both sides must always be examined, balanced, and placed against each other.
>
> (Tacey 1997: 15)

In psychoanalytic terms, for Tacey this involves neither the pro-feminist tendency of 'killing off the father' and overthrowing his authority through the demonization of the masculine and concomitant idealization of the feminine (cf. John Stoltenberg's *Refusing to be a Man*), nor the recuperative masculinist desire to mythologize the masculine and 'redeem the father'. Rather the essential task is, as Tacey quotes James Hillman, 'to redeem the father by surpassing him' (Tacey 1997: 45). Boys must not be alienated from their 'masculine heritage', but neither should they uncritically accept that 'heritage' via the 'father's authority'. Their role is to accept the reality of their masculine inheritance along with the responsibility to (post)modernize its expression in line with the pressing issues of their time. The strength of the recuperative masculinist position in the 'What about the boys?' debate has therefore been in affirming boys' right to their 'masculine heritage', while the strength of the pro-feminist position has been to submit this heritage to critical appraisal and to recognize the need for its (post)modernization in line with the reality of the changes in sexual politics brought about by feminist theory and practice.

In choosing to place programmes for boys in schools within a gender equity framework, there is an acknowledgement that the distinctions between masculinities and femininities, the public and private spheres, and the roles of men and women are becoming increasingly blurred. None the less this acknowledgement does little to allay the fears of recuperative masculinists that the needs of boys cannot be clearly seen through a framework developed from an initial focus on girls in schooling. For instance, Vogel (1998: 1) argues that 'gender equity policy is based on the premise that females are oppressed by males, so it is impossible for boys to be disadvantaged'. However, we would argue strongly that it is in no sense valid to say that boys are disadvantaged because of their sex in a manner parallel to that of girls, but there certainly is a case to be made that specific groups of boys are disadvantaged, even in relation to girls in the same situation. As the analysis of school performance data in Chapter 4 showed, working-class boys and black boys are not faring well and do need assistance in overcoming the specific disadvantages they face. Once we get past the recuperative masculinist mistake of treating boys as an homogenous group and recognize boys in their diversity, then the concerns they raise about boys loses some of its backlash character and becomes instead an important resource in addressing the needs of boys who do need help.

So we can ask questions such as: How can we encourage boys to elect to study subjects like English, languages, history, music, visual arts and drama in greater numbers? Why are boys grossly overrepresented in remedial classes? Why do disciplinary problems in schools overwhelmingly involve boys? Why do boys seem to lack motivation and self-confidence? Why don't boys read as well as girls? These questions have been put on the agenda by recuperative masculinists and need to be recast by also asking which boys is it that these questions specifically relate to.[2] When the same approach is applied to questions more commonly put by pro-feminists such as: Why do boys resort to physical and verbal abuse so readily? Why do boys continue to sexually harass girls and persecute effeminate and/or gay boys? Why do boys seem to be intolerant and lacking in empathy? We are able to deflect the recuperative masculinist criticism that pro-feminists caricature boys (as a category) as toxic problems for girls and masculinity as a pathology to be overcome. After all, if we are to take seriously the notion of a hierarchy of masculinities it seems illogical to tar all boys with the same brush.

While this may make some feminists and pro-feminists nervous in relation to macro-level arguments that address boys' continuing economic and social advantage over girls, it must be realized that if we are to argue that recuperative masculinist claims for boys are invalid on the basis of an essentialist bias that overlooks the complexities of categories such as class, race, ethnicity and sexuality, we cannot also continue to treat boys as a single category with respect to macro-level claims by pro-feminists as to boys' relations of social power over girls. The poststructuralist move of strategic essentialism that Spivak (1992), for instance, argues for has obvious advantages for certain feminist arguments. However, strategic essentialism cuts both ways in the context of the 'What about the boys debate?' and in masculinity politics more generally. As just mentioned, it is not possible on the one hand to deny the recuperative masculinists' claims to boys as a single category and on the other hand allow its use for pro-feminist arguments. How then is it possible for pro-feminists to maintain the feminist insight that men and boys *in general* are socially, economically and culturally privileged in relation to women and girls, as well as make use of the notion of the social construction of a masculini*ties* in order to forestall the recuperative masculinist strategy of essentializing maleness and/or masculinity? How is the need for strategic essentialism to be paired with the need to acknowledge the diversity and fluidity of masculine expressions – a kind of 'strategic pluralism' as Blackmore (1999) has put it in relation to feminism and women?

Now the experience since the late 1960s of feminist activism has shown that it is possible for at least some women to gain their share of the social, economic and cultural privileges that have traditionally accrued to men – gender convergence as Walby (1997) has put it. In this sense we might argue that there are no formal barriers for women in the public realm as long as they are willing to adopt and live by the masculine codes of behaviour that have traditionally defined that sphere: that is, if they are willing to develop the powers and capacities of their bodies in a direction more amenable to the demands of the masculine public realm. However, if we accept Gaten's (1996) argument as mentioned in Chapter 1, that there is a real difference in the social and cultural reception of masculine modes of action performed by a female body as compared to a male body, then we might doubt the possibility of women ever fully participating as men do in the public realm as currently constituted. But then how does this argument relate to the acknowledgement that traditional distinctions such as masculine/feminine and public/private are becoming increasingly blurred? The 'blurring' that has taken place is a testament to the success of feminist reforms, and of the current and historical necessity for women to live in two worlds – the public and the private – if they are to have social and economic independence. Men *as men* have not been confronted with the same demands, although men in marginalized positions are faced with similar difficulties on the basis of their sexuality, race, class and ethnicity. What this means, then, is because we have not witnessed to any real extent either an effective challenge to the identification between the 'masculine' and the public realm, or a broadening of the social and cultural prestige ceded the feminine and its role in the private sphere, that boys and men will retain their social and economic advantage over women and girls as long as dominant expressions of masculinity remain tied to success in the public realm and ignore the possibilities and responsibilities that exist in the private sphere. In other words, the social and economic advantage that men and boys have over women and girls exists in and through the historical affinity between masculinity and the public sphere, in that the powers and capacities of male bodies have been constructed in tandem with and in service to the changing demands of the public realm. This understanding provides a basis from which to approach 'What about the boys issue?' within a gender equity framework, as the general approach must be predicated upon encouraging boys to broaden their modes of expression to encompass what has been traditionally seen as feminine, instead of progressively limiting their options as they attempt to continue to define themselves in contrast to girls, women, and their identification with the feminine. This will become more crucial to boys and men as more women and girls take up positions in traditionally masculine preserves, and as more service and information oriented occupations replace more labour intensive ones.

Recuperative masculinist refusals to accept this inevitability result in fears over the 'feminization of society' and the supposed marginalization of men as mentioned at the beginning of Chapter 2. However, men are marginalizing themselves by not accepting that the changes that have been wrought by feminist reforms in combination with the drastic alterations to the structure of the economy require them to change as well. We are not serving the needs of boys in schooling well if we attempt to reinstitute increasingly outmoded notions of masculinity and manhood, when what is required is the (post)modernization of both. The real issue in the 'What about the boys?' debate is 'What can we do to better prepare boys for a world very different from their fathers?' and not 'How can fathers imbue their sons with modes of masculine expression with which the former are familiar and comfortable?' The insights of recuperative masculinists are valuable to some extent, but must be interpreted through the lens of gender equity if we are to prepare boys for their futures. Some groups of boys are disadvantaged (as are some groups of girls) and if we are to be guided by the social justice principles that inform a gender equity approach then their needs should be addressed. But boys as a whole are not disadvantaged in any sense that might be equated to the situation with girls in schooling. However, they are limited by a continued adherence to increasingly outmoded and limiting expressions of masculinity, and if we are to address boys in general in any way then it must be to encourage them to realize the necessity for expanding and not contracting their options.

This is a difficult task given that cultural prestige tends to be equated

with the economic success that a masculine embodiment as currently constituted promises access to. This approach is also likely to encounter some
resistance in school communities, given that the opinions and beliefs of
many parents and teachers are predicated upon notions of sexual difference
formed in quite different times and circumstances. For this reason, it is not
uncommon for the arguments of recuperative masculinist to strike an
immediate chord with members of school communities (particularly male
teachers), offering as they do simple and seemingly commonsense answers
to complex issues. For instance, recuperative masculinists such as Steve Biddulph in Australia have argued for the 'empowerment' of boys, mirroring
the language used in the focus on girls in schooling and in doing so ignoring the different relations that boys and girls have with respect to the socio-
economic power that resides in the public realm. A more appropriate but
more difficult goal for programmes for boys in schools is to encourage the
notion of *respect* – both for boys in relation to themselves and others, and
for the facilitators of such programmes in seeking to create 'respectful practices' with the boys they are working with (cf. Denborough 1996; McLean
1997; Mills 1998a, 1998b). This approach can be justified in at least three
ways: first, it acknowledges the advantageous positioning of boys in comparison to girls with respect to the public realm; second, it recognizes that
boys do not need to be encouraged any more than they traditionally have
been by the reproduction of dominant expressions of masculinity to pursue
independence and their share of social power – if anything this needs to be
mediated by greater feelings of empathy and community; and third, it
addresses the very real need that many boys have to develop a more positive vision of themselves and others.

In arguing that we need to address the needs of boys within a gender
equity framework, this chapter has also stressed the importance of form-
ing responses to the 'What about the boys?' debate that move beyond the
current divide between pro-feminist and recuperative masculinist positions. At the level of general principles, this has involved an acknowledgement that we need to incorporate the insights that recuperative
masculinists have into the needs of boys into an understanding of boys'
experiences that takes account of their advantageous positioning in
relation to the public realm. However, this positioning exists as the *potential* that boys have, given the current constitution of expressions of dominant masculinities, to develop the powers and capacities of their bodies in
the direction of achieving socioeconomic power, while the *reality* is that the
outcome of this process is extremely variable. Accordingly, there are
groups of boys who are socially, economically and educationally disadvantaged and it is important that their needs be addressed. More
broadly, though, the issue that boys in general face is their tendency to contract their options as girls expand theirs. This can be overcome only if boys
cease constructing themselves in opposition to girls and femininities, and

begin to expand their range of expressions by developing the powers and capacities of their bodies in directions traditionally denied them. In order to encourage boys to expand themselves in such a way, programmes in schools must address the powers and capacities of boys' bodies in more direct ways than has been the case with the dominant pro-feminist model of conscious and rational change through pedagogical methods such as 'conversation' – however this may be construed. (Kenway *et al.* 1997a) have demonstrated the heavy emotional load of gender reform work in schools for both girls and boys and female and male teachers.) Here again pro-feminists have something to learn from the recuperative masculinist acknowledgement of boys' emotional and physical attachment to traditional and dominant expressions of masculinities. Forms of embodiment are the site of our most stubborn behavioural patterns, prejudices and fears, and the most obvious enjoyment that many men and boys gain by expressing themselves through an aggressive physicality demonstrates only that this energy cannot be ignored, but must be allowed a multiplicity of avenues through which to express itself beyond the limitations of contemporary masculine norms. Modes of creative expression such as theatre and dance can not only provide such avenues, but also address in a more direct way than 'conversation' the embodied prejudices and fears that lead to the harmful behaviours, both for themselves and others, that many boys display. In combination with programmes that teach 'skills for living' such as cooking, cleaning, washing and ironing, childcare and shopping along the lines of the Hackney Downs initiative (see p. 143), then, we can begin to see how programmes in schools can provide opportunities for boys to develop in ways that expand their own options without inhibiting the rights of girls to full participation in the public realm.

Such an approach must also reject the zero-sum construction of boys' and girls' interests and related 'competing victims' syndrome accounts. In Chapter 2 we suggested that such programmes and their desired goals would work against the 'narrowly defined economic and political interests of men' (Messner 1997: 110) and in so doing, expand the range of acceptable practices of masculinity for boys and men. This project is inevitably (and desirably) intertwined with the empowerment of girls and women. We concur with his observation and see this as a goal of educational programmes underpinned by the framework we have sought to outline which moves beyond a simple divide. Such an approach attempts to pull together the notions of difference and equality and works strategically at system, school and classroom levels in relation to both social and academic goals. Programmes in schools must deal with boys and girls in complementary ways for both social and academic outcomes, while always recognizing the inequality inherent in the current gender order, a recognition central to the pro-feminist position, but lacking and often derided in recuperative approaches.

Notes

1 Sedgwick (1993) provides evidence of this horrible reality for the USA.
2 For good analyses of the links between constructions of masculinity and literacy and subject English in schools, see Martino (1995a, b) and Alloway and Gilbert (1997). For good analyses of these links in school science, see Letts (1997, 1998).

6 Towards a pro-feminist politics of alliance ·

> For men to support feminism, it seems to me, means acknowledging men's experience of powerlessness, which often makes feminist women uneasy, while placing it within a context of men's aggregate power – the power of men as a group over women as a group, and the power of some men over other men. Disaggregating the term masculinity into its plural masculinities is one way to address the second dimension of power. Some men are disempowered by virtue of class, race, ethnicity, sexuality, age, able-bodiedness. But all men are privileged *vis-à-vis* women.
>
> (Michael Kimmel 1998: 64)

> . . . men will have to work against our narrowly defined economic and political interests. But men also have a stake in the movement for social justice. In rejecting hegemonic masculinity and its rewards, we also may become more fully human. For I am convinced that the humanisation of men is intricately intertwined with the empowerment of women.
>
> (Michael Messner 1997: 110)

Introduction

Throughout this book we have argued that since the mid-1960s men have had to respond to feminisms in one way or another, both in relation to their participation in the public sphere of work and politics, as well as in terms of relations within the private sphere of the home. We used Kimmel's work in Chapter 1 to speak of the impact of feminist projects on changes in work, the home, and intimate relations, and the recognition now that men too have a gender and that gender is a centrally important element in social arrangements. Men have responded in various ways to feminisms; most men, however, have not organized politically in relation to them. This is probably true of male teachers in schools as well. None the less, since the 1970s there has been a pro-feminist men's movement which has sought to support feminism, while also seeking to change men and hegemonic masculinities.[1] Debate among pro-feminists has turned on the emphasis given to either of these goals, supporting feminist reforms or changing men. Feminism from the outset also recognized that men had to change if feminist goals were to be reached, even though there were more separatist elements that denied the possibility of men changing at all. The question of men generally then was fairly low in the initial political priorities of feminism and most feminists were fairly sceptical of pro-feminist men.

The political context of feminism and men's responses to it has changed considerably since the initial impact of the second wave of the women's movement in the 1960s and 1970s. Feminism has become more diverse and fragmented, both theoretically and politically; the triumvirate of liberal, radical and socialist feminisms has been joined by a range of what we might call post-feminisms which seek to speak to difference and which recognize the fragmentation and reconsideration of both Enlightenment and modernist goals. Thus we now also have poststructuralist and postcolonial feminisms. This proliferation of feminisms of course raises the question of which feminism pro-feminist men should be pro. Our position, as suggested in Chapter 1, has been that we need to take account of both the newer feminisms of difference and those older perspectives of feminisms of equality. As Fraser (1995) has argued, contemporary progressive politics is about working these two sets of goals together, what she refers to as politics of recognition (difference) and politics of redistribution (equality). However, and as noted in Chapters 1 and 3, the nation-state, its political goals and administrative structures, have been changed – narrowed – since the heyday of 1960s and 1970s progressive politics, under pressures from globalization and the dominance of market liberal ideology. These changes to the character and remit of state policies have made the achievement of progressive goals generally, as well as those associated with feminism, more difficult to accomplish. Along with the effects of globalization – restructured labour markets, high levels of unemployment, pervasive insecurity, the growth in inequality and so on – this new politics has also provided fertile ground for a politics of backlash.

In the new global, post-Cold War era, governments have taken up policies of economic rationalism, and at the same time some, for example Labor governments in Australia (1983–96), also pursued policies of social rationalization, seeking to create a meritocracy where gender (and race, ethnicity, sexuality, able-bodiedness and so on) were not to be factors in opportunities available through education and careers. While taking up such a politics of recognition, these same governments shied away from policies of redistribution, evident in meaner welfare policies and a smaller public sector. In such a context, we have seen continuing and high levels of unemployment and the growth in social inequality. Rapid change has been everywhere and insecurity has also been pervasive in relation to employment security, but also in most other dimensions of social life. It is almost as if globalization has seen a real divide created between educated elites whose skills are required by the emergent economic structures and globalizing labour markets and then others who appear to be excluded, and condemned, at best, to employment in secondary and peripheral labour markets, or at worst, to unemployment and social exclusion. The participation of women in the workforce has grown across this time; however, much of the growth has been in part-time work in the service sector. Women's employment growth has been greater than that for men, but many more men still participate in full-time employment. The result of these changes has been that some middle-class men are challenged by some middle-class women for career preferment. Yet the extent of this challenge is usually very much overstated in the anti-feminism of recuperative masculinist politics. Walby (1997) has referred to this challenge as 'gender convergence'. At the same time there has been what Walby calls 'gender polarization' occurring. She suggests that polarizations among females have occurred between those with higher education qualifications and careers and both older women who did not have the same opportunities, and younger women who did not do well at school. For men, many blue-collar working-class jobs have disappeared, changing and challenging the transitions between school and work and adulthood for many working-class boys. Youth unemployment remains high and is most often experienced by those from the most disadvantaged homes. Willis's lads (1977) now learn not to labour, while with the credential spiral those who continue in education have to compete for longer. There are thus also polarizations between groups of men.

It is in that political context that backlash politics and resentment have emerged. Often these focus upon government policies which seek to redress disadvantages experienced by women or by other so-called minority groups. Backlash national chauvinisms have also emerged which peddle new forms of racism and which in the Australian context seek to reduce expenditure on the most disadvantaged groups, including indigenous Australians, and which also want reductions in migration and in specific programmes for those from non-English speaking backgrounds. Programmes attempting to break down barriers to women's participation in careers have also been criticized, and at the same time childcare funding has been reduced as part of the meaner and leaner state. Social rationalization has thus come under attack in the context of economic rationalization and the insecurities and uncertainties of a new globalized world. In that context, conservative politicians have sought the electoral support of male members of the disaffected working class and underclass; some have attempted to constitute men as the new disadvantaged. We have already mentioned the pro-feminist men's movement which developed from the 1970s in relation to feminism. In this new political context of backlashes and resentment, other varieties of masculinity politics emerged and appeared to gain more support among men, with more than a little help from the media. By and large these recuperative men's groups were not pro-feminist and displayed varying degrees of hostility towards feminism, as we have outlined in Chapter 2. Many of them believed that feminism generally had achieved its goals. Some blamed feminism for the problems that men and boys were facing. The recuperative masculinists soon turned their attentions to education and that raft of policies and changed practices which were the result of the feminist engagement with schooling since the 1970s. As argued in Chapter 3, the emphasis of restructured educational systems upon performance indicators provided bodies of evidence regarding differential male/female performance through schooling, as did the always readily available exam results at the end of secondary schooling. Utilizing a somewhat crude reading of these data, some attempted to constitute an essentialized category of boys as the new disadvantaged. Such evidence was also used in the 'What about the boys?' debate to the effect of reframing the thinking of many in schools in respect of gender equity questions. Policy was also reframed, while many conservative politicians articulated the need for a focus on boys in schooling. As mentioned earlier in this book, the *National Policy for the Education of Girls in Australian Schools* became *Gender Equity: A Framework for Australian Schools*, with the policy now including boys within its remit.

As we have shown in Chapter 4 in some detail, the evidence on differential male/female performance in schooling is much more complex and nuanced than both the media and recuperative men's groups have suggested. One has to ask which boys and indeed which girls? Our reading is that some middle-class girls are doing the more 'masculinist subjects', for example physics, chemistry and maths, in greater numbers and doing well at them and thus challenging middle-class boys. There is also a way in which the discourse surrounding these data also naturalizes an assumption of good performance by boys and is surprised by good performance by girls. At the same time, working-class and minority boys are not doing well, particularly in literacy testing which most school systems have now put in place. Further, boys' results are more spread across the spectrum than is the case for girls, that is, some boys do very well, and some boys do very badly. Working-class girls appear to be doing better at literacy than their male counterparts, but we have known about this discrepancy for a long time. Further, we noted how a narrow reading of the feminist project for girls in schooling, which saw the major goal as getting more girls into those masculinist subjects, also played into backlash politics. The evidence also suggested that girls do a broader range of subjects than boys and participate in a broader range of extra-curricular activities. We also showed how boys were involved in anti-school behaviour in much greater numbers than girls; they also participated more in risk taking behaviours. We also noted the high suicide rates for adolescent boys, and also suggested that homophobia and questions of sexuality were significant factors in many of these suicides.

The new recuperative men's groups have read the data in a variety of ways, but have most often suggested that feminism has achieved its goals in schooling and it is now time for a focus on the boys. The uglier versions usually blame feminism (and indirectly, women) for all the problems that boys are now facing, including blaming female teachers and the feminization of pedagogy. In Chapter 5 we outlined the stances of pro-feminism and recuperative men's politics to the contemporary situation for boys in schooling and the related debates. We suggest that pro-feminists tend to emphasize the need to change and challenge hegemonic masculinities, as these restrict boys' schooling, and the schooling of other boys, of many girls, and the working lives of many teachers. Pro-feminists usually work within a social construction of gender framework. On the other hand, recuperative men's groups tend to emphasize the poor academic performance, as well as poor social outcomes, for boys, and in response seek to reassert particular forms of masculinity through schooling. They also call for more male teachers to assist the passage of boys to manhood. Pro-feminists see the need to challenge dominant constructions of masculinity as a way to improve the situation for both boys and girls in both academic and social terms, while the recuperative men's groups see the need to affirm the positives of masculinity. We reiterate our point made many times throughout this book that we need to be careful of essentializing both boys and girls in this debate. It is poor and marginalized boys who are not doing well academically at school and working-class girls are not doing too well either. And girls from all backgrounds are still often subject to harassment by boys of all backgrounds.

It should be clear from the argument presented throughout this book that our stance is pro-feminist. However, we have also pointed out the shortcomings, both theoretical (Chapter 1) and practical (Chapter 5) that pro-feminism, as currently expressed, exhibits. The two quotes at the beginning of this chapter as generally representative of pro-feminist standpoints are a good case in point. First, Kimmel's (1998) assertion that 'all men are privileged *vis-à-vis* women' needs some qualification, as we must recognize that, for instance, affluent white women in the west are not only better off financially than many men in the developing world, but also better off than some men in their own countries. It is for this reason that Chapters 2 and 5 argued that men's social privilege stems from the historical and cultural association of the construction of the powers and capacities of male bodies with the public sphere. This allows us to recognize both the hierarchies within masculinities, recognize some women's advantage over some men, but still understand how men retain privileges in relation to women in similar socioeconomic circumstances. We acknowledge that this may well be asserting far too much, given the continuing sense of solidarity among men and their presumptions of collective entitlement both in relation to the public sphere and to women. Second, Messner's (1997) argument that, 'in rejecting hegemonic masculinity and its rewards we also may become more fully human', recalls the criticisms of pro-feminist theory in Chapter 1 with respect to the limitations inherent in the reliance on a sex/gender distinction, particularly when confronted with the need to positively acknowledge difference. Just what does 'more fully human' mean and how can it be posited beyond some ahistorical essence that exists prior to not only the distinction between mind and body, but also the central pro-feminist commitment to the social construction of gender? Rather, we are dealing with a politics of possibility that will lead us into unchartered territory as we exhort men to reconstitute their masculinities in ways comparable to women's explorations in response to feminisms. All of this reinforces the need to tie a pro-feminist commitment to equality with poststructuralist, postcolonial and queer theories' analyses of difference in order to provide a theoretical framework from within which men can critically engage with the political necessity to seek social equality through a positive recognition of difference. Such an approach requires a politics of alliance with other groups (e.g. feminist, gay and lesbian, anti-racists, redistributive politics) seeking similar ends around specific issues rather than a global pro-feminist men's politics.

From such a perspective, we believe that there *is* a need to consider issues to do with boys in schooling and a need to focus on both the social construction of masculinities and their destabilization, as well as issues of boys' narrow subject choices, the poor academic performance of some groups of boys, and boys' participation in a narrow range of extra-curricular activities. Boys have been disadvantaged, even though they probably do not see it that way, by their very narrow subject choices and very little has been done in schools to alter this situation. Something needs to be done. We recognize, however, the inherent difficulties in such a project, given the differential valorization of various subjects within the school curriculum and their linkages to post-school success in the public sphere; and that boys' narrow subject choices have traditionally advantaged them in vocational terms. We would stress that the limited success for girls in school resulting from feminist projects has been largely within that framework, leaving largely unchallenged extant subject hierarchies, as just one instance of the social and historical association of the masculine with the public sphere. We also need to do something about homophobia in schools (see Epstein and Johnson 1998) and its manifestations in a high incidence of verbal and physical harassment of gay and lesbian students, often leading to their self-exclusion from schools and at the extreme to suicide. Taking all this into account, we believe that any focus on boys needs to be located within a broader gender equity framework informed by a commitment to social justice. We take this stance for a number of reasons. We reject the view that feminism has achieved its goals for girls through schooling. That is an absurd observation when placed against the evidence, including the amount of harassment experienced by girls. We also reject a zero-sum account of boys' and girls' issues in schooling and concomitant competing victims' accounts. We have always felt uneasy when discussions have turned to the horrendously high suicide rates among young males, when the response has been that girls attempt suicide in the same numbers but are not as successful. We see both sets of statistics as totally unacceptable with immediate action required to attempt to do something about this shocking situation. A commitment to social justice demands no less. Thus to reiterate we believe a focus on boys should be framed by both a gender equity policy informed by social justice, while acknowledging that social justice has no essentialist meaning and now has to be concerned with both equality and difference.

We need both strategic essentialism and strategic pluralism in our approaches. As argued in Chapter 5, some programmes need to focus on all boys, based on the acknowledgement of the historical and cultural connections between the construction of the powers and capacities of male bodies and the public sphere, while other approaches need to focus on specific groups of boys, particularly in relation to school performance and post-school options. We also need to encourage many variant practices of masculinity, indeed of gender more generally, what Connell (1995) calls 'gender multiculturalism'. Feminist goals for girls need to be continued and continually rethought as theory develops. The goal of gender equity policies and programmes in schools should be more equal gender relations in both the public and private spheres leading to their reconstitution – that is, the goal is that of a more equitable gender order. The education of boys thus needs to be broadened so that it prepares them better for full participation in work outside the home, in domestic work and within politics and culture. Currently, boys' education seems to be narrowly focused upon preparation for paid work, while the more extensive subject selections and broader extra-curricular participation of girls seem to be better suited to achieving this range of goals. Developing more equitable gender regimes in schools is just one step in the direction towards a more equal gender order and we would stress, therefore, that the goal of any focus on boys in schooling must be driven by the need to prepare boys for a future very different from that of their fathers.

This brings us to the place of teachers, both men and women, in such a politics. Chapter 3 demonstrated how structural backlash has regendered educational systems, ensuring a more masculinist 'hard core' in systemic policy making and a more feminized 'periphery' in schools – the retraditionalization of masculinities and femininities. In contrast, feminist projects and pro-feminism have been about detraditionalizing both masculinities and femininities. We support calls for more male teachers in schools, but not so as to reinforce dominant constructions of masculinity and extant gender regimes, that is, we think there ought to be more male teachers but we vehemently reject the common backlash justifications for such calls. Rather, we would hope that some of these men would work for the goals of gender justice we have outlined above, as some already do, and we strongly believe that men have a responsibility to work on these issues towards a reconstruction of masculinities and more equal gender relations. At the same time, we would stress that there is a very real need to continue the push to get more women – feminist women – into senior positions in schools and within educational systems. Those recuperative men who call for more male teachers are always deadly silent about the impact of structural backlash on opportunities for women. The worst elements of recuperative masculinist politics actually also want to dismantle equal employment opportunity and affirmative action programmes for women. A further reason for supporting more male teachers is that we believe men have a responsibility to work with boys to construct a more gender equitable future. Some evidence would suggest that female teachers are more likely to take up the issues we have been dealing with in this concluding chapter than males (Mills 1998a, b). This is particularly so when questions of masculinity are dealt with in human relations and pastoral care programmes. There is the danger here of women again being responsible for doing emotional work for boys and men, for developing 'nurturant pedagogies' for males, as Kenway (1995) has put it. However, the strategy of men working with boys should not be justified on the grounds that men will have more authority and influence over boys than women in the same situation. The work of Reay (1990) in England with primary school boys shows how women can work in positive and successful ways with boys on gender projects. Nor does the goal of empowerment, familiar from the focus on girls in schooling, have a place in men's work with boys. Rather, the goal should be one of fostering respect and empathy as important elements in reconstructed expressions of masculinities. In our view, this probably requires a more sympathetic consideration of the various forms of masculinity inherited by boys than most pro-feminists have usually conceded. Reiterating Tacey's (1997) point elaborated in Chapter 5, this heritage must be both acknowledged, and subjected to critical appraisal, in order to provide boys with the best possible grounding for the difficult, but necessary, project of reformulating masculinities for a society within which the roles of men and women will be less clearly demarcated. This is a project which must be undertaken by boys themselves and whose outcomes will no doubt surprise pro-feminists and masculinists alike.

We are aware that the political context is not conducive to the sorts of goals we are talking about, particularly given the prevalence of backlash and the rejection of notions of group disadvantage in both popular politics and within public policy. Some have even argued that equity is too expensive in these economic rationalist times where efficiency takes precedence. We would counter with the observation that in the long run inequity is even more expensive. At one level, for example, backlash politics is a response to growing social inequality. However, the issues we are concerned with here are not going to go away. Indeed, we find in our visits to schools and talking with teachers, administrators, policy makers and gender equity workers that the issues remain of central importance – questions to do with both boys and girls, but as we have noted throughout this book, now with much more concern over boys' underachievement. What is more, schools are creating policies and developing strategies around the media constructed panic about boys and fears that masculinity is under threat. In our view the sort of framework we have sketched here is much more likely to have success and work than approaches which operate within any sort of recuperative or backlash framework. And teachers tend to be practical and decent people: they want solutions that have some efficacy but within an equitable framework. It has been said, in Australia at least, that female teachers have been the heartland of feminism. We think it necessary that teaching also become the heartland of pro-feminism in relation to the issue of boys' schooling.

Schools are developing programmes for boys as the media-constructed accounts feed back into schools and often push school policies and practices ahead of systemic responses. In Chapter 3 we utilized the notion of policy as palimpsest to refer to the way centrally determined policies implemented in a top-down fashion are always rewritten and reread in schools, inadvertently giving female teachers some power over implementation of gender policies. Indeed, we would argue that such policy is continually being rewritten in the ongoing practices of schools. Kenway *et al.* (1997a) refer to this as the gap between hope and happening. While recognizing these problems of 'implementation', we would still stress the importance of systemic policies; indeed we believe a strong systemic commitment to social justice and to gender equity (covering both boys and girls) becomes even more important in restructured and devolved educational systems where schools apparently have more policy autonomy. A central problem with *Gender Equity: A Framework for Australian Schools* is that it is not particularly user friendly and anyway systems have weakened their commitment to this policy, given the changed political context. The research by Collins *et al.* (1996) demonstrates quite emphatically the significance of such central policies in relation to girls' schooling. It is in the state of South Australia that reform for girls' schooling has been engaged with in a serious fashion for a prolonged period. This has had a positive effect on the extent of the 'embeddedness' of changes for girls in schooling. The degree of embeddedness of girls' issues will be an important factor in the nature of schools' take-up of boys' issues – whether they are taken up in a pro-feminist or recuperative fashion. However, these top-down systemic policies are not the only policies operating in schools, for schools are closer to direct social pressures than are central offices and thus often do respond in policy terms well before systems have done so. With devolved systems this will become more and more the case. This is exactly what appears to be happening with the issue of boys and schooling.

Recently we came across a newspaper article outlining developments for boys in a high school in a Queensland provincial city, Maryborough. This school also has a web site on the school's initiatives for boys. As we shall show, that school's approach is a mixture of feminist, pro-feminist and recuperative discourses. We would stress that we do not deal with this school's approach because we want to be critical. Rather, we see what the school is attempting as a call for help and we believe many other schools and teachers are in a similar situation. Thus we use this example to try to pull together the arguments of this book concerning men's engagement with feminisms and we do so in the open-ended spirit that we talked about in Chapter 1. We see our contribution as part of a continuing conversation about the issues. We also use this example to demonstrate our view that the 'What about the boys?' discourse can be appropriated for progressive educational and political ends.

One school's policy and programmes for boys

The Maryborough State High School 'Boys in Education' programme provides a good example of how the debate around boys in schooling has become equated with the issue of 'boys' underachievement', and how the context in which this takes place assumes the success of the feminist agenda for girls in schools. A newspaper article reporting on the 'Boys in Education' programme, entitled 'Boys take back seat at school' (*Sunday Mail*, 7 June 1998: 32), opens with the claim that 'Girl power has triumphed in Queensland schools – and teachers are worried'. Teachers are apparently worried because 'Boys are being swamped by a new generation of assertive, high-achieving girls'. This sentiment is repeated in the Introduction to the web site set up by Maryborough State High School to describe the programme.

> Due to a concern that boys within the school environment were not achieving academically or socially to their full potential, a group of Parents and Teachers have attempted to address the problem. It would appear that the boys have been left behind in the race for gender balance. So successful has been the equity campaign that the boys have taken the soft option in terms of leadership and participation.

The similarity in the framing of the issue of boys in schooling by both the newspaper article and the school itself reflects the argument of Chapter 1 with respect to the 'bardic function' of simplistic media representations of the 'What about the boys?' debate, and demonstrates the extent to which it is widely accepted that the focus on girls in schooling has been not only successful, but also too successful inasmuch as boys have been left wallowing in the wake of 'girl power'. The overstatement of the success of girls expresses a deeper cultural fear of the loss of male hegemony, and reinforces the belief that gender equity is a zero-sum game, with girls' gains coming at the expense of boys. It also speaks to a concern that masculinity is under threat. Furthermore, the media representation in this specific case, but also in many other articles, almost 'reinscribes men as the centrepiece of the feminist project' (Kimmel 1998: 66) in so far as some men interpret feminism as nothing more than an attempt to 'get at' men. We believe that we need to determine what the gains for girls have actually been, and when we have that answer we ought to celebrate these successes, while also trying to understand what still needs to be done for girls in schools. We suspect that the gains are smaller than many representations of them would suggest and apply only to specific groups of girls. This is backlash in Faludi's (1991) terms, where small gains are read as being more substantial than they really are. This does not mean that we ought not be concerned with boys, but to recognize that the feminist project for girls has not achieved all of its goals which were always broader than simply getting more girls into masculinist subjects.

An examination of the performance data included in the Maryborough web site provides little support to the claim that boys' academic performance has suffered as a result of gender equity strategies. Rather it supports the arguments of Chapter 4 with respect to an ongoing gender segmentation of subject choice, a mild challenge to boys in physics, and a continuation of the traditional predominance of girls in the humanities. The newspaper article mentioned above also cites the preponderance of girls receiving subject awards – 80 per cent – even in subjects such as manual arts and marine studies. However, without a consideration of the overall performance of boys and girls in relation to their respective participation rates, this statistic does nothing more than alert us to the fact that some girls have taken up 'non-traditional' options and excelled in the process. As noted earlier in this chapter, we think there is a cause for concern in the fact that boys have not moved into non-traditional domains in the same ways as girls. There needs to be some focus on this in schools. This does not appear to be a concern in the Maryborough 'Boys in Education' strategy.

Even though the framing of the Maryborough 'Boys in Education' programme falls very much in line with typical recuperative masculinist claims in relation to boys in schooling, and is therefore subject to the qualifications and critiques presented throughout this book, the available details of the programme demonstrate a mixture of discourses, with feminist and pro-feminist concerns also taken into account. For instance, the aims of the programme belie the zero-sum sentiment of the Introduction in stating the need to: 'Address disadvantages that face boys whilst continuing to work on barriers that face girls'; 'Assist boys in challenging aggressive behaviour to eliminate sex based harassment, violence, bullying and victimization'; and produce strategies to give 'boys the message that it's ok to be careful, to show emotions, and discuss masculinity issues'. However, the conversion of these aims into approaches made familiar by the focus on girls in schooling and uncritically translated into boys' programmes fails to account for the very different social positionings of girls and boys. This can be seen in the choice of strategies such as assertiveness and conflict resolution programmes, school mentoring systems to promote boys' involvement in school leadership positions (interestingly with the rider of 'using appropriate male teachers'), and the use of 'outside' speakers to encourage non-traditional career options. When these are combined with typical recuperative masculinists' concern with styles of pedagogy 'adapted to suit the learning styles of boys', it is difficult to see just how the feminist and pro-feminist concerns mentioned above are to be addressed. There is also a concern for critical literacy approaches for boys; this is a concern of progressive theorists in contemporary debates about literacy, but in those debates a critical literacy approach is deemed to be appropriate for both boys and girls. And to be fair to the school this might be their approach as well. So despite the recognition of the need to both continue to address gender equity issues in relation to girls and confront the problems associated with boys' overly aggressive and abusive behaviours, it seems that the overall framing of the programme as a separate boys' strategy does not allow for an appropriate response to these concerns. This conclusion is further reinforced by the observation by the deputy principal in the newspaper article that the boys' strategy also seeks 'to promote the positive aspects of being male'. This demonstrates a recuperative masculinist reading of the situation without the necessary pro-feminist rider that boys' 'masculine heritage' must also be subject to critique and reconstitution. Again we can see how a gender equity framework provides a more balanced and complete response to the issue of boys in schooling.

It is interesting, then, to note that the (female) deputy principal of the school is quoted in the above mentioned article as saying that, 'Some feminists may see the new focus on boys as a nightmare, but I believe we need to change the lives of boys to make the lives of girls better'. The nightmare for feminists and pro-feminists alike is not so much in the focus on boys *per se*, for both have argued consistently that boys and men must change if the goal of equitable social relations between the sexes is to become a reality. Rather, the nightmare is spawned by an *exclusive* focus on boys outside of a broader gender equity framework that is *inclusive* of both boys and girls. When an exclusive focus on boys is combined with the influence of recuperative masculinist analyses of 'boys' disadvantage', specifically its inability to theorize social power and its assumption that the feminist project has already succeeded, there is little scope for a genuine consideration of either an ongoing commitment to girls in schooling, or a pro-feminist approach to the needs of boys.

One might argue that the shortcomings of the Maryborough 'Boys in Education' programme may well stem from a combination of factors: the ubiquity of the recuperative masculinist reading of the 'What about the boys?' debate in the media and its concomitant 'bardic function'; familiarity with strategies used in the focus on girls in schooling; the low profile of pro-feminist boys' programmes; and the difficulty of confronting the 'naturalized' associations between masculinity and social privilege and hegemony. However, this programme has been initiated and developed within a policy environment, at both state and federal levels, that has accepted the arguments in favour of a gender equity framework. As we have noted at various points in this book, the conversion of the *National Policy for the Education of Girls in Australian Schools* into *Gender Equity: A Framework for Australian Schools* was the result of a policy tussle between feminists and pro-feminists on the one side and those calling for a specific boys' policy on the other. The resulting policy settlement, while perhaps not the desired outcome by either side, located both girls' and boys' issues within a gender equity framework. Why then has the policy-level commitment to addressing the needs of boys within such a framework been ignored at the school level? We cannot simply blame disaffected and/or ill-informed male staff at the school as the programme has been promoted by a female deputy principal, who we assume would be familiar with the appropriate policy documents. We can only surmise that the influence of the broader school community in a politically conservative area has played some role, and that the dismantling of state gender equity networks due to reduced funding (typical of 'structural backlash') has meant that schools are left to find their own way with these issues. Further, school-based management within a framework of devolution has also sponsored a view that schools are autonomous agents with the right to develop their own policy frameworks and the media has done a good job in telling schools and their communities that they should be concerned about boys. In that context, and in our view, schooling systems still need to take responsibility for feminist goals for girls' schooling and pro-feminist goals for boys, both framed within a gender equity policy.

Conclusion: men and pro-feminism

While Maryborough High School's 'Boys in Education' programme demonstrates quite neatly the shortcomings of separate boys' policies, and hence the importance of addressing boys' needs in schooling within a gender equity framework, it also highlighted the difficulties involved in instituting such a response to the 'What about the boys?' question in the current political climate. At the very same time as there is a backlash against the notion of group disadvantage, recuperative masculinists are seeking to constitute men and boys as a new disadvantaged group, while operating from a position of presumptive equality in respect of the broader power relations between the genders. The media regularly echoes this stance. We understand the difficulty in getting some men, some male teachers and some boys to recognize the advantages accrued to males over females within the current political climate. Not all men do feel powerful and some clearly are not. This need to work with the contradictory situation of male advantage and power and many males' feelings of powerlessness is a central conundrum of moving towards pro-feminist programmes for boys in schools. However, we would agree with Kimmel (1998) concerning the *potential* of a pro-feminist position to work effectively with this contradiction. As he puts it:

Pro-feminism, a position that acknowledges men's experience without privileging it, possesses the tools to bring those levels together, to both adequately analyse men's aggregate power, and also describe the ways in which individual men are both privileged by that social level of power and feel powerless in the face of it.

(Kimmel 1998: 64)

Pro-feminism recognizes differences among men and masculinities, while also acknowledging the ways in which social class, race, ethnicity, sexuality and so on intersect with masculinity and complicate the picture further. Kimmel argues there is another important element in some men's feelings of powerlessness and that relates to the notion of entitlement, men's feeling of their right to preferment and power within the public sphere which is clearly challenged by feminism (1998: 65). (Much of the debate about boys' performance in schools reads as a response to the challenge from some females to such entitlement and much the same could be said about women's movement into the workplace.) However, we need to reiterate the difficulty that a pro-feminist politics has had in coming to terms with men's pain and agree with the arguments of Seidler (1997), Tacey (1997) and Flood (1997a) that a critical approach to masculinity needs to be combined with a recognition of the underlying stubborn, yet not immutable, bodily and emotional attachments of men to their masculine heritage in order to facilitate its reconstitution. There is the added dimension here of the negative impact of globalization on many men's lives and this no doubt adds to their sense of powerlessness.

Pro-feminist work by men often carries with it certain suspicions from both feminist women and from other men. We would argue, though, that some feminists are now prepared to accept the genuineness of the stance of some pro-feminist men. In Chapter 2 we quoted Gloria Steinem to the effect that women did want a men's movement, but a men's movement of a particular kind – pro-feminist rather than recuperative in orientation. The edited collection by Digby (1998), entitled *Men Doing Feminism*, contains a number of essays by feminists supporting male pro-feminism. In the foreword, for example, Bartky (1998: xii) suggests that, given 'the antiquity, power, depth, and breadth of patriarchy' women alone cannot overthrow it. She makes an analogy between pro-feminist men and antiracist whites, while also adumbrating all the difficulties and conundrums that such stances raise. Kimmel (1998) in that collection points out how, when he gives public lectures in universities in the USA on the need for pro-feminism, he is usually challenged by both feminists and what he calls 'angry-white-men-in-training' (1998: 59). This male challenge usually works through attempts to cast doubts on his masculinity and sexuality, the inference being that he loses his credibility as a man if he is gay. Kimmel's experience has also been reflected in the experience of the authors and of Mills (1998a) in his research. It seems that the problematization of masculinities in discussions with men and boys is often sidelined as being a gay issue, rather than one to be considered by 'real' men or 'real' boys. Much of this we believe turns on naive and 'common sense' notions of the relationship between masculinity and sexuality, notions which need to be deconstructed by pro-feminist work and work against homophobia more generally. And again we would emphasize the most effective way for pro-feminists to address such issues is through a politics of alliance, given that any mass men's movement is more likely to be recuperative rather than progressive in character. The focus needs to be on the dismantling of men's solidarity, rather than its reconstitution.

Just as there has been a struggle for feminists working in schools, it will not be easy for pro-feminists working with boys. In the current climate when there is so much attention being focused on boys, it is very important for men to approach this work in schools within a gender equity framework, as this also demands a continuing focus on girls. It has been our argument throughout this book that men committed to social justice have a responsibility to work with boys in a pro-feminist way and we have attempted to outline what this might mean. We would also argue that the sort of pro-feminist project outlined throughout the book would be of benefit to both boys and girls, both men and women. Schooling should be about the interests of both towards a more gender equal future.

Note

1 We realize that there has been some engagement by male theorists with feminist ideas for a much longer period. However, in this book we are dealing basically with the recent past and the present. Kimmel and Mosmiller (1992), for example, have traced a pro-feminist politics in the USA from 1776 to 1990 in their book, *Against the Tide: Profeminist Men in the United States, 1776–1990. A Documentary History.* Martin Mills brought this point to our attention.

Bibliography

Acker, S. (1995) Gender and teachers' work, in M. W. Apple (ed.) *Review of Research in Education* 21, 1995–6. Washington, DC: American Educational Research Association.

Adair, M. (1992) Will the real men's movement please stand up?, in K. Leigh Hagan (ed.) *Women Respond to the Men's Movement: A Feminist Collection*. San Francisco, CA: Pandora.

Ainley, J., Graetz, B., Long, M. and Batten, M. (1997) *Socioeconomic Status and School Education*. Canberra: Australian Government Publishing Service.

Allen, J. R. and Bell, E. J. (1996) *Changing Populations and Changing Results: Gender Differences in Senior Studies 1987–95*. Brisbane: Board of Senior Secondary School Studies, Queensland.

Alloway, N. (1995) Playing at gender? Young children struggling to get it right, in Ministerial Advisory Committee on Gender Equity in Education (MACGEE), *Proceedings of the Challenging Perspectives, Building Partnerships Conference*. Brisbane: Queensland Department of Education.

Alloway, N. and Gilbert, P. (1997) Boys and literacy: lessons from Australia. *Gender and Education* 9(1): 49–59.

Appadurai, A. (1996) *Modernity at Large: Cultural Dimensions of Globalization*. Minneapolis, MN: University of Minnesota Press.

Apple, M. W. (1986) *Teachers and Text*. New York: Routledge.

Austin, D., Clark, V. and Fitchett, G. (1971) *Reading Rights for Boys: Sex Role in Language Experience*. New York: Appleton-Century-Crofts.

Australian Education Council (1991) *Listening to Girls*. A report of the consultancy undertaken for the review of the national policy for the education of girls in Australian schools. Carlton: Curriculum Corporation.

Australian Education Council (1992) National Action Plan for the education of girls 1993–97. Carlton: Curriculum Corporation.

Baca Zinn, M. and Dill, B. T. (1996) Theorizing differences from multiracial feminism. *Feminist Studies* 22: 321–31.

Ball, S. J. (1990) *Politics and Policy Making in Education: Explorations in Policy Sociology*. London: Routledge.

Ball, S. J. (1994) *Education Reform: A Critical and Post-structural Approach*. Buckingham: Open University Press.

Barber, L. (1998) The bare essentials. *Weekend Australian Review*, March 14–15, p. 23.

Barker, P. (1991) *Regeneration*. Harmondsworth: Penguin.

Barker, P. (1993) *The Eye in the Door*. New York: Plume.

Barker, P. (1995) *The Ghost Road*. London: Viking.

Bartky, S. (1998) Foreword, in T. Digby (ed.) *Men Doing Feminism*. London: Routledge.

Bauman, Z. (1997) *Postmodernity and its Discontents*. Cambridge: Polity Press.

Baumli, F. (ed.) (1985) *Men Freeing Men: Exploding the Myth of the Traditional Male*. Jersey City, NJ: New Atlantis.

Bhabha, H. (1994) *The Location of Culture*. London: Routledge.

Biddulph, S. (1995) Foreword, in R. Browne and R. Fletcher (eds) *Boys in Schools: Addressing the Real Issues – Behaviour, Values and Relationships*. Sydney: Finch.

Biddulph, S. (1994) *Manhood: A Book about Setting Men Free*. Sydney: Finch.

Biddulph, S. (1997) *Raising Boys*. Sydney: Finch.

Biddulph, S. (1998) The Cotswold Experiment, Certified Male homepage, http://www.pnc.com.au/~pvogel/cm/.

Bittman, M. and Pixley, J. (1997) *The Double Life of the Family: Myth, Hope and Experience*. Sydney: Allen & Unwin.

Blackmore, J. (1993) Towards a 'post masculinist' institutional politics, in D. Baker and M. Fogarty (eds) *A Gendered Culture: Educational Management in the Nineties*. St. Albans, Vic.: Victoria University of Technology.

Blackmore, J. (1996) Doing 'emotional labour' in the education market place: stories from the field of women in management. *Discourse* 17(3): 337–49.

Blackmore, J. (1997a) Disciplining feminism: a look at gender-equity struggles in Australian higher education, in L. Roman and L. Eyre (eds) *Dangerous Territories: Struggles for Difference and Equality*. New York: Routledge.

Blackmore, J. (1997b) Gender restructuring and the emotional economy of higher education. Conference paper, Annual Conference of the Australian Association for Research in Education, Brisbane, 1–4 December.

Blackmore, J. (1997c) Institutional schizophrenia: self governance, performativity and the self managing school. Conference paper, Annual Conference of the Australian Association for Research in Education, Brisbane, 1–4 December.

Blackmore, J. (1997d) Worried, weary, overworked or just plain worn out? Gender, restructuring and the emotional economy of higher education. Paper presented to Gender Equity Forum, University of Queensland, 9 September.

Blackmore, J. (1999) Localisation/globalisation and the midwife state: strategic dilemmas for state feminism and education? *Journal of Education Policy* 14(1).

Blackmore, J. with Kenway, J., Willis, S. and Rennie, L. (1996) Putting up with the put down? Girls, boys, power and sexual harassment, in L. Laskey and C. Beavis (eds) *Schooling and Sexualities Teaching for a Positive Sexuality*. Geelong, Vic.: Deakin University Press.

Blankenhorn, D. (1996) *Fatherless America: Confronting Our Most Urgent Social Problem*. New York: HarperCollins.

Bly, R. (1988) *When a Hair Turns Gold: Commentary on the Fairy Tale of Iron John, Part Two*. St Paul, MN: Ally Press.

Bly, R. (1991) *Iron John: A Book about Men*. Shaftesbury: Element.

Board of Studies (1996) *The Report of the Gender Project Steering Committee*. Sydney: New South Wales Board of Studies.

Bordo, S. (1997) *Twilight Zones: The Hidden Life of Cultural Images from Plato to O.J.* Berkeley, CA: University of California Press.

Bourdieu, P. (1984) *Distinction: A Social Critique of the Judgement of Taste.* London: Routledge & Kegan Paul.

Boyle, T. Coraghessan (1995) *The Tortilla Curtain.* New York: Penguin.

Brod, H. (1998) To be a man, or not to be a man – that is the feminist question, in T. Digby (ed.) *Men Doing Feminism.* London: Routledge.

Brooks, A. (1997) *Postfeminisms: Feminism, Cultural Theory and Cultural Forms.* London: Routledge.

Browne, R. and Fletcher, R. (eds) (1995) *Boys in Schools: Addressing the Real Issues – Behaviour, Values and Relationships.* Sydney: Finch.

Butler, J. (1990) *Gender Trouble: Feminism and the Subversion of Identity.* New York: Routledge.

Carrigan, T., Connell, R. and Lee, J. (1985) Towards a new sociology of masculinity. *Theory and Society* 5(14): 551–602.

Cerny, P. (1990) *The Changing Architecture of Politics: Structure, Agency and the Future of the State.* London: Sage.

Cheng, C. (ed.) (1996) *Masculinities in Organizations.* London: Sage.

Christian, H. (1994) *The Making of Anti-Sexist Men.* London: Routledge.

Clarke, J. and Newman, J. (1997) *The Managerial State.* London: Sage.

Clarke, J., Cochrane, A. and McLaughlin, E. (eds) (1994a) *Managing Social Policy.* London: Sage.

Clarke, J., Cochrane, A. and McLaughlin, E. (1994b) Mission accomplished or unfinished business? The impact of managerialization, in J. Clarke, A. Cochrane and E. McLaughlin (eds) *Managing Social Policy.* London: Sage.

Clatterbaugh, K. (1997) *Contemporary Perspectives on Masculinity: Men, Women, and Politics in Modern Society.* Boulder, CO: Westview Press.

Cockburn, C. (1991) *In the Way of Women.* New York: ILR Press.

Cole, E. L. (1982) *Maximized Manhood: A Guide to Family Survival.* Springdale, PA: Whitaker House.

Collins, C., Batten, M., Ainley, J. and Getty, C. (1996) *Gender and School Education: A Project Funded by the Commonwealth Department of Employment, Education, Training and Youth Affairs.* Canberra: Australian Government Publishing Service.

Connell, R. W. (1987) *Gender and Power: Society, the Person and Sexual Politics.* Sydney: Allen & Unwin.

Connell, R. W. (1990) The state, gender and sexual politics. *Theory and Society* 19: 507–44.

Connell, R. W. (1993) Men and the women's movement. *Social Policy* summer: 72–8.

Connell, R. W. (1995) *Masculinities.* Sydney: Allen & Unwin.

Connell, R. W. (1996) Teaching the boys: new research on masculinity, and gender strategies for schools. *Teachers College Record* 98(2): 206–35.

Considine, M. (1988) The corporate management framework as administrative science: a critique. *Australian Journal of Public Administration* 47(1): 4–19.

Coser, L. A. (1974) *The Greedy Institution: Patterns of Undivided Commitment.* New York: Free Press.

Court, M. (1995) Good girls and naughty girls: rewriting the scripts for women's anger, in B. Limerick and B. Lingard (eds) *Gender and Changing Educational Management*. Sydney: Hodder.

Cox, E. (1996) *Leading Women*. Sydney: Random House Australia.

Crook, S., Pakulski, J. and Waters, M. (1992) *Postmodernization*. London: Sage.

Czarniawska, B. (1997) *Narrating the Organisation: Dramas of Institutional Identity*. Chicago: University of Chicago Press.

Dale, R. (1989) *The State and Education Policy*. Milton Keynes: Oxford University Press.

Daly, M. (1978) *Gyn/Ecology: The Metaethics of Radical Feminism*. Boston, MA: Beacon Press.

Daniels, H., Hey, V., Leonard, D. and Smith, M. (1995) Gendered practice in special educational needs, in L. Dawtrey, J. Holland, M. Hammer and S. Sheldon (eds) *Equality and Inequality in Education Policy*. Clevedon, PA: Multilingual Matters.

Dansky, S., Knoebel, J. and Pitchford, K. (1977) The effeminist manifesto, in J. Snodgrass (ed.) *A Book of Readings for Men Against Sexism*. Albion, CA: Times Change Press.

David, M., West, A. and Riddens, J. (1994) *Mothers' Intuition? Choosing Secondary Schools*. London: Falmer.

Davis, M. (1997) *Gangland: Cultural Elites and the New Generationalism*. Sydney: Allen & Unwin.

Daws, L. (1995) Challenging perspectives, building partnerships. Keynote address, Third Conference of MACGEE, Girls and Boys: Challenging Perspectives, Building Partnerships, Brisbane Girls' Grammar School, April.

de Beauvoir, S. (1952) *The Second Sex*. New York: Bantam.

Denborough, D. (1996) Step by step: developing respectful and effective ways of working with young men to reduce violence, in C. McLean, M. Carey and C. White (eds) *Men's Ways of Being*, Boulder, CO: Westview Press.

Department of Employment, Education and Training (DEET) (1995) *No Fear: A Kit Addressing Gender Based Violence*. Canberra: Curriculum and Gender Equity Policy Unit, DEET.

Digby, T. (ed.) (1998) *Men Doing Feminism*. London: Routledge.

Douglas, P. (1994) 'New men' and the tensions of profeminism. *Social Alternatives* 12(4): 32–5.

Douglas, P. (1996) The body and social theory in Connell's *Masculinities*. *Discourse* 17(1): 107–14.

Drabble, M. (1996) *The Witch of Exmoor*. London: Viking.

Dwyer, P. (1996) Outside the educational mainstream: foreclosed options in youth policy. *Discourse* 18(1): 71–85.

Economist (1996) Tomorrow's second sex, *The Economist*, 28 September: 23.

Eisenstein, H. (1991) *Gender Shock: Practising Feminism on Two Continents*. Sydney: Allen & Unwin.

Eisenstein, H. (1996) *Inside Agitators: Australian Femocrats and the State*. Sydney: Allen & Unwin.

Elias, N. (1978 [1939]) *The History of Manners: The Civilizing Process,* vol. 1. New York: Pantheon.

Elias, N. (1982 [1939]) *State Formation and Civilization: The Civilizing Process,* vol. 1. Oxford: Blackwell.

Elwood, J. (1995a) Gender, equity and the gold standard: examination and coursework performance in the UK at 18. Conference paper, American Educational Research Association Conference, San Francisco, CA, April.

Elwood, J. (1995b) Undermining gender stereotypes: examination and coursework performance in the UK at 16. *Assessment in Education* 2(3): 283–303.

Epstein, D. and Johnson, R. (1994) On the straight and narrow: the heterosexual presumption, homophobias and schools, in D. Epstein (ed.) *Challenging Lesbian and Gay Inequalities in Education*. Buckingham: Open University Press.

Epstein, D. and Johnson, R. (1998) *Schooling Sexualities*. Buckingham: Open University Press.

Faludi, S. (1991) *Backlash: The Undeclared War Against Women*. London: Vintage.

Farrar, S. (1990) *Point Man: How a Man Can Lead a Family*. Portland, OR: Multnomah.

Farrell, W. (1975) *The Liberated Man: Beyond Masculinity*. New York: Bantam.

Farrell, W. (1986) *Why Men Are the Way They Are: The Male–Female Dynamic*. New York: McGraw-Hill.

Farrell, W. (1993) *The Myth of Male Power: Why Men Are the Disposable Sex*. New York: Simon & Schuster.

Fine, M., Weis, L. and Addelston, J. (1998) On shaky grounds: constructing white working class masculinities in the late twentieth century, in D. Carlson and M. W. Apple (eds) *Power/Knowledge/Pedagogy: The Meaning of Democratic Education in Unsettling Times*. Boulder, CO: Westview Press.

Fine, M., Weis, L., Addelston, J. and Marusza, J. (1997) (In)secure times: constructing white working class masculinities in the late 20th century. *Gender and Society* 11(1): 52–68.

Fineman, S. (1993) Organisations as emotional arenas, in S. Fineman (ed.) *Emotion in Organisations*. London: Sage.

Fletcher, R. (1995) Changing the lives of boys, in R. Browne and R. Fletcher (eds) *Boys in Schools: Addressing the Real Issues – Behaviour, Values and Relationships*. Sydney: Finch.

Flood, M. (1997a) Frequently asked questions about pro-feminist men and pro-feminist men's politics, unpublished paper. Australian National University.

Flood, M. (1997b) Responding to men's rights. *XY: Men, Sex, Politics* 7(2): 37–9.

Flood, M. (1997c) Pro-feminist publishing: delights and dilemmas. *Social Alternatives* 16(3): 14–17.

Foley, D. (1990) *Learning Capitalist Culture: Deep in the Heart of Texas*. Philadelphia, PA: University of Pennsylvania Press.

Foster, V. (1994) 'What about the boys!' Presumptive equality, and the obfuscation of concerns about theory, research, policy, resources and curriculum in the education of girls and boys. Conference paper, Australian Association for Research in Education Conference, Newcastle University, NSW, November.

Foster, V. (1996) Space invaders: desire and threat in the schooling of girls. *Discourse* 17(1): 43–63.

Foucault, M. (1974) *The Archaeology of Knowledge*. London: Tavistock.

Frank, L. (1996) A white boy is being beaten, in P. Smith (ed.) *Boys' Masculinities in Contemporary Culture*. Boulder, CO: Westview Press.

Franzway, S. (1986) With problems of their own: femocrats and the welfare state. *Australian Feminist Studies* 3: 45–57.

Fraser, N. (1995) From redistribution to recognition? Dilemmas of justice in a post-socialist age. *New Left Review* July–August (212): 68–93.

Freebody, P., Ludwig, C., Gunn, S. *et al.* (1995) *Everyday Literacy Practices In and Out of Schools in Low Socio-economic Urban Communities.* Nathan, Qld: Faculty of Education, Griffith University.

French, M. (1992) *The War Against Women.* London: Hamish Hamilton.

Fuss, D. (1989) *Essentially Speaking.* New York: Routledge.

Gallop, J. (1982) *The Daughter's Seduction: Feminism and Psychoanalysis.* Ithaca, NY: Cornell University Press.

Gard, M. (1998) Concepts of masculinity: dancing as a career option for rural and regional Australian males. Conference paper, American Educational Research Association Conference, San Diego, CA, 13–17 April.

Gardiner, G. (1997) Aboriginal boys' business: a study of indigenous youth in Victoria in relation to educational participation and contact with the juvenile justice system. *Journal of Intercultural Studies* 18(1): 49–61.

Garner, H. (1995) *The First Stone.* New York: Free Press.

Gatens, M. (1996) *Imaginary Bodies: Ethics, Power and Corporeality.* London: Routledge.

Gender Equity Taskforce (1997) *Gender Equity. A Framework for Australian Schools.* Canberra: Ministerial Council for Employment, Education, Training and Youth Affairs.

Gewirtz, S., Ball, S. and Bowe, R. (1995) *Markets, Choice and Equity in Education.* Buckingham: Open University Press.

Giddens, A. (1990) *The Consequences of Modernity.* Stanford, CA: Stanford University Press.

Giddens, A. (1991) *Modernity and Self-Identity: Self and Society in the Late Modern Age.* Cambridge: Polity Press.

Giddens, A. (1992) *The Transformation of Intimacy: Sexuality, Love and Eroticism in Modern Societies.* Cambridge: Polity Press.

Giddens, A. (1994) *Beyond Left and Right: The Future of Radical Politics.* Stanford, CA: Stanford University Press.

Gilbert, P. (1994) *Divided by a Common Language? Gender and the English Curriculum.* Melbourne: Curriculum Corporation.

Gilbert, R. and Gilbert, P. (1998) *Masculinity Goes to School.* Sydney: Allen & Unwin.

Gilder, G. (1973) *Sexual Suicide.* New York: Bantam.

Gilder, G. (1986) The sexual revolution at home. *National Review,* 10 October: 30–4.

Gillborn, D. (1997) Young, black and failed by school: the market, education reform and black students. *International Journal of Inclusive Education* 1(1): 65–87.

Goldberg, H. (1976) *The Hazards of Being Male: Surviving the Myth of Masculine Privilege.* New York: Signet.

Goldberg, H. (1979) *The New Male.* New York: Signet.

Goldberg, S. (1974) *The Inevitability of Patriarchy.* New York: William Morrow.

Grace, G. (1995) *School Leadership: Beyond Education Management: An Essay in Policy Scholarship.* London: Falmer.

Grant, J. and Tancred, P. (1992) A feminist perspective on state bureaucracy, in A. J. Mills and P. Tancred (eds) *Gendering Organizational Analysis.* London: Sage.

Greer, G. (1991 [1970]) *The Female Eunuch*. London: Paladin.

Gruneau, R. and Whitson, D. (1993) *Hockey Night in Canada: Sport Identities and Cultural Politics*. Toronto: Garamond.

Gutterman, D. S. (1994) Postmodernism and the interrogation of masculinity, in H. Brod and M. Kaufman (eds) *Theorizing Masculinities*. Thousand Oaks, CA: Sage.

Hagan, K. L. (ed.) (1992) *Women Respond to the Men's Movement: A Feminist Collection*. San Francisco, CA: Pandora.

Hall, S. (1996) New ethnicities, in D. Morley and K. Chen (eds) *Stuart Hall: Critical Dialogues in Cultural Studies*. London: Routledge.

Harding, S. (ed.) (1994) *The 'Racial' Economy of Science*. Bloomington: Indiana University Press.

Harding, S. (1998) *Is Science Multicultural? Postcolonialisms, Feminisms and Epistemologies*. Bloomington: Indiana University Press.

Hearn, J. and Collinson, D. L. (1994) Theorizing unities and differences between men and between masculinities, in H. Brod and M. Kaufman (eds) *Theorizing Masculinities*. Thousand Oaks, CA: Sage.

Hearn, J., Sheppard, P., Tancred-Sheriff, P. and Burrell, G. (eds) (1989) *The Sexuality of Organisation*. London: Sage.

Heath, S. (1987) Male feminism, in A. Jardine and P. Smith (eds) *Men in Feminism*. New York: Routledge.

Heath, S. (1999) Watching the backlash: the problematisation of young women's academic success in 1990s Britain. *Discourse* 20(2).

Henry, M. and Taylor, S. (1993) Gender equity and economic rationalism: an uneasy alliance, in B. Lingard, J. Knight and P. Porter (eds) *Schooling Reform in Hard Times*. London: Falmer Press.

Henry, M., Lingard, B., Rizvi, F. and Taylor, S. (1999) Working with/against globalisation in education. *Journal of Education Policy* 14(1).

Hillman, J. (1990) The great mother, her son, her hero and the power, in P. Berry (ed.) *Fathers and Mothers*, 2nd ed., Dallas: Spring Publications.

Hochschild, A. R. (1983) *The Managed Heart: Commercialization of Human Feeling*. Berkeley, CA: University of California Press.

Hocking, C. (1983) *Men Facing Difficult Times: Report of an Inservice on 'Developing Interrelating Skills in Adolescent Boys'*. Melbourne: Equal Opportunity Unit, Department of Education, Victoria.

Hood, C. (1991) A public management for all seasons. *Public Administration* 69: 3–19.

Hood, C. (1995) Contemporary public management: a new global paradigm. *Public Policy and Administration* 10(2): 104–17.

hooks, b. (1984) *Feminist Theory: From Margins to Centre*. Boston, MA: South End Press.

hooks, b. (1992) Men in feminist struggle: the necessary movement, in K. L. Hagan (ed.) *Women Respond to the Men's Movement: A Feminist Collection*. San Francisco, CA: Pandora.

Houtz, J. (1995) In her face! *Seattle Times*, 10 January.

Hughes, R. (1993) *The Culture of Complaint: The Fraying of America*. Oxford: Oxford University Press.

Industry Task Force on Leadership and Management Skills (1995) *Enterprising*

Nation: Renewing Australia's Managers to Meet the Challenges of the Asia-Pacific Century (Karpin Report). Canberra: Australian Government Publishing Service.

Inner London Education Authority conference (n.d.) Equal Opportunities – What's in it for the Boys? Caister: Whylde.

Kaufman, M. (1994) Men, feminism, and men's contradictory experience of power, in H. Brod and M. Kaufmann (eds) *Theorizing Masculinities*. Newbury Park, CA: Sage.

Keen, S. (1991) *Fire in the Belly: On Being a Man*. New York: Bantam.

Kenway, J. (1987) Left right out, Australian education and the politics of signification. *Journal of Educational Policy* 2(3): 189–203.

Kenway, J. (1990) *Gender and Education Policy: A Call for New Directions*. Geelong, Vic.: Deakin University Press.

Kenway, J. (1994) Submission to Inquiry into Boys' Education 1994 (O'Doherty Report). On behalf of Women in Education, New South Wales.

Kenway, J. (1995) Masculinities: under siege, on the defensive and under reconstruction? *Discourse* 16(1): 59–81.

Kenway, J. (1996) Reasserting masculinity in Australian schools. *Women's Studies International Forum* 19(4): 447–66.

Kenway, J., Willis, S., Blackmore, J. and Rennie, L. (1997a) *Answering Back: Girls, Boys, and Feminism in Schools*. Sydney: Allen & Unwin.

Kenway, J., Willis, S., Blackmore, J. and Rennie, L. (1997b) Are boys victims of feminism in schools? Some answers from Australia. *International Journal of Inclusive Education* 1(1): 19–35.

Kerfoot, D. and Knights, D. (1993) Management, masculinity and manipulation: from paternalism to corporate strategy in financial services in Britain. *Journal of Management Studies* 30(4): 659–77.

Kickert, W. (1991) Steering at a distance: a new paradigm of public governance in Dutch higher education. Conference paper, European Consortium for Political Research Conference, University of Essex, March.

Kimmel, M. (ed.) (1995) *The Politics of Manhood: Profeminist Men Respond to the Mythopoetic Men's Movement (And the Mythopoetic Leaders Answer)*. Philadelphia, PA: Temple University Press.

Kimmel, M. (1996a) *Manhood in America: A Cultural History*. New York: Free Press.

Kimmel, M. (1996b) Try supporting feminism!, in T. Lloyd and T. Wood (eds) *What Next for Men?* London: Working with Men.

Kimmel, M. (1998) Who's afraid of men doing feminism?, in T. Digby (ed.) *Men Doing Feminism*. London: Routledge.

Kimmel, M. and Kaufman, M. (1995) Weekend warriors: the new men's movement, in M. Kimmel (ed.) *The Politics of Manhood: Profeminist Men Respond to the Mythopoetic Men's Movement (And the Mythopoetic Leaders Answer)*. Philadelphia, PA: Temple University Press.

Kimmel, M. and Mosmiller, T. (1992) *Against the Tide: Profeminist Men in the United States, 1776–1990. A Documentary History*. Boston, MA: Beacon.

Kindler, H. (1993) *Maske(r)ade: Jungen – und Mannerarbeit für die Praxis*. Schwabisch Gmund und Tubingen: Neuling Verlag.

Kirk, D. and Wright, J. (1995) Health issues and the construction of gender. *Proceedings of the Promoting Gender Equity Conference*. Gender Equity Taskforce of the Ministerial Council for Education, Employment, Training and Youth Affairs (MCEETYA), 22–4 February, Canberra, ACT Department of Education.

Kivel, P. (1992) *Men's Work: How to Stop the Violence that Tears Our Lives Apart.* Center City, MN: Hazeldon.

Kivel, P. (1996) *Making the Peace.* Alameda, CA: Hunter House and Oakland Men's Project.

Knight, J. and Lingard, B. (1997) Ministerialisation and politicisation: changing structures and practices of educational policy production, in B. Lingard and P. Porter (eds) *A National Approach to Schooling in Australia? Essays on the Development of National Policies in Schools Education.* Canberra: Australian College of Education.

Kruse, A. (1996) Approaches to teaching girls and boys: current debates, practices and perspectives in Denmark. *Women's Studies International Forum* 19(4): 429–45.

Letts, W. (1997) Five male secondary science teachers: dis/playing gender. Paper presented to the Australian Association for Research in Education Annual Conference, Brisbane, 30 November–4 December.

Letts, W. (1998) Boys will be boys (if they pay attention in science class). Paper presented to the American Educational Research Association Conference, San Diego, April.

Limerick, B. (1991) *Career Opportunities for Teachers in the Queensland Department of Education with Special Reference to the Under-representation of Women in Senior Management Positions.* Brisbane: Queensland Department of Education.

Lingard, B. (1993) Corporate federalism: the emerging approach to policy-making for Australian schools, in B. Lingard, J. Knight and P. Porter (eds) *Schooling Reform in Hard Times.* London: Falmer.

Lingard, B. (1995) Gendered policy making inside the state, in B. Limerick and B. Lingard (eds) *Gender and Changing Educational Management.* Sydney: Hodder.

Lingard, B. (1998) The disadvantaged schools programme: caught between literacy and local management of schools. *International Journal of Inclusive Education* 2(1): 1–14.

Lingard, B. and Limerick, B. (1995) Thinking gender, changing educational management, in B. Limerick and B. Lingard (eds) *Gender and Changing Educational Management.* Sydney: Hodder.

Lingard, B. and Porter, P. (eds) (1997) *A National Approach to Schooling in Australia? Essays on the Development of National Policies in Schools Education.* Canberra: Australian College of Education.

Lingard, B., Knight, J. and Porter, P. (eds) (1993) *Schooling Reform in Hard Times.* London: Falmer.

Lingard, B., Ladwig, J. and Luke, A. (1998) School effects in postmodern conditions, in R. Slee, G. Weiner and S. Tomlinson (eds) *Effective for Whom? School Effectiveness and the School Improvement Movement.* London: Falmer.

Linn, M. (1992) Gender differences in educational achievement, in *Sex Equity in Educational Opportunity, Achievement and Testing: Proceedings of the 1991 ETS Invitational Conference.* Princeton, NJ: Educational Testing Service.

Lloyd, T. (1985) *Working with Boys.* London: National Youth Bureau.

Ludowyke, J. (1997) *Improving the School Performance of Boys.* North Melbourne: Victoria Association of State Secondary School Principals.

Luke, A. (1997) New narratives of human capital: recent redirections in Australian educational policy. *Australian Educational Researcher* 24(2): 1–21.

Luke, A., Land, R., van Kraayenord, C. and Elkins, J. (1997) *Report of an Intrinsic Critical Appraisal of the Year 2 Diagnostic Net Continua and Associated Teacher Support Materials undertaken for the Queensland Schools Curriculum Council*. Brisbane: University of Queensland.

Luke, C. (1996) ekstasis@cyberia. *Discourse* 17(2): 187–207.

Lyotard, F. (1984) *The Postmodern Condition*. Minneapolis, MN: University of Minnesota Press.

Mac an Ghaill, M. (1994) *The Making of Men: Masculinities, Sexualities and Schooling*. Buckingham: Open University Press.

Mac an Ghaill, M. (ed.) (1996) *Understanding Masculinities: Social Relations and Cultural Arenas*. Buckingham: Open University Press.

Mac an Ghaill, M. and Haywood, C. (1997) Masculinity and social change: rethinking sexual politics. *Social Alternatives* 16(3): 11–13.

MacCann, B. (1993) *Sex Differences in Participation and Performance at the NSW Higher School Certificate: A Method Which Adjusts for the Effects of Differential Selection*. Sydney: New South Wales Board of Studies.

MacCann, B. (1995) *A Longitudinal Study of Sex Differences at the Higher School Certificate and School Certificate: Trends over the Last Decade*. Sydney: New South Wales Board of Studies.

Mahony, P. (1985) *Schools for the Boys? Co-education Reassessed*. London: Hutchinson.

Mahony, P. (1996) Changing schools: some international feminist perspectives on teaching girls and boys. *Women's Studies International Forum* 19(4): 1–2.

Mahony, P. (1997a) Talking heads: a feminist perspective on public sector reform in teacher education. *Discourse* 18(1): 87–102.

Mahony, P. (1997b) The underachievement of boys in the UK: old tunes for new fiddles? *Social Alternatives* 16(3): 44–50.

Mahony, P. and Hextall, I. (1997a) Problems of accountability in reinvented government: a case study of the teacher training agency. *Journal of Education Policy* 12(4): 267–83.

Mahony, P. and Hextall, I. (1997b) Teaching in the managerial state. Conference paper, Australian Association for Research in Education Conference, Brisbane, November.

Mann, S. (1997) Emotional labour in organisations. *Leadership and Organisational Development Journal*. 18(1): 4–12.

Martinez, L. (1994) *Boyswork: Whose Work? The Changing Face of Gender Equity Programs in the 90s*. Brisbane: Queensland Department of Education.

Martino, W. (1995a) Critical literacy for boys. *Interpretations* 28(2): 18–32.

Martino, W. (1995b) Gendered learning practices: Exploring the costs of hegemonic masculinity for girls and boys in school. Proceedings of the *Promoting gender equity* Conference, 22–4 February, Canberra. ACT Department of Education: 343–64.

Mauss, M. (1973 [1934]) Techniques of the body. *Economy and Society* 2: 70–88.

McCarthy, C. (1998) *The Uses of Culture: Education and the Limits of Ethnic Affiliation*. New York: Routledge.

McGaw, B. (1996) *Their Future Options for Reform of the Higher School*

Certificate. Sydney: Department of Training and Education Coordination, New South Wales.

McLean, C. (1995) The cost of masculinity: placing men's pain in the context of male power. Proceedings of the *Promoting gender equity* Conference, 22–4 February, Canberra ACT Department of Education.

McLean, C. (1996) The politics of men's pain, in C. McLean, M. Carey and C. White (eds) *Men's Ways of Being: New Directions in Theory and Psychology*. Boulder, CO: Westview Press.

McLean, C. (1997) The costs of masculinity: placing men's pain in the context of male power, in Ministerial Council for Education, Employment, Training and Youth Affairs (MCEETYA) (ed.) *Gender Equity: A Framework for Australian Schools*. Canberra: ACT Government Printer.

McLeod, J. (1998) Out of the comfort zone: feminism after the backlash. *Discourse* 19(3): 371–8.

Mead, J. (ed.) (1997) *Bodyjamming: Sexual Harassment, Feminism and Public Life*. Sydney: Vintage.

Meade, C. (1987) *The Him Book*. Sheffield: City Libraries.

Meadmore, P. (1996) Male teachers as role models: a quick-fix? *Perspectives on Educational Leadership*, 6(8): 1–2.

Mellor, P. and Shilling, C. (1997) *Re-forming the Body: Religion, Community and Modernity*. London: Sage.

Men Against Sexual Assault (MASA) (written by Brook Friedman) (1996) *Boys-Talk: A Program for Young Men about Masculinity, Non-violence and Relationships*. Adelaide: Kookaburra Press.

Men's Issue Page (1997) Promise Keepers. http://www.vix.com/men/orgs/promise-keepers/desc.html, January.

Messner, M. (1997) *Politics of Masculinities: Men in Movements*. Thousand Oaks, CA: Sage.

Messner, M. and Sabo, D. (1994) *Sex, Violence and Power in Sports: Rethinking Masculinity*. Freedom, CA: Crossing.

Millet, A. (1995) *Times Educational Supplement*, 8 September.

Milligan, S., Ashenden, D. and Quin, R. (1994) *Women in the Teaching Profession*. Canberra: Australian Government Publishing Service.

Mills, A. J. and Tancred, P. (eds) (1992) *Gendering Organizational Analysis*. London: Sage.

Mills, M. (1997) Wild men: looking back and lashing out. *Social Alternatives* 16(4): 11–14.

Mills, M. (1998a) Challenging violence in schools: disruptive moments in the educational politics of masculinity, unpublished PhD thesis. University of Queensland.

Mills, M. (1998b) Issues in implementing boys' programs in schools: male teachers and empowerment, unpublished paper. University of Queensland.

Mills, M. and Lingard, B. (1997) Masculinity politics, myths, and boys' schooling: review essay. *British Journal of Educational Studies* 45(3): 276–92.

Moore, R. (1996) Back to the future: the problem of change, and the possibilities of advance in the sociology of education. *British Journal of Sociology of Education*, 17(2): 145–61.

Morris, E. (1996) Boys will be boys? Closing the gender gap. Labour Party Consultation Paper, November.

Mortimore, P., Sammons, P., Stoll, L., Lewis, L. and Ecob, R. (1988) *School Matters: The Junior Years*. Wells: Open Books.

National Coalition of Free Men (NCFM) homepage (1997) http://www.ncfm.org, January.

National Organization for Men Against Sexism (NOMAS) homepage (1997), http://www.csbsju.edu/mm22/suite/nomas.html, January.

Newmann, F. and Associates (1996) *Authentic Achievement: Restructuring Schools for Intellectual Quality*. San Francisco, CA: Jossey-Bass.

Novogrodsky, M., Kaufman, M., Holland, D. and Wells, M. (1992) Retreat for the future: an anti-sexist workshop for high schoolers. *Our Schools/Our Selves* 3(4): 67–87.

O'Doherty, S. (chair) (1994) *Changes and Opportunities: A Discussion Paper*. Report to the Minister for Education, Training and Youth Affairs on the Inquiry into Boys' Education 1994 by the New South Wales Government Advisory Committee on Education, Training and Tourism. Sydney: NSW Government.

Oerton, S. (1996) *Beyond Hierarchy: Gender, Sexuality and the Social Economy*. London: Taylor & Francis.

Offe, C. (1975) The theory of the capitalist state and the problem of policy formation, in L. Lindberg, R. Alford, C. Crouch and C. Offe (eds) *Stress and Contradiction in Modern Capitalism*. Lexington, MA: D. C. Heath.

Orr, E. (1994) *Australia's Literacy Challenge: The Importance of Education in Breaking the Poverty Cycle for Australia's Disadvantaged Families*. Camperdown: The Smith Family.

Ozga, J. (ed.) (1993) *Women in Educational Management*. Buckingham: Open University Press.

Ozga, J. and Lawn, M. (1988) Schoolwork: interpreting the labour process of teaching. *British Journal of Sociology of Education* 9: 323–36.

Ozga, J. and Walker, L. (1995) Women in educational management: theory and practice, in B. Limerick and B. Lingard (eds) *Gender and Changing Educational Management*. Sydney: Hodder.

Pease, B. (1997) *Men and Sexual Politics: Towards a Profeminist Practice*. Adelaide: Dulwich Centre Publications.

Pusey, M. (1991) *Economic Rationalism in Canberra: A Nation-Building State Changes its Mind*. Melbourne: Cambridge University Press.

Putnam, L. and Mumby, D. (1993) Organisations, emotion and the myth of rationality, in S. Fineman (ed.) *Emotion in Organisations*. London: Sage.

Ramsay, C. (1996) Male honor: on David Cronenberg, in P. Smith (ed.) *Boy's Masculinities in Contemporary Culture*. Boulder, CO: Westview.

Ramsay, E. (1995) Management, gender and language: who is hiding behind the glass ceiling and why can't we see them?, in B. Limerick and B. Lingard (eds) *Gender and Changing Educational Management*. Sydney: Hodder.

Ramsay, E. (1997) Feminism and the future, sisterhood and the state. *Discourse* 18(3): 479–89.

Reay, D. (1990) Working with boys. *Gender and Education* 2(3): 269–82.

Richards, G. and Sproats, A. (1996) 'An overview of gender trends in tertiary aggregate scores across Australia'. Sydney: New South Wales Board of Studies.

Riddell, S. (1998) Boys and underachievement: the Scottish dimension. *International Journal of Inclusive Education* 2(2): 169–86.

Robins, D. and Cohen, P. (1978) *Knuckle Sandwich: Growing up in the Working Class City*. Harmondsworth: Penguin.

Roman, L. and Eyre, L. (eds) (1997) *Dangerous Territories: Struggles for Difference and Equality*. New York: Routledge.

Rowan, J. (1987) *The Horned God: Feminism and Men as Wounding and Healing*. London: Routledge & Kegan Paul.

Rowbotham, S. (1997) *A Century of Women: The History of Women in Britain and the United States*. London: Viking.

Ryan, J. (1998) Boys to men, *San Francisco Chronicle*, 22 March: 1, and *Sunday Examiner and Chronicle*: 4.

Sadker, M. and Sadker, D. (1994) *Failing at Fairness: How Our Schools Cheat Girls*. New York: Touchstone.

Salisbury, J. and Jackson, D. (1996) *Challenging Macho Values: Practical Ways of Working with Adolescent Boys*. London: Falmer.

Sammons, P. (1995) Gender, ethnic and socio-economic differences in attainment and progress: a longitudinal analysis of student achievement over 9 Years. *British Educational Research Journal* 21(4): 465–85.

Sawer, M. (1990) *Sisters in Suits: Women and Public Policy in Australia*. Sydney: Allen & Unwin.

Scheerens, J. (1992) *Effective Schooling: Research, Theory and Practice*. London: Cassell.

Schools Commission (1987) *The National Policy for the Education of Girls in Australian Schools*. Canberra: Australian Government Publishing Service.

Sedgwick, E. K. (1990) *Epistemology of the Closet*. Berkeley, CA: University of California Press.

Sedgwick, E. K. (1993) *Tendencies*. Durham, NC: Duke University Press.

Segal, L. (1990) *Slow Motion: Changing Masculinities, Changing Men*. London: Virago.

Seidler, V. (1990) Men, feminism and power, in J. Hearn and D. Morgan (eds) *Men, Masculinities and Social Theory*. London: Unwin Hyman.

Seidler, V. (1991) *Recreating Sexual Politics: Men, Feminism and Politics*. London: Routledge.

Seidler, V. (1994) *Unreasonable Men: Masculinity and Social Theory*. London: Routledge.

Seidler, V. (1997) *Man Enough: Embodying Masculinities*. London: Sage.

Sexton, P. (1969) *The Feminized Male: Classrooms, White Collars, and the Decline of Manliness*. New York: Random House.

Shakespeare, S. (1998) *Daily Mail*, 5 January.

Sheffield Men Against Sexual Harassment's SMASH pack (originally published in 1984 and revised in 1987).

Skuja, E. (1995) Performance of the Australian university sector in access and equity, in G. D. Postle, J. R. Clarke, E. Skuja, D. D. Bull, K. Batorowicz and H. A. McCann (eds) *Towards Excellence in Diversity*. Toowoomba, Qld: USQ Press, University of Southern Queensland.

Slattery, L. (1998) What's the snag for 90s men: misogynist predator or feminist victim? *Weekend Australian*, 4–5 April: 5.

Slee, R., Weiner, G. and Tomlinson, S. (eds) (1998) *Effective for Whom? School Effectiveness and the School Improvement Movement*. London: Falmer.

Smalley, G. and Trent, J. (1994) *The Hidden Value of a Man: The Incredible Impact of a Man on His Family.* Colorado Springs, CO: Focus on the Family.

Smedley, S. (1997) Men on the margins: male student primary teachers. *Changing English* 4(2): 217–27.

Snodgrass, J. (ed.) (1977) *A Book of Readings for Men Against Sexism.* Albion, CA: Times Change Press.

Spivak, G. C. (1992) French feminism revisited, in J. Butler and J. W. Scott (eds) *Femininists Theorize the Political.* New York: Routledge.

Steinem, G. (1992) Foreword, in K. L. Hagan (ed.) *Women Respond to the Men's Movement: A Feminist Collection.* San Francisco, CA: Pandora.

Stobart, G., Elwood, J. and Quinlan, M. (1992) Gender bias in examinations: how equal are the opportunities? *British Educational Research Journal* 18(3): 261–76.

Stoltenberg, J. (1988) *Refusing to be a Man: Essays on Sex and Justice.* Portland, OR: Breitenbush.

Stronach, I. and MacLure, M. (1997) *Educational Research Undone: The Postmodern Embrace.* Buckingham: Open University Press.

Summers, A. (1986) Mandarins and missionaries: women in the federal bureaucracy, in L. Grieve and A. Burns (eds) *Australian Women.* Melbourne: Oxford University Press.

Tacey, D. J. (1997) *Remaking Men: The Revolution in Masculinity.* Ringwood, Vic: Viking.

Taylor, S., Rizvi, F., Lingard, B. and Henry. M. (1997) *Educational Policy and the Politics of Change.* London: Routledge.

The GEN (The Gender Enquiry Network) (1993) *But the Girls are Doing Brilliantly!* Canberra: DEET.

Teese, R. (1995) Educational and economic indicators of regional disadvantage amongst young people in Victoria, 1992–1994, unpublished paper. University of Melbourne.

Teese, R., McLean, G. and Polesel, J. (1993) *Equity Outcomes: A Report to the Schools Council's Task Force on a Broadbanded Equity Program for Schools.* Canberra: Australian Government Publishing Service.

Teese, R., Davies, M., Charlton, M. and Polesel, J. (1995) *Who Wins at School? Girls and Boys in Australian Secondary Education.* Melbourne: University of Melbourne Departments of Education Policy and Management.

Thompson, C. (1988) Education and masculinity, in A. O'B. Carelli (ed.) *Sex Equality in Education: Readings and Strategies.* Springfield, IL: Charles C. Thomas.

Thompson, E. (1991) Democracy undermined: reforms to the Australian Public Service from Whitlam to Hawke. *Australian Quarterly* winter: 127–42.

Throop, D. (1996) Men's movement history, in Men's Issue Page, http://www.vix.com/men/history/accounts/throop5.html, 12 February.

Tolson, A. (1977) *The Limits of Masculinity.* London: Tavistock.

Vogel, P. (1997) Review of *Boys-Talk: A Program for Young Men about Masculinity, Non-violence and Relationships,* posted on boysed@halibut.pnc.com.au, 14 February.

Vogel, P. (1998) Boys' education: is equity enough?, Certified Male homepage, http://www.pnc.com.au/~pvogel/cm/.

Von Hoffman, T. (1997) *Big Damn Book of Sheer Manliness.* Santa Monica, CA: General Publishing Group.

Walby, S. (1997) *Gender Transformations*. London: Routledge.

Walker, J. (1988) *Louts and Legends: Male Youth Culture in an Inner-City School*. Sydney: Allen & Unwin.

Walkerdine, V. (1986) Progressive pedagogy and political struggle. *Screen* 27(5): 54–60.

Wark, M. (1997) *The Virtual Republic: Australia's Culture Wars of the 1990s*. Sydney: Allen & Unwin.

Waters, M. (1995) *Globalization*. London: Routledge.

Weiner, G. (1995) A question of style or value? Contrasting perceptions of women as educational leaders, in B. Limerick and B. Lingard (eds) *Gender and Changing Educational Management*. Sydney: Hodder.

Weiner, G., Arnot, M. and David, M. (1997) Is the future female? Female success, male disadvantage and changing gender patterns in education, in A. H. Halsey, H. Lauder, P. Brown and A. Stuart Wells (eds) *Education Culture Economy Society*. Oxford: Oxford University Press.

Weldon, F. (1997a) Pity the man of today, *Guardian Weekly*, 21 December.

Weldon, F. (1997b) *Big Women*. London: Flamingo.

West, P. (1995) Giving boys a ray of hope: masculinity and education, discussion paper. University of Western Sydney.

Whitehead, S. (1999) From paternalism to entrepreneurialism: the experience of men managers in UK postcompulsory education. *Discourse* 20(1).

Wilkinson, I. (1997) Closing the gender and home–language gaps in reading literacy. *Set Special: Language and Literacy* (5): 1–4.

Williamson, T. (1985) A history of the men's movement, in F. Baumli (ed.) *Men Freeing Men: Exploding the Myth of the Traditional Male*. Jersey City, NJ: New Atlantis.

Willis, P. (1977) *Learning to Labour*. Farnborough: Saxon House.

Wilson, W. J. (1997) *When Work Disappears: The World of the New Urban Poor*. New York: Vintage.

Yates, L. (1985) Is 'girl friendly schooling' really what girls need?, in J. Whyte, R. Deem, L. Kant and M. Cruikshank (eds) *Girl Friendly Schooling*. London: Methuen.

Yates, L. (1993) *The Education of Girls: Policy, Research and the Question of Gender*. Melbourne: Australian Council for Educational Research.

Yates, L. (1996) Understanding the boys' issues: what sort of challenge is it? Conference paper, American Educational Research Association Conference, New York, April.

Yates, L. (1997) Gender equity and the boys debate: what sort of challenge is it? *British Journal of Sociology of Education* 18(3): 337–47.

Yates, L. and Leder, G. (1996) *Student Pathways: A Review and Overview of National Databases on Gender Equity*. Canberra: Australian Capital Territory Department of Education and Training.

Yeatman, A. (1990) *Bureaucrats, Technocrats, Femocrats: Essays on the Contemporary Australian State*. Sydney: Allen & Unwin.

Yeatman, A. (1994) *Postmodern Revisionings of the Political*. London: Routledge.

Young, I. M. (1997) Unruly categories: a critique of Nancy Fraser's dual systems theory. *New Left Review* 222: 147–60.

Index